ART OF MODERN JOURNALISM

Shahzad Ahmad

ANMOL PUBLICATIONS PVT. LTD.
NEW DELHI - 110 002 (INDIA)

ANMOL PUBLICATIONS PVT. LTD.
4374/4B, Ansari Road, Daryaganj
New Delhi - 110 002
Ph.: 23261597, 23278000
Visit us at: www.anmolpublications.com

Art of Modern Journalism

First Published, 2005

PRINTED IN INDIA

Published by J.L. Kumar for Anmol Publications Pvt. Ltd., New Delhi - 110 002 and Printed at Mehra Offset Press, Delhi.

Contents

Preface

In Modern world, Journalism is one discipline, which attracts people like any thing, but, it is equally challenging and drastic in cases. Particularly, under the new world order and in current global scenario, its value has increased manifold.

Apart from being a glorious profession, Journalism, today is a full-fledged subject, mastery of which leads one to a successful career and an all powerful status in society.

As a discipline, Journalism requires proper training and a comprehensive course, if possible. Although, there is no defined qualification for appointment as a journalist, in any capacity, in any media organisation, yet it is always better to be properly qualified and well-equipped with all essential knowledge.

Of course, there are books on Journalism but not in a great number. And, if one goes selective, then only a few books would rest in hand, as there is still a dearth for exclusive and exhaustive books on several streams of Journalism.

This series of books on Journalism is an effort to fill the abovesaid vaccum only. Here are books on all subjects and topics, related to Journalism. The undersigned is confident enough that this humble endeavour would prove to be worthy on the basis of its merits and receive a warm acceptance by students of journalism, scholars and the working journalists, as well.

— **Editor**

1

Introduction

Long before the mass media were invented, Plato may have provided the opening round in the controversy over the social costs and benefits of mass culture. In his commentary on the training of the children who were to become the leaders of his ideal Republic, he saw the mass culture of his day as posing a threat to the minds of the young:

Then shall we simply allow our children to listen to any stories that anyone happens to make up, and so receive into their minds ideas often the very opposite of those we shall think they ought to have when they are grown up?

No, certainly not [replies, Glaucon].

It seems, then, our first business will be to supervise the making of fables and legends, rejecting all which are unsatisfactory; and we shall induce nurses and mothers to tell their children only those which we have approved... Most of the stories now in use must be discarded.

This theme-popular entertainment is harmful to the minds of the young has been a consistent one from the beginnings of mass communication. It has been claimed from time to time that such charges can be validated by scientific evidence, but repeatedly this evidence has turned out to be difficult to interpret and therefore controversial. Social sciences insist that any important conclusions about the effects of the media be supported by solid evidence. Because of such insistence upon data rather than emotion, they sometimes find themselves in the awkward position of seeming to defend the media when actually they are simply refusing to accept the inadequately supported claims of critics.

Nevertheless, the insistence that conclusions be based on adequate evidence has never deterred the literacy critic from charging the media with a deep responsibility for society's problems. Most nineteenth-century American writers at some point in their careers took time to criticize and condemn the newspaper for superficiality and distortion. The following excerpts from the pens of well-known and influential literacy figures are samples of the climate of opinion prevailing among the literary during the time when the mass newspaper was diffusing through the American society:

Henry David—The penny-post is, commonly, an institution through which you seriously offer a man that penny for his thoughts which is so safely offered in jest. And I am sure that I have never read any memorable news in a newspaper. If we read of one man robbed, or murdered, or killed by accident, or one house burned, or one vessel wrecked, or one steamboat blown up, or one cow run over on the Western Railroad, or one mad dog killed, or one lot of grasshoppers in the winter we never need read of another. If you are acquainted with the principle, what do you care for a myriad instances and applications? To a philosopher all news, as it is called, is gossip, and they who read it and edit it are old women over their tea.

Samuel Clemens—That awful power, the public opinion of this nation is formed and modelled by a horde of ignorant self-complacent simpletons who failed at ditching and shoemaking and fetched up in journalism on their way to the poorhouse.

Stephen Crane—A newspaper is a collection of half-injustices which bawled by boys from mile to mile, Spreads its curious opinion to a million merciful and sneering men, while families cuddle the joys of the fireside when spurred by tale of lone agony. A newspaper is a court where everyone is kindly and unfairly tried by a squalor of honest men. A newspaper is a market where wisdom sells it freedom and melons are crowned by the crowd.

A newspaper is a game where his error scores the player victory, while another's skill wins death.

A newspaper is a symbol; it is a feckless life's chronicle, a collection of loud tales concentrating eternal stupidities, that in remote ages lived unhaltered, roaming through a fenceless world.

One remarkable aspect of these statements is that you could simply substitute the word "television" for "newspaper" and obtain a rather parallel version of the hostility and attacks primarily directed at television by critics today.

The tenacity and stability of the mass media generally in the face of such a long history of criticism by powerful voices needs explanation. The problem at first seems deceptively simple: the media appeal to the masses and the masses want the kind of content they get and so the media continue to give it to them.

Many social scientists, such as Skornia, have exposed the inadequacy of this explanation by nothing the old chicken-and-egg problem. It is difficult at best to know if the public taste determines the media fare or if the media fare determines public taste. The answer probably lies somewhere in between with public taste being both a cause and effect of media fare. The relationship between public taste and media fare thus becomes a circular one which, in terms of the chicken-egg analogy, is an ongoing process of chickens producing eggs and eggs producing chickens.

The structural functional analysis of social systems (or "functional analysis" for short) concerns itself with the patterns of action exhibited by individuals or subgroups who relate themselves to one another within such systems. A social system is, for this reason, an abstraction—but one not too far removed from the observable and empirically verifiable behaviours of the persons who are doing the acting. The social system, then, is a complex of stable, repetitive, and patterned action that is in part a manifestation of the culture shared by the actors, and in part a manifestation of the psychological orientations of the actors (which are in turn derived from that culture). The cultural system, the social system, and the personality systems (of the individual actors), therefore, are different kinds of abstractions made from the same basic data, namely, the overt and symbolic behaviours of individual human beings. They are equally legitimate abstractions, each providing in its own right a basis for various kinds of explanations and predictions. Generally speaking, it may be difficult or nearly impossible to analyse or understand fully one such abstraction without some reference to the others.

But, granted that the term "social system" is a legitimate scientific abstraction, how does this general conceptual strategy help in understanding the mass media of communication? To answer this question, we need to set forth in greater detail exactly what is meant by the term social system, and what type of analysis it provides. To aid in providing such an explanation we turn briefly to several ideas that are important aspects of the study of social systems. One of the most important of these ideas is the concept of the "function" of some particular repetitive phenomenon (set of actions) within such a system. The fact that such content has long survived the jibes of influential critics was said to require explanation. One form of explanation will be provided by noting the function of such a repetitive phenomenon within some stable system of action. The term "function" in the present context means little more than "consequence." To illustrate briefly, we might hypothesize that the repetitive practice of wearing wedding rings on the part of a given married couple has the function (consequence) of reminding, them as well as others that the two are bound together by the obligations and ties that matrimony implies. This practice thereby contributes indirectly to maintaining the permanence of the marriage, the stability of that particular social system. The practice is in a sense "explained" by noting its contribution to the context within which it occurs. A comparison of a number of such systems with and without this particular item (but in other respects matched) would test the assertion.

In the above example, the social system is a relatively simple one. There are only two "components," and each of these happen to be the behaviour pattern of an individual. Their patterns are derived both from the individual psychological makeup of the partners and from the cultural norms concerning marriage prevailing in their community, social class, and society. It is a miniature system whose stability is dependent upon satisfaction of its "needs." For example, such a system requires that the partners perform roles that meet the expectations each has of the other and the expectations the community has of married couples. This can be thought of as a "need" for adequate role performance, without which the stability of the system would be endangered. Other "needs," related to economic matters and emotional satisfactions, could be cited.

More complex illustrations of social systems can easily be pointed to, where the "components" of the system are not the actions of individual persons but subsystems. A department store, for example, is a complex social system consisting of the actions of managerial personnel, buyers, salespersons, the clerical staff, customers, transportation workers, a janitorial team, and security employees. Each of these components is a smaller system of action within the broader system of the store itself, and it in turn is a complex system of action carried out within the context of the external social conditions of the community. In spite of the complexity, any given set of repetitive actions might be analysed in terms of their contribution to maintaining or undermining the system's stability. Granting to employees the right to buy merchandise at cost could have the function (consequence) of maintaining their morale and loyalty, and thus would contribute fairly directly to the maintenance of the system. Rigid insistence on the observance of petty rules, such as docking the pay of an employee who on rare occasions was late for work, might be disruptive of morale and loyalty, and by contributing to labour turnover it could be dysfunctional. Instead of contributing to the maintenance of the system, it could cause disruptions and instability. Such inductively derived conclusions would be subject to testing for validity, of course, but the functional analysis would have generated the hypothesis to be tested (an important role of theory).

A "functional analysis," then, focuses on some specific phenomenon occurring within a social system. It then attempts to show how this phenomenon has consequences that contribute to the stability and permanence of the system as a whole. The phenomenon may, of course, have a negative influence, and if so, it would be said to have "dysfunctions" rather than "functions." The analysis is a strategy for inducing or locating hypotheses that can be tested empirically by comparative studies or other appropriate research methods.

The analysis of social system is extremely difficult, No infallible rules specify precisely how to locate and define the exact boundaries of a given social system, particularly if it is relatively complex. As yet, no completely agreed upon criteria exist for establishing linkages between the components of a system, and no standard formulas can uncover the precise contribution that a given repetitive form of action makes to the stability of a system. A functional analysis of the contribution of some item to the stability of a system, then, is a procedure that is somewhat less than rigorous. But in spite of this source of potential criticism, this strategy has proved useful in our attempts to understand complex social phenomena, such as the mass media.

How can this type of analysis be applied to the mass media? First, we can identify that portion of the content of the mass media that is in "low" cultural taste or provides gratifications to the mass audience in such a manner that it is widely held to be potentially debasing as the "relatively persistent trait or disposition" of the mass media we seek to explain. It would be difficult in practice to construct a set of categories under which to analyse the content of the media so that material of "low" cultural taste can be identified readily. It would be difficult, but actually it would not be impossible. Excessive violence, the portrayal of criminal techniques, horror and monster themes, open pornography, suggestive music, and dreary formula melodramas are typical categories of content that arouse the ire of critics. Considerable disagreement would probably occur as to the exact content that should be included in any given category. There would also be debates over the number of categories used. There would also be debates over the number of categories used. Nevertheless, it is theoretically possible to identify the content of any given medium that is most objected to by the largest number of critics. We will assume that given sufficient time and resources, and using survey techniques, preference scales, attitude measuring instruments, and other research procedures now available that the content of any given medium could be divided roughly into something like the following three categories:

Low-taste Content—This would be media content widely distributed and attended to by the mass audience, but which has consistently aroused the ire of critics. Examples would be crime dramas on television that emphasize violence, openly pornographic motion pictures, day time, confession magazines, crime comics, suggestive music, or other content that has been widely held to contribute to a lowering of taste, disruption of morals, or stimulation toward socially unacceptable conduct. Whether or not such charges are true.

Non-debated Content—This would be media content, widely distributed and attended to, about which media critics have said very little. It is not an issue in the debate over the impact of the media on the masses. Examples would be television weather reports, some news content, music that is neither symphonic nor popular, magazines devoted to specialized interests, motion pictures using "wholesome" themes, and many others. Such content is not believed either to elevate or lower taste, and it is not seen as a threat to moral standards.

High-taste Content—This would be media content sometimes widely distributed but not necessarily widely attended to. It is content that media critics feel is in better taste, morally uplifting, educational, or in some way inspiring. Examples would be serious music, sophisticated drama, political discussions, art films, or magazines devoted to political commentary. Such content is championed by critics as the opposite of the low-taste material, which they see as distinctly objectionable.

Of course, the first of the above categories is the one to which we wish to direct most of our attention. It is the repetitive phenomenon whose contribution to the media (as a social system) needs analysis. Nevertheless, it would also be possible to study the other two categories with somewhat parallel perspectives, but this will receive relatively little attention in the present discussion.

We need now to begin to identify the components and boundaries of the social system within which low-taste content occurs so that eventually the contribution it makes to the system can be inductively hypothesized.

Rather than develop a purely descriptively scheme that will apply only to a single medium, it will be more fruitful to attempt to develop a general conceptual scheme into which any or all media could be placed, with suitable minor modifications in details. Such a general scheme will emphasize the similarities between media, particularly in terms of relationships between the components in the system.

Audience—The first major component of the social system of mass communication is the audience. This is an exceedingly complex component. The audience is stratified, differentiated, and interrelated in the many ways that social scientists have studied for years. Some of the major variables that play a part in determining how this component will operate within the system are the major needs and interests of audience members, the various social categories represented in an audience, and the nature of the social relationships between audience members. These variables point to behavioural mechanisms that determine the patterns of attention, interpretation, and response of an audience with respect to content of a given type.

Research Organisations—The rough typology of content suggested is in some degree related to the characteristics of the audience. Organizations devoted to research, to measuring the performances of media audiences, or to various forms of market research provide information to those responsible for selecting the categories of content that will be distributed to the audience. There is a link, then, between the audience as a component in the system and the market research-rating service organizations as a second component. In purely theoretical terms, both components are role system themselves and are thus actually subsystems. This is in a sense a one-way link. For very minor (or usually no) personal reward, audience members selected for study provide data about themselves to such an agency, but very little flows back. This linkage between components is by comparison relatively simple.

Distributors—The content itself, of whatever type, flows from some distributor to the audience. The role system of the distributor component varies in detail from one medium to another. In addition, several somewhat distinct subsystems exist within this general component. First, there are local outlets, which are likely to be in the most immediate contact with the audience. The local newspaper, the local theatre, the local broadcasting station play the most immediate part in placing messages before their respective audiences. But inseparably tied to them are other subsystems of this general component. Newspaper syndicates, broadcasting networks, or chains of movie theatres pass content on to their local outlets. The link between these two subsystems is a two-way one. The local outlet provides money, and the larger distributor supplies content. Or the link age may be that the local outlet provides a service, and the distributor (who is paid elsewhere) provides money.

The relationship between audience and distributor seems at first to be mostly a one-way link. The distributor provides entertainment content (and often advertising), but the audience provides little back in a direct sense. However, it does provide its attention. In fact, it is precisely the attention of the audience that distributors are attempting to solicit. They sell this "commodity" directly to their financial backer or sponsor. In addition, the audience supplies information to the research component and this is indirectly supplied to distributors in the form of feedback so that they may gauge the amount of attention they are eliciting. The linkages between components grow more complex as we seek the boundaries of the system.

Producers and their Sponsors—To the audience, the research, and the distributing component, we may add the role system of the producer of content. This component's primary link is with the financial backer (or sponsor) component and with the distributor, from whom money is obtained and for whom various forms of entertainment content are manufactured. A host of subsystems are included in this producer component, depending upon the particular medium. Examples are actors, directors, television producers, technicians, foreign correspondents, wire-service editors, film producers, labour union leaders, publishers, copyeditors, clerical staff, and many, many more.

Advertising Agencies—Linking the sponsor, distributor, producer, and research organization are the advertising agencies. Paid primarily by the sponsor, this component provides (in return) certain ideas and services. For the most part, it provides the distributor with advertising messages. It may have links with the research component as well.

Subsystems of Control—Over.this complex set of interrelated components, there are other subsystems that exert control. The legislative bodies, at both the state and national level, which enact regulative statutes concerning the media, constitute an important part of such a control component. Another important part of this role subsystem is the official regulative agencies, which implement the policies that have been legislated. The link between the legislative body (control component) and the audience is, course, one of votes and public opinion, to which the component is presumably sensitive and dependent. Information lines between audience, legislative bodies, and regulatory agencies are more or less open.

To the regulatory components whose role definitions are found in legal statute can be added the private voluntary associations that develop "codes" and to some degree serve as a control over the distributors. Such distributors provide them with money, and they in turn provide surveillance and other services.

The regulatory subsystems draw definitions of permissible and non-permissible content from the general set of external conditions within which this extremely complicated system operates. Surrounding the entire structure as an external condition are our society's general norms concerning morality, and the expressions that these find in formal law. Similar, although less likely to be incorporated into law, are our general cultural norms and beliefs regarding what will be likely to entertain or otherwise gratify Americans. Thus, we seldom see traditional Chinese opera but frequently see western horse opera. We seldom hear the strains of Hindu temple music but frequently hear the "strains" and other noises of the latest singer whom teenagers admire. If our interests run to more serious fare, we are likely to hear the music of a relatively small list of European or American composers who created their works within a span of about three centuries. Or we are likely to view ballet, opera, drama, and so on, of a fairly limited of artists whose products are defined by our society as classics or as innovative new approaches.

Each of the several media will fit into this general model of a social system in slightly different ways. A complete description of each of the media separately would be tedious. Indeed, each could well occupy the contents of an entire book. Two decades ago, Opotowsky attempted just such a detailed analysis of the television industry, although he did not use the social system concept.

To add to the complexity of this conceptual scheme, it must be remembered that although each medium constitutes a somewhat separate social system in itself, the media are also related to one another in systematic ways. Thus, we may speak of the entire set of communication media, including those which have not been specifically analysed in the present volume, as the mass communication system of the United States.

The structure of this mass communication system has been heavily influenced by the general social, political, economic, and cultural conditions that were current during the period when our mass media were developing and remain as important socio-cultural forces in the society within which they operate. Because of their importance for understanding our mass media as they are today. Our free enterprise beliefs, our views of the legitimacy of the profit motive, the virtues of controlled capitalism, and our general values concerning freedom of speech constitute further external conditions (in addition to those related to moral limits and cultural tastes) within which the American mass communication system operates.

Within the system itself, the principal internal condition is, of course, a financial one. Most of the components in the system are occupational role structures, which motivate their incumbent personnel primarily through money. To obtain money, they are all ultimately dependent upon the most central component of all-the audience. Unless its decisions to give attention, to purchase, to vote, and the like, are made in favourable ways, the system would undergo service strain and would eventually collapse.

Almost any dramatic change in the behaviour of the audience would cause the most severe disruption in the system for any given medium. The consequences of attention loss to the motion picture theatre as a mass medium was shown to be severe.

Such disruptions are infrequent, but they do occur. The key to heading off dramatic changes in audience behaviour, of course, is to provide entertainment content that will satisfy and motivate the largest possible number of audience members to carry out their roles in accord with the needs of the system. Such content will, in other words, maintain the stability of the system. The ideal, from the standpoint of the system, is content that will capture audience members' attention, persuade them to purchase goods, and at the same time be sufficiently within the bounds of moral norms and standards are not provoked.

The entertainment content that seems most capable of eliciting the attention of the largest number of audience members is the more dramatic, low-taste content. Since the most central media system goal is economic profit, sex and violence or any other attention-getting and attention-maintaining content is functional in the sense that even though it may be of low-taste, it maximizes the size of the audience exposed to advertisements. In general, the larger the audience, the more the distributor and producer can charge for advertising. For example, ads in prime-time television periods cost substantially more than those aired during relatively low-audience-size periods, such as early in the morning.

The assumption made by many media personnel and advertisers that low-taste content appeals primarily to the relatively uneducated, who still constitute a majority of the potential audience, may be false. In an early study Wilensky found that educated people said that they preferred and exposed themselves to high-taste content more often than did the relatively uneducated. But when observations were made of what the educated and educated actually aid, there was little difference between their levels of exposure to low-taste media content.

There is a great deal of evidence to show that the relatively uneducated spend more time than the educated being exposed to the mass media. It may be misleading to conclude that they do so only because the uneducated relish low-taste content. The relatively uneducated majority also have relatively low incomes, which probably means they have less choice than their more educated and wealthier counterparts in how they spend their non-working hours. The mass media may be more appealing to the relatively uneducated and poor in large part because the media are relatively inexpensive forms of leisure. Moreover, as Baker and Ball point out, it is probably superficial to think that the only reason people in general spend time with the media is because of the inherent appeal of their content. Any number of need-fulfilments and gratifications, over and above those related to entertainment or staying informed, are provided by the media. Babysitting and companionship (even when it is electronic companionship) are examples.

When all is said and done, however, it is still true that low-taste content sells and sells big. This fact establishes it as the key element in the social system of the media. It keeps the entire complex together by maintaining the financial stability of the system. Critics who provoke public attention by denouncing media content or by proclaiming that a casual connection exists between media content and socially undesirable behaviour may temporarily receive some recognition, they may also achieve some temporary disturbance in the system, or if they are persistent enough, they may ultimately even displace some specific from of low-taste content from a given medium altogether. Examples from the past are quiz shows that were found to be "rigged," and popular disc jockeys who were receiving "payola" (a fee for repeatedly playing a song to make it popular). In such cases the audience may be temporarily disaffected, low-taste content comes in such a variety of forms that the temporary or even permanent absence of one minor form does not alter the major picture. Critics have been complaining about newspaper concentration on crime news for a century, yet there has been no noticeable abatement in the reporting of such stories. Critics of the soap opera may have breathed a sigh of relief several years ago when these programs at last disappeared from radio. Their joy must have been short-lived when such daytime serials turned out to be quite popular with television viewers, so popular in fact that soap operas now appear during prime evening hours. Analyses of the level of violent television content show that it goes down slightly after federal government investigations on the effects of television violence or widespread campaigns by voluntary associations (e.g., the P.T.A.), only to return shortly after the public outcry has subsided.

When a formula is discovered for eliciting attention and influencing purchasing decisions from any large segment of the audience, it will be abandoned by the media only with great reluctance, if at all. The broadcast ballgame, the war movie, the star comedian, the family situation comedy, the western thriller, the detective story, the adventures of the secret agent, the drama of the courtroom—all are beginning to rank with such time-honoured formulas as the sob story, the funnies, the sex-murder account, the sports page, and disclosure of corruption in high places as attention-getting devices that can bring the eye or ear of the consumer nearer to the advertising message.

In short, the social system of the mass media in the United States is becoming more and more deeply established. Some future change can be expected in the kind of content it will produce to maintain its own stability. At present, however, the function of what we have called low-taste content is to maintain the financial stability of a deeply institutionalized social system that is tightly integrated with the whole of the American economic institution, the probability that our system of mass communication in this respect can be drastically altered by the occasional outbursts of critics seems small indeed.

Far more likely than media system change brought about by periodic attacks on low-taste media content is media system change brought about by trends in the economic system such as the emergence of a "post-industrial" society. Because the media system is also a subsystem in the larger economic system, it will have to adapt to such changes if it is to survive. If Bell's forecast that systems in the business of producing, processing, and transmitting information will become increasingly involved in key economic sectors of our society is valid, then we would expect significant changes in the nature of the mass media system. One change would surely be a marked increase in the knowledge and technical information of "non-debated" media content will rise sharply with a corresponding decline in low-taste media content.

But as is usually the case when talking about changes in social systems, such future developments in the nature of the

that creates understanding, facilitates work, and strengthens collective living among people.

The primary function of communication is to inform, educate, entertain and influence people to make them function smoothly. It also has a secondary function to perform as well through debates and discussion, cultural promotion and integration; it fosters creativity and understanding among people, groups, and societies so that they live in peace and harmony. These functions have been discussed below:

Information—Information is regarded as power. The more informed you are, the more powerful you become. Communication provides us enormous information about the environment in which we live. Information such as news of war, danger, crisis, famine etc., is important for that helps us in taking appropriate steps to safeguard our interests.

Instruction—Instructing, educating and socializing the members of the society is one of the major functions of communication. Communication creates awareness, provides a fund of knowledge, expertise and skills, gives direction and opportunity to people so that they can become an active member of the society.

Persuasion—With the passage of time this has become one of the major functions of communication. Persuasion helps in reaching decision on public policy in order to make possible to control and govern.

Entertainment—Entertainment is the need of every individual in order to break the monotonous routine of daily life and to divert their attention from the troubles and tensions. It not only revitalise our personality but also educate us. Communication provides entertainment through films, music, drama, art, literature, comedy, sports etc.

Debate and Discussion—Debate and discussion are the two ways in media through which public can clarify different viewpoints on issues of public interest and come to a general agreement on matters that concern all.

Integration and Cultural Promotion—Communication is a great integrating tool. It enables different individuals, groups or cultures to come to know each other, and appreciate others, way of life. It also provides opportunity for culture to be preserved and promoted.

Different Formats

All of us are engaged in a variety of communication acts. There are:

Intrapersonal Communication—It is talking to oneself, listening to oneself and relating one to oneself. This helps us contemplating, conceptualizing and formulating our thoughts or ideas before we actually indulge in overt communication.

Interpersonal Communication—This is the universal form of communication that takes place between two individuals. It is person-to-person contact, which includes everyday exchanges that may be formal or informal by means of words, sounds, facial expressions, gestures, postures etc.

There is face-to-face interaction between two persons in interpersonal communication and so it becomes very effective because one gets immediate feedback. It is also possible to influence the other person and persuade him or her to accept your point of view. It also has an emotional appeal and can motivate, encourage and coordinate work in a much effective manner than any other form of communication.

Group Communication—This is an extension of interpersonal communication, where more than two individuals are involved in exchange of ideas, thoughts, skills and interests. This kind of communication provides an opportunity for people to come together and discuss topics of common interest.

Communication in a group serves many goals like collective decision making, self expression, increasing one's effect, elevating one's status, relaxation etc. On the other hand it also has many limitations, as it is time consuming and often inefficient. In addition imbalances in status, skills and goals may distort the process and the outcome sharply.

Mass Communication—Another form of communication which involves communication with mass audience in Mass communication and the channels through which this kind of communication takes place are referred to as mass media. But both mass media and mass communication are generally considered synonyms for the sake of convenience.

Any mechanical device that multiplies messages and takes it to a large number of people simultaneously is called Mass Communication.

Thus, it is clear from the above definition that mass communication is a special kind of communication in which the nature of the audience and the feedback is different from that of interpersonal communication.

The two main components of mass communication are thus audience and feedback.

Audience—Whosoever is the recipient of mass media content constitutes its audience. Here the audience is large, heterogenous and anonymous in character. Heterogenous in the sense that messages are sent to people in all walks of life, each person with unique, characteristics. By anonymous, we mean that the receivers of the messages tend to be strangers to one another and to the source of those messages.

Feedback—Feedback in mass media is slow and weak. It is not direct as in face to face exchange and is invariably delayed. Considerable time and money are required to process the feedback received from the audience.

Different Streams

Mass media is broadly divided into print media and electronic media. Print media has a history of about 500 years. Whereas the electronic media are products of the 20th century.

Print Media—It includes newspapers, magazine, books and

other printed matter. Their growth was slow in the beginning but as the demand for education and information increased, they evolved quickly and flourished greatly.

Electronic Media—It includes radio, television, satellite TV, cinema etc. They provide instantaneous communication and their impact is greater. This differentiate it from print media. Electronic media are quicker than print media as the latter takes more time for mass production and delivery to a widely dispersed population.

Radio—Time of its inception is in 1920s. And since then its network has expanded a great deal. One of the best advantages that radio has over other media is that it can serve and entertain an audience which is otherwise occupied. However, the radio has suffered a setback in the recent times because of TV, which has attracted especially the urban population.

Television—With a modest beginning in the 1930s, it has become a powerful media of mass communication. It has grown into a massive network of mass information and mass entertainment.

The newer development in network technologies is that of satellite-Cable television. Audiences now have multiple choices ranging from news and information to entertainment of wide variety.

Films—Films are considered a major mass medium because of their mass appeal and influence on society. They set trends in styles and tastes, dominate the popular radio and television entertainment programmes.

There has been rapid expansion of mass media all over the world in recent times. People now have more access to mass media whose reach is getting wider due to technological advancement. The mass media are now not limited to urban population but have made inroads into small towns and villages. People now have more access to information and thus have become better and more informed and educated. However, despite the growth of media, its reach is largely limited to urban areas in India.

The Print Media, although a powerful means of communication cater only to audiences that are literate. There are about 20,000 newspapers and other printed matter produced in major metropolitan and big cities in the country but only a small fraction of reaches the rural masses.

The television network has also increased tremendously covering 80 percent of the, population. But again TV is out of reach of the majority of the rural masses. Only the few in the village have access to it. The new development in this direction have been the linking of satellites via cable to the TV at home. Again even if audiences in small towns and villages have access to these sophisticated media, the messages are lost on them because they are not area specific and lack local cultural flavour and relevance, which is very necessary for audience to identify with and understand.

Radio is one of the significant media of mass communication. Government owned All India Radio covers 80% of the area and 90% of the country's population. But again the broadcast receiving facilities are limited. There is also a vast imbalance between the availability of radio sets in rural and urban areas. Inspite of the imbalance, radio is the only medium which is said to be truly a mass medium in India because it is a low cost mobile means of communication.

Films has become a major medium of popular entertainment. But again film exhibition facilities in the country are limited. Most of the cinema houses are in the metropolitan cities and towns.

Real Effect

Our age is the age of mass communication and mass communication performs certain functions that are useful to us. Millions are exposed to a variety of messages each day. But the question is what is the extent and nature of its impact?

By and large mass communication messages are positive i.e., Pro-communal harmony, anti-drugs, anti-AIDS, anti-war, anti-terrorism, pro-national and so on. Infact, it has helped in promoting national integration and has created awareness among people about the socio-economic and political development of the country.

But the adverse effects of mass communication have also been felt and that to not so much from print media as from television and cable T.V. and overdose of T.V. is bad and gives ideas about a materialistic culture that doesn't exist.

A model is an abstracted representation of a reality. It only represents the reality of communication for better understanding of the communication process and is not a reality. Models are based on assumption that theorists make as to how communication functions and what effect it has upon individual and society.

Development of Models—The earlier models of communication were simple but inadequate. Aristotle constructed a model which had only-speaker-speech-audience-these three were elements, and the basic function of communication was to 'persuade the other party'.

By 1950s models became more elaborate and adequate. The universally applicable models of communication are those of Shannon and Weaver's.

Some Examples

Harold D. Lasswell's Model (1948)—Lasswell presented a strictly verbal model which takes the form of a question-

Who

Says what

In which channel

To Whom

With what effect?

Identification of source, analysis of message content, choice of channel, characteristics of audience and evaluation of effects

are the 5 components of communication process. It is the 'effect' that the model emphasizes the most change in one of these elements will lead to a change in the effect.

Claud Shannon and Warren Weaver's Model (1949)—They were the first to develop an engineering model of human communication based on telephone communication. In this model communication begins with an information source who creates the message, he transmits it by means of his vocal apparatus which acts as a transmitter, through the air as the channel with noise interference to the hearing mechanism of the person he is communicating with acting as the receiver which recreates the message so that another person, a receiver, can receive it.

Their model is important as it introduces the concept of 'Noise'. Noise refers to channel that may interfere with the signals transmitted and produce different signals.

Charles E. Osgood's Model (1954)—His model is different from the earlier attempts in the sense that it doesn't follow the conventional pattern of communication from source to channel to receiver.

He emphasized the point that each participant in the communication process sends as well as receives messages and as such encodes, decodes and interprets messages. This is particularly true in interpersonal communication.

Wilbur Schramm's Model (1971)—He adopted Shannon and Weaver's model and introduced two concepts of encoder, decoder, redundancy, feeback and noise into his model. He stressed the importance of feedback and noise, where feedback refers to response that a receiver makes to a source's communication.

According to him in a conversation between two people, one is constantly communication back to the other. The feedback obtained in such situation plays a very important role in the communication process as it tells the source how his messages are being received and interpreted. The 'Noise' may contaminate the message and make communication ineffective. In many instances a message is likely to suffer deterioration before it is decoded and interpreted by a receiver.

Wilbur further viewed the communication process as a complex one in the context of personal, social and cultural factors. Communication, according to him is a process of sharing of experience. The source can encode and the destination can decode only in terms of experience each has had; for e.g., if we have never learned German, we can neither encode nor decode in that language.

He further elaborated this model by bringing into focus the frames of reference of persons participating in the communication process. A (source) and B (destination) have the same kind of situation, have the same social resources and face similar constraints. If the destination decides that the message is interesting and promising enough, he selects some of it or all of it, interprets it according to his frame of reference and disposes it according to his needs, values, social imperatives and constraints.

George Gerbner's Model (1956)—In his model communication is seen as a transmission of messages. There are three stages in his model. The first stage is horizontal. It starts with an event E as perceived by M (Human being directly or through a Machin). M selects E according to his perception of the event. Thus, the process involves interaction and negotiation.

In the 2nd stage, which is vertical dimension, converts whatever we have perceived into a signal. This is called message. Here, it is also important to select the appropriate 'means'-the medium channel of communication.

The 3rd stage is again horizontal. Here the meaning of the message is not 'contained' in the message itself, but is the result of an interaction or negotiation between the receiver and the message.

Theodore M. Newcomb's Model (1953)—This model tries to explain the role of communication in a society or a social relationship. According to it, communication maintains equilibrium within the social system. This model assumes significance in the light of people's increasing need for information. Infact, in a democracy people need adequate information about their social environment so that they can identify their problems and share with their group, and know how to react.

Bruce H. Westley's & M.S. Maclean's Model (1957)—This model is an extension of Newcomb's model and specifically adapted for the mass media. It is based on the assumption that messages in mass communication pass through check points called 'gatekeeper' before they are actually received by audience. They decide on which messages are to be transmitted and how their content are to be modified. Thus, the audience's exposure to an event's reality is in the gatekeeper's hands.

But this model also has a drawback and that is that it applies only to mass media and fails to take account of the relationship between the mass media and the other systems through which we fit into society like family, work, friendships, school, trade unions etc.

Every communication order is ultimately conditioned or influenced by the political system and cultural milieu and the ends and purposes for which it is to be used. What could India's freedom mean to the concept of mass communication? What could be the type of new orientation for individual media, their functional roles and dimensions, their goals and priorities?

With the dawn of freedom, the Indian media were delinked from the apron-strings of British political and cultural imperialism. As part of the sovereign national system, they could now be used to serve the people and the nation according to new visions and national goals, policies and targets set by the new architects of the nation, the media managers and experts.

However, when the Britishers left, India was emaciated by the Partition and was left at the lowest level, politically, economically, socially and communication wise. There were yawning gaps in the communication infrastructure. India's tryst with its new density was therefore very uncertain.

Politically, the Constitution of India, enforced on 26 January 1950, the first Republic Day, had granted to every citizen and media the freedom of speech and expression and to every adult the right to vote and elect legislators. The establishment of a representative system of government, gave the right to every citizen to be informed, that is to have reasonable access to social, political, aesthetic, normal and other ideas and information vital for the grooming of enlightened voters and inculcation of democratic citizenship. It also implied the right to reasonable access to competitive sources of information and media. These rights which flowed out of democratic citizenship enjoined new obligations on the communication media and government to inform and educate the citizens and children of the country and at the same time stimulate awareness about fundamental and other civic and social duties. It was generally agreed that mass media of communication would have a key role in the building of our democratic polity and illumination of our social fabric.

With the beginning of the era of planned development since 1950-51, another role of the media of mass communication came to the forefront. It would provide communication support to the plans and inform people about the philosophy and objectives of plans, about the targets and benefits accruing to them as also about their responsibilities involved in the planned efforts. The other demand on communicators was to enthuse and involve people by removing ignorance and superstitions, by changing their negative attitudes and motivating them into purposeful action, all through persuasive and two-way communication. The dimension of their task was underlined by the Study Team on Mass communication sponsored by Ford Foundation, which observed that "India's development task is so great and her population so large that only by the most efficient possible programme of public information necessarily emphasising mass communication can communicators hope to reach people often enough and effectively enough to activate, on the needed scale, discussion process and subsequent action in the cities, towns and villages." In this context, the Vidyalankar Committee stated that the principal aim of publicity or communication was to prepare the minds of the people to meet the challenges of these new problems.

On the basis of studies on development and communication done in India, UNESCO and various developing countries, as also on the basis of field-based experience and communication and promotional research studies and surveys, a new professional thinking on the concept, role and process of relevant communication gradually emerged. Broadly speaking, the purpose of communication came to be understood as (1) politically to create, inform and enlighten public opinion, the basis of a democratic developing society to create awareness among individuals as also about their fundamental duties and obligations to promote scientific temper and national cohesion in society and inculcate the spirit of cooperative partnership among all sections of people, and to foster the establishment of feedback loops and research methodologies to assess public opinion and interpret it; (2) economically, to act as an activist in the extension of technology transfer among various sections of farmers, workers and other members of the working force, to provide a supporting pad to efforts at modernization and economic growth, afford market and tourist information and to stimulate advertising and promotional campaigns; and (3) culturally to foster individual and community expression, discovery, enrichment, creativity and enlightened reaction.

This type of purposeful and dynamic communication system couldn't grow out of the mass media-oriented Western concepts, models and theories, which were not very relevant to rural areas in India or any other developing country. It had to be evolved out of a process of trial and error, experimentation and deliberation. Conceptually it had to be envisaged and shaped by professional committees or bodies especially to be set up for the purpose and reinforced by the directions and guidelines of intentional, regional, national and local seminars, conferences or memorial lectures.

Such a system could not grow it was sustained and nurtured by the committee, trained and socially and professionally oriented practitioners and their managers as also by a competent research base. But above all, none of these things would happen unless the efforts in this direction get the policy backing and financial and administrative support of the government and proper appreciation and cooperation of the media and their organisations and the people.

General View

After Independence, challenges and experimental opportunities came in quick succession. Rehabilitation of refugees, the problem of integrating the recognised states, the Kashmir issue, green revolution, communal disturbances, strikes, inflation, abject poverty, colossal unemployment, malpractices in the public distribution system, corruption, shortage of essential commodities and housing facilities, wars, local and general elections, student unrest, gheraos, walkouts and many more problems constituted serious challenges. Fortunately, policy support and communication aid sanctions flowed from the dynamic and supporting leadership of the various Indian Prime Minister's and their governments. New dimensions of importance were given by these personalities. As a supporting measure professional introspection, trend setting and guidelines came from the various mass communication and professional bodies and media commissions and committees set up by the government from time to time. Eminent among the bodies which left their impress on the communication scene of India included the first Press commission, UNESCO sponsored Evaluation Study Team on TV, the Study Team on Mass Communication sponsored by the Ford Foundation, the Vidyalankar Committee for the Study of Five Year Plan Publicity, the Chanda Committee on Broadcasting and Information Media. All these bodies were set up or functioned in the sixties and seventies. The Verghese Committee on Autonomy for Akashvani and Doordarshan, the Kuldip Nayar Committee on News Agencies, the second Press Commission, Satellite Instructional Television Experiment evaluation teams and the

Joshi Panel on TV Software deliberated and submitted professional guidance emerged from the numerous UNESCO or international, regional and national communication and media seminars, conferences and evaluation and promotional surveys and reports undertaken by various research teams.

Political View

A look into the visions and dynamic and supporting leadership of the various Indian Prime Ministers and their governments would reveal that without them many Indian communication systems and patterns or strategies of mass communication would have remained still-born. In fact, the individual trend and directional setting in the communication process by each Prime Minister has been pronouncedly significant. For instance, Pandit Jawaharlal Nehru, India's first Prime Minister, sought to make mass communication a process of dialogue more than a merely to and fro communication, and certainly more than downward communication. A builder of modern India, he was also a builder of the communication system and media in our country. His package contribution was the laying of the foundation, securing extension a modernization of media, introducing professionalism, tempering of media freedom with social responsibility and giving a rural and research orientation. The second Prime Minister, Lal Bahadur Shastri, reinforced Pandit Nehru's directional and managerial model by adding a focus on professional integrity and dedicated service. The third Prime Minister, Indira Gandhi and her government have provided a thrust for sophisticated multi-media technology. Blending and balancing with the resurgent indigenous technology, it aimed to ultimately strengthen and streamline the entire communication network to make it more rural service worthy, elastic and effective enough to offer services of international standard to prestigious international meets in India as also to provide communication support to the implementation of the 20-point programme. The new technology helped in rearing the confidence building-role of the electronic media which operate in the public sector. Smt. Gandhi's government also recognised the importance of a free press but insisted on its responsible functioning and observance of a code of ethics in the discharge of its professional and social responsibilities. There was a focus on the need of the Indian media and practitioners to play a leading role in the New World Information and Communication Order to seek a balanced and two-way flow of information in the world, so as to contribute to the maximum extent possible to the South to South cooperative communication efforts and programmes. There was an emphasis on using media for national unity and integration. Liberalisation of the import policy for facilitating media machinery and material for faster mechanisation of the media units, ensued while offering encouragement to communication research and training and media development programmes. The fourth Prime Minister, Morarji Desai and his government sought to emphasise on autonomy of media, including that of Akashvani and Doordarshan, austerity and professional integrity. The fifth Prime Minister, Choudhary Charan Singh and his government, during his short tenure, endeavoured to bend the functioning of the media primarily for the benefit of rural areas and agriculturists. The seventh and the present Prime Minister and his government are additionally focusing on the application of computer and other modern technologies and are emphasising on open university educational aspect of mass media and better professionalism and programming.

There is a consensus of media experts, however, that the real architects of India's present modernised, multimedia, integrated, development oriented system of communication were Pandit Nehru and Indira Gandhi—as a matter of coincidence father and daughter. If India has entered the satellite, electronic and modern visual communication age, it is primarily for the vision and dynamic leadership of these two Prime Ministers. If our country has developed and revitalized traditional and other indigenous media, and made them in conjunction with modern mass media as instruments of innovative and development communication, specially in the areas of family welfare, health, agricultural extension and eradication of illiteracy, the credit for this too goes primarily to the incisiveness and initiative of these two leaders and their governments.

Apart from bequests of national leaders, there are existent visible and invisible contributions of several other professional and individual entrepreneurs, exponents, trainers and researchers who have helped individually and co-operatively in making our communication system what it is.

Modern View

Since Independence, the concept of mass communication in India has been transformed. From the Western theories-based hypotheses it has now become most flexible, relevant and development-oriented. Now, a participatory type has been envisaged by the 7th Plan for a decentralised form of planning system at the district level. Four stages have marked this transition in our country:

(1) communication considered as a process of transmitting information, ideas, thoughts, feelings and attitudes to large anonymous audiences with an accompanying hypodermic model of who says what in which channel to whom with what effect;

(2) a distinction being made between informational communication and persuasive communication seeking to influence the behaviour or attitudes of the respondents;

(3) focus in media strategies shifting from mass media to media mix or relevant communication technologies. Experience and research revealing that with literacy, financial and technical problems rampant in a country, there could be very little success by adòpting only big media strategies. Attention thus started being fixed on low cost small media such as low powered radios and indigenous or folk form of channels as well;

(4) communication being accepted as a multi-disciplinary science or a distinct discipline supported by its own hypotheses, systematic knowledge, research methodologies and trend and case studies.

This nebulous concept of positive, multi-lateral promotional communication of participatory type came to be known by different names, such as development communication, development support; communication, integrated rural communication, participatory communication and the like. The philosophy behind these themes was to provide a meaningful system in developing countries to harmonise development and communication efforts aimed at giving the rural and urban people a better deal. While the relationship between the two was accepted by all, the issue of cause and effect has remained still unresolved. In other words, which is the mover and which is the moved, remains a chicken and egg question. Whatever the perception, both development and communication are now considered engaged in a reactory system, one helping the other, complementing and supplementing each other in the process of fostering balanced growth and progress. If people have access to mass media, and the messages are segmented and relevant, even rural people with low literacy rates and per capita incomes can be sensitised, motivated and changed.

Being considered different from terms like advertising, public relations, propaganda, agriculture extension, rural communication, promotion, marketing communication and even the Western concept of mass media-oriented communication, the term 'development communication', in the Third World countries has acquired a more positive and pragmatic role and result-oriented connotation. As explained by Nora Quebral of Indonesia, this brand of communication implies "the art and science of human communication applied to the speedy transformation of a country and the mass of its people from poverty to a dynamic state of economic growth that makes possible greater social equality and the larger fulfilment of human potential." This development support concept of mass communication is thus dynamic, purposive, practical and promotional in approach and nature. It is a new hope for development and social change in the Third World. Though not a panacea for all ills, it is one of the vital components in any development planning and implementation. This science and art of communication views an individual, a society or a nation in its totality, transcending thereby from a piecemeal or a segmented view of rural or urban society, economic and human development. In our country development communication combines in it the philosophy of humanism of Pandit Nehru, intending to achieve a better, richer and fuller way of life, along with the growth and development of the country as a whole. Another strand of the concept which is typically Indian is that development communication should grow mostly out of people's participation and people's satisfaction, the essential ingredients of which are:

(a) a sense of feeling to have actively participated;

(b) a sense of pride in evolving co-operative solutions to the problem in hand;

(c) a sense of achievement, reflected in the concrete betterment of poorer sections of the people and of backward areas.

Research studies based on Western models ascribe to mass communication different roles in development, varying from nil to the enthusiastic, from a cautious to a pragmatic position. Lloyd Sommerlad a UNESCO expert projected a balanced and pragmatic picture about the role which communication can play in national development. In his view "communication is an important element in the matrix of influences which lead to innovation and modernisation of a society. If used constructively, the media can help create an environment favourable for change and development. They can enlarge horizons, bring information about the experience of others, raise aspirations and help to provide the motivation for improved practices and social conditions. They are part of the process of teaching new and better ways of working and living. The extent to which communication, both interpersonal and mediated, contributes to development depends on the policies and strategies adopted and the skill with which the tools are used. Essential will be the planned use of extension services and the media, co-ordination of the parallel channels of communications, co-operation between various government and private agencies involved in the development; a programme appropriate to the cultural background and provision of participation, feedback and a multilateral flow of information."

The communication revolution in India is experiencing the confluence of three stages of technological growth: wire, wireless and integrated. True to its tradition of assimilation of foreign and indigenous elements, India is pressing into service the earlier and modern media and using high cost and low cost communication technologies. Her Song and Drama Division, Field Publicity units and extension agencies, padyatras, folk media and human activist system on the one hand and satellite, colour TV, video, cassette, computer, electronic and digital technologies used in press communications and telecommunications on the other indicate the balance the country holds so as to meet the needs of her mammoth, multi-media mass communication exercises, movements and campaigns. Some of the innovative multi-media programmes involved in the green and white revolutions in the northern states, TV coverage during the course of SITE, Kheda, on-going SITE and INSAT—IB experiments and the 9th Asiad, 7th Non-aligned and recent Commonwealth Summit and Namedia meets are pointers to the evolution of the spirit and urge for innovation and experimentation. Similar trends were visible in the video technology based experiment for intercommunity communication near Delhi, the Farms School programme of All India Radio and the newspaper communication support for Chattera Village initiated by the Hindustan Times, a Delhi English daily.

Apart from these illustrations, the government sector publicity media units provide more robust and wider display of media mix. For instance, outside publicity done through Field Publicity units undertake a variety of publicity programmes like film shows, group discussions, talks, seminars, song and drama programmes and photo displays. These pertain to major national themes like national integration adult education, child welfare, family welfare, agriculture and agro-based small-scale industries. Similar programmes are also organised to make people aware of social evils like untouchability and drinking. The Song and Drama units utilise live entertainment media to make the masses aware of the various national programmes and objectives. It has a wide range of stage forms like puppet shows, plays, dances, dramas, ballads, harikathas and sound and light shows.

The mix used by the Directorate of Advertising and Visual Publicity is a visual package. It comprises press advertisements, illustrated printed material like posters, folders, leaflets, cinema slides, metallic tablets, radio and television spots and photographic exhibitions.

Another set of print medium mix for mass circulation is brought out by the Publications Division of the Ministry of Information and Broadcasting comprising books, pamphlets and journals in Hindi, English and other Indian languages on a wide range of subjects including art and culture, history and tradition, political evolution, democratic process, economic development and social resurgence.

Thus we see that whether it is the sphere of agriculture, family planning or government publicity India has been pursuing the policy of appropriate mix of media and technologies. This has entailed the use of face to face, group, written, printed, visual, folk, computerized electronic, outdoor or even a mix of them. The approach has been multi-media and cross-disciplinary, goal and result oriented. Centralisation in core programmes have been successful in so far as it has sought to stimulate unity in basic plan programmes or achieving integration in national cultural programmes, but it has equally underlined the importance that at grassroots level the development programmes should be localised and area specific and implemented as far as possible by the involvement of local people, but you need to support decentralisation which has inherent value, by an integrating system. Here the challenge to media practitioners and managers is in finding ways of making satellite and other big media an integrating force, at the same time making them help to knit together several decentralised activities at the grassroots level.

The family planning communication package is an example. It envisages an all out effort at dovetailing of population education in the formal educational system as also in the non-formal training programmes of functionaries of development departments. It has centralised programmes integrated with decentralised activities. Its media package is wide complexioned and involves a still more dynamic package comprising radio, TV, colour films in 16 mm film strips, cinema slides, exhibitions, tape recorders, newspapers, magazines, posters, folders, brochures, leaflets, hoardings, wall paintings, bus boards, match box labels, dramas, puppet shows and other local folk art media. Its symbols and slogans are splashed all over, from mud walls in villages to telephone and telegraph poles in cities, reminding people that family planning is an intrinsic part of the environmental scene and an aid to family welfare.

Alongwith discovering new media mixes, strategy of field publicity or extension is also changing. The necessity of people's involvement and obtaining their feedback is calling for modification in the strategies known by various names as area approach, pooling plans or district-level decentralised plans.

India has made use of another multi-dimensional, multimedia and demonstrational audio-visual aid called exhibition. In size, stature and character it varies from stationary to mobile or even exhibition on wheels; from simple village exhibitions, trade fairs and a seasonal market to very big, modernly designed multi-levelled complexes, known as national and international exhibitions or world trade fairs. These exhibitions use a package of communication media ranging from spoken word, exhibits or visuals to video, TV, films, radio, projectile aids, traditional media, promotional literature, outdoor publicity aids, balloons, neon light and sky splashed advertisements. Cumulatively these exhibitions draw large crowds and their impact differ from creating awareness and publicity to more dramatic results in terms of transfer of technology and sale of goods and machinery. Policies and programmes of government are also publicised through photographic exhibitions. Art exhibitions and gallaries promote education about art forms of various kinds.

Whatever form that these innovatory types of communication strategies may take-person-to-person or group, written, printed, visual, folk or electronic, indoor or outdoor, hot or cold, or even a mix of them-the basic feature is that these programmes are goal oriented, research fed, professionally planned and executed and assessed. They are pragmatic and multi-media and disciplinary in approach. They are fairly sensitive and alive to criticism and suggestions and in a sense quite responsive and flexible.

The dimensions of integrated communication system which are found relevant to rural India warrant closer relationship between the administrative and communication agencies; credible and knowledgeable sources; segmentation of messages for different audiences; linkage of information to the felt needs of the people; and projection of timely usable, solution-oriented and people-beneficiary messages. The other requisite preconditions of a successful system of communication are management decentralisation for effective participation of people and the inculcation of the philosophy of empathy among the media practitioners and managers and policy makers.

Despite a large measure of success in mass communication, one big lesson that emerges out of the Indian scene of communication is that we must continuously rediscover the goals and dimensions of mass communication and its media. To this end, our communication system, our postulates, our media's role and their functions need to be periodically or as a part of inbuilt research, assessed, modified or revamped. This would help us realise our cherished dreams of a sunny future without being swept off our feet or alienating us from our fundamental values. Here the application of feedback research is significant. So is the contribution of a professionally and media-oriented and socially activising training system, which can strengthen the country's capacity for attracting to the communication, advertising and public relations professions, man of vision, integrity, independent judgement and professional aptitude. This would help equip them with media climated and field based knowledge and skill to serve our society.

3

Career in Journalism

A professional journalist is easily identified: he is on the payroll of a journal; he reports for his paper, or he may write features or editorials or edit copy. He is known by different names: Reporter, Feature Writer, Special Correspondent, Sub-Editor, Assistant Editor, Sports Editor, City Editor, Commercial Editor, News Editor etc.

The range of work he does is as wide as the world around him. He may report on crime, law and order, political developments, the courts, the Executive, the Legislature, people, fashions, art, music, drama, literature indeed, whatever makes news.

A journalist does more than that he edits what others write, he comments and criticizes and he puts together the news.

Primarily, it is a profession for the man trained to do the particular job in the complex business of bringing out a journal. It is definitely not for amateurs.

Time was when it used to be said that a journalist is born, not made, that you could not push a man through a journalism school and he would emerge at the other end a journalist. Mahatma

Gandhi never saw the inside of a journalism school. Neither did Bal Gangadhar Tilak. Nor did a score of distinguished editors since James August and Hicky brought out the first full-fledged printed newspaper in India, *The Bengal Gazette* on 29 January 1780. Yet, they were men who brought much honour to the profession.

But those were different times. It was sufficient, then, for any one with a sense of mission, to declare himself a journalist, buy or hire a printing press and bring out a journal. Today, however, things are quite different, more complicated. And while, no doubt, some are born journalists, they would be even better if they attended a course in journalism.

This fact, indeed, was recognized as early as in 1920 by none other than Dr. Annie Besant, founder of the National University at Adyar, Madras. The University was launched under the auspices of the Theosophical Society and its first chancellor was Rabindranath Tagore. Dr. Besant was the Pro-Chancellor and Sir C. P. Ramaswamy Iyer, Vice-Chancellor. The University had courses in arts, science and commerce and the subject of journalism was added to the Arts Faculty and was part of the English Department. Dr. James H. Cousins was the Head of the Department of English and Journalism. The subjects taught were: History of journalism, press laws, editorial practice and newspaper administration. Though the Degree Course was closed down at the end of five years it is interesting to note that the importance of adequate training had been recognised as long ago as 1920 and that among the first teachers of journalism were such men of note as N. S. Rama Rao, C. S. Trilokekar, Yadunath Sarkar, and Seshagiri Rao.

We may, therefore, concede for the moment that to be a good journalist it is important to receive adequate and obviously the right kind of training. But-and here we may enter a caveat-not everyone who aspires to be a journalist necessarily becomes one merely by receiving a diploma. Which makes us turn to the next question: What makes a journalist?

There are as many answers to the question as there are leaders of journalism.

"Vitality" according to James Reston of the *New York Times.*

"Hustling" according to Paul Miller of the Gannett group of newspapers in the United States.

"Ferreting out the truth" according to another distinguished editor, Herbert Brucker.

Of course, a journalist should be fun of energy, must be able to get at the truth, if necessary by hustling, but these are partial answers. More things go into the making of a journalist than mere energy or the drive to do a job. Yet, there is much sense in what Mr. Reston once said in a talk to the Columbia School of Journalism: I am a strong advocate of education and specialized training for newspapermen. Yet on the Washington staff of the *New York Times* we have men with multiple degrees from universities.and other men who did not complete their higher education for-one reason or other... Both do well. In going over their records, I am struck by the fact that all of them have this one great quality-vitality, drive, aliveness-call it what you will.

It occurs to me, therefore, that the most thorough education and the finest training in some speciality are of no avail to make a newspaper man outstanding unless he also had the necessary vitality to get on with the job.

S. Sadanand, founder editor of the *Free Press Journal* fits Reston's description to a T. Sadanand never went to college and yet-all those who knew him would concede that he was a great journallst. He was a man of tremendous vitality and what Reston called "aliveness" and "drive". And what he was, he sought in others. The point about such a man is that, while he may not have come to his profession with a university degree, he would have enough-energy and initiative to provide himself with the kind of education needed to be a good-and successful-journalist. In the old days men with the necessary drive got themselves jobs as journalists and educated themselves as they went along. They were largely self-taught men. Today, however, with competition being what it is for the few openings available to aspiring men and women, the wise among them would acquire the necessary preeducation before applying for a post.

The student of journalism must have, to start with, a good degree whether it be in the arts, sciences or commerce. This presumes that he can write grammatically and is familiar with the structure of a sentence. It is advisable that a student who had graduated in a non-English medium take a special course in English to get the utmost benefit from studies in jonrnalism imparted in that language.

This does not mean that a student not proficient in English cannot benefit from a course in journalism. The essentials of journalism hold good whether the future journalist works for an English or an Indian-language newspaper. Accuracy, honesty and sensitivity to news are universal assets. In the absence of journalism courses in the Indian languages there is only one way in which an aspirant can learn his trade: by attending courses in the English language.

What is essential is that whichever be the language in which the journalist intends to pursue his calling he be well versed in it. Journalists deal in facts; but facts are expressed in words, whether they are in English, Hindi, Marathi, Malayalam or Tamil. A journalist who is not proficient in the language of his choice cannot possibly hope to make an impact on his readers.

This leads to the issue of proficiency not just in one language, but several. The more languages one knows, the more one's chances of landing a job, especially these days when states vie with one another to conduct their business in the regional languages. Even in the thirties, forties and fifties, the reporter who understood and was conversant with Hindi, Urdu, Gujarati and Marathi, not to speak of Telugu and Tamil had a head start over others, especially while covering All India Congress Committee meetings. What was true of past years is even more true today.

As an addendum it may be stated that the journalist who is conversant with a foreign language such as French, German, Russian or Arabic stands a better chance of being selected for posts abroad than one who knows only English. Is journalism a business, profession, craft or trade? It is fashionable to say that journalism is a profession like law or medicine or engineering. A profession it is, but, at the same time, it is a craft that has to be learnt. And woe to the publisher journalist who is ignorant of the principles of business management. Sadanand was a great journalist but a poor business manager and, in the end, was a sad failure. He would' have been a better journalist if he was a better business manager.

Successful journalism is not necessarily good journalism but good journalism needs to be successful journalism as well. The primary purpose of a journalist is to communicate and a journal that does not sell is a journal that fails of its primary purpose. To say, therefore, that journalism is a lofty profession and not a trade or a craft is a bit of snobbery that one can usefully do without.

Good writing is taught not only because excellence by itself is a desirable asset but also because it sells. And a sub-editor who is sound lay-out man is worth his weight in gold. To say that making a lay-out is a profession and not an art is not to understand the meaning of words. Journalism no doubt is a profession, but a journalist who limits himself to his profession is more likely to find that he has that most unenviable of talent un saleable Knowledge. The history of journalism is littered with the lives of men whose snobbery would not permit them to see themselves as businessmen and traders as well.

A professional is a man who has had training in his particular field. An individual is not allowed to practice medicine unless he is certified by a duly recognized medical school. Lawyers, chartered accountants and in some countries even barbers and "beauticians" have to acquire a certificate that recognizes their competence. It would be in the fitness of things, therefore, if news papermen too acquire adequate recognition of their professional talent from their competeters. However, in the absence of institutional recognition a journalist in India acquires professional respectability by the very fact of being on a journal's payroll. The belief, obviously, is that if a person is on the payroll he must be-competent.

In the circumstances the only way to distinguish a professional from the amateur is to find out whether the person is actively employed on a full-time basis by a newspaper or journal. If he is, he literally qualifies himself to be known as a professional. The free-lance journalist-one who is not regularly employed but is a frequent contributor-is just that a free-lance journalist.

The Random House Dictionary of the English language defines a free-lance as a person who works as a writer, designer, performer etc., but not on a *regular* salary basis for anyone employer, organization or the like. The description or definition obviously stems from the fact that in the middle ages, military adventurers,.often of knightly rank, offered their mercenary services to who ever paid them best. Their lances were, so to speak, available to the highest bidder.

The term is now applicable to writers, designers and all who sell their work to whoever offers them the best terms. They may be amateurs or professionals who have retired but whose work is deemed worthy of acceptance. Among the best-known free-lancers, surely, is Ruskin Bond, the short-story writer who contributes widely and is considered a success.

Free-lancing, however, is not an easy way to make a living, especially in India where magazines and journals are not known to be good paymasters. The free-lance writer with demonstrated ability to produce acceptable work, of course may eventually hope to reach the status of a contract writer, assured of a regular in come. Such a status assumes that the writer is on contract to write a set series of articles for editors. Should a writer be commissioned to do a piece, the editor would be morally bound to accept it, unless it is downright hopeless. An editor, however, is not bound to print the piece though he is bound to pay for it. Frequently editors accept articles "for possible use" or lay down their own conditions beforehand that give them freedom to reject a commissioned article.

Free-lancing for a beginner is a precarious way to make a living. A person willing to free-lance must either be willing to live on a subsistence level or have sufficient financial means to stay alive without having to depend on income from writing. Many free lancers have regular jobs that guarantee them their bread and butter Jagjit Singh, the distinguished science writer, was a railway administrator.

Few writers can expect to launch a successful full-time career in free-lancing until they are thoroughly competent and *well-known*. Too often competence is not enough; they must be recognised as competent. The recognition factor, in the case of free-lancers is just as important as the competence factor. A. G. Noorani, the lawyer is frequently commissioned to write in-depth articles from as varied a lot as *The Illustrated Weekly of India* or *Sunday* because he is a regular writer for the *Indian Express*. N. J. Nanporia is, similarly, a frequent contributor to various magazines on the strength not only of his unquestioned competence but because he is recognised as an authority on international affairs.

Another free-lance writer of repute is Chanchal Sarkar who is a Director of the International Press Institute. *Science Today* has an entire stable of free-lance writers who write knowledgeably on science subjects.

Unless he is very well known, a free-lancer is wise to specialize in a field where he has little or no competition. Noorani is a lawyer who can write competently on law-he has few competitors in his particular field. Many astrologers in India make a respectable earning by turning out astrology columns which are invariably popular. A free-lancer who is in great demand rapidly acquires status. Requests have gone to them from editors to produce quick copy when regular staff members are fully engaged or are not adjudged sufficiently competent to contribute on special subjects. On the roster of the *Illustrated Weekly of India's* contributors are such distinguished names as K. P. S. Menon, C. N. Vakil or Nikhil Chakravarthy.

There is one note of warning to the young man or woman who wants to be a journalist. You will not from your first week in office be writing stories which make politicians humble and governments shake. It will be a long time before you get a by-line. The only way up is hard work and merit will first have to be proved. Because you write good essays in school is no guarantee that you will make a good journalist.

Journalism, as Profession

The career of a journalist is very interesting and full of vast opportunities. It is gaining much importance and prestige in the modern society. With the manifold increase in the circulation of newspapers and magazines as well as start of newspapers and journals, there is a great scope for the young men and women who want to join the profession of journalism.

There are hundreds of openings each year for the new entrants. The increase in the circulation of newspapers has created the need for the addition of more staff, both for the larger and the smaller newspapers. The proliferation of magazines and periodicals has also led to the proliferation of jobs in the field of journalism. There is no doubt that an ambitious man or woman possessing the necessary qualifications, can find a suitable opening in the newspaper media.

The career of a journalist demands a wide range of qualities and skilis. There is no doubt that this career is highly rewarding, but a journalist has to work very hard for this. He has to know something of everything. The person who wants to reach the top has to master the techniques of journalism and go through the mill. He should also possess a flair for writing, sound judgement, personal integrity, yearning for facts and an expert knowledge of all branches of journalism.

The men or women who work for newspapers, come from many backgrounds and are of many temperaments. Those in the editorial departments, need a strong sense of curiosity about their fellow-beings and a sympathy for them. The other qualifications include a good command of English (or any other language in which the paper is printed), an interest in politics and the government, a desire to know why things happen, a high respect for accuracy and an aptitude for personal communication with other people in order to obtain news from them. A reporter must be both a willing listener and an alert poser of questions.

Now-a-days newspapers generally seek employees for all editorial and journalistic jobs, who have had at least some college education. Many editors insist upon a graduation degree as the minimum educational requirement for all reporters they hire. The diploma in journalism is desirable, but is not absolutely essential. Nevertheless, an applicant who is well trained in liberal arts, with emphasis on English (or the language of the newspaper) and political science, is welcome in most newspapers. Some of those who join this career can also specialise in a particular branch of journalism like news reporting, editorial work, photography, feature writing, sports, writing for T.V. or Radio, criticism, magazine writing etc.

In fact, there are two main divisions of newsroom work, reporting and desk-work. Reporting includes gathering and writing news and feature stories. Desk-work includes the selection and preparation for printing of the written material and photographs submitted by the reporters, photographers and the news agencies. The men who do the desk-work are called the editors.

Sense of Power

Some men and women find their greatest satisfaction in being reporters all their lives probing for information, being close to events as they happen and mingling with the people who make news. Few laymen have any concept of the inside workers of a newspaper who really put the paper together. In fact, even the desk experience is quite necessary for the top jobs. Similarly, few desk men are successful unless they have had a thorough grounding in reporting. Only in this way they can know the problems—a reporter faces on a story and can give him useful suggestions.

A beginner can start as a city hall beat reporter for small daily, he may also start as the telegraph editor handling the news wire and writing headlines. If he chooses the reporting path and sticks to reporting, then he may graduate eventually to a metropolitan reporting staff. If he selects the editing path, he may advance to a large paper copy desk. Or, in either capacity, he may remain with the small daily and soon rise to the editorial management status.

Some persons prefer to become specialists and do their reporting in one specific field itself. The women's page of a modern daily offers many opportunities for stimulating writing; the sports page has also been a great attraction for young reporters. Business news is also a speciality of many papers. Some big papers also offer oportunities to critical reviewers of film, television, the drama and books. There are also many opportunities to specialise in one of the broader general news areas; politics, science, labour, religion, urban problems, social work and public help. Although news reporting is the most glamourous and best publicised part of newspaper work, there are many other opportunities available for young men and women on the editorial page, advertising and sales, copy-writing, circulation, photograph, promotion, public relations etc. in a newspaper.

Many youngmen and women join certain small newspapers or magazines even to do the subordinate or secretarial work. After obtaining a foothold in the newspaper work they rise up to high posts due to their merits and qualifications, because after working in the offices of these newspapers or magazines they acquire a lot of practical experience in the field of journalism. Some persons, while working in subordinate positions, increase their educational and professional qualifications by attending part time evening courses or through correspondence courses.

Although academic or professional education is not an essential requirement for a successful career in journalism, yet some academic qualification is desirable as a minimum so that a person can write correctly and fluently. Possession of a university degree may be quite advisable for those who want to achieve rapid progress in the field of journalism or who want to reach the top jobs. Some newspapers also demand a minimum qualification of B.A.. degree or its equivalent for the new entrants.

Practical Aspects

A young man or woman who possesses the minimum educational qualification and the aptitude for journalistic-work should apply for a job to some newspaper or magazine office. If a person has already done some writing work, it will be considered as an additional qualification. There is no doubt that a brilliant person possessing a good educational qualification and an aptitude for writing work, will not find much difficulty in securing a position or job in some newspaper or magazine office. Some newspapers may also offer the post of a trainee or a junior reporter in the beginning for six months or one year. If you want to join this profession, you may accept even this offer. To start with the salary offered may not be very high, but as a person gathers experience and proficiency in writing, he will be able to obtain rapid promotions and a good salary due to his ability and hard work.

Demands of Profession

A successful journalist has to know something of everything and in a way everything of something. He should have some knowledge of law, religion, war, science, business, politics, economics etc. He should also be interested in philosophy, music, painting and other cultural activities. In fact, a journalist should have a vast general knowledge, because the more the general knowledge he possesses, the better equipped he will be for the journalistic work.

A journalist should be a voracious reader of newspapers, journals, periodicals etc. In fact there is no end to the knowledge and as far as the knowledge of a journalist is concerned, sky is the limit. Therefore, he should try to learn every new thing which comes in his way. He should have a very strong desire for learning new subjects and new things to increase his knowledge. Only then he can go far in this profession.

Farsightedness and Resourcefulness : A person who wants to become a successful journalist must be far-sighted and resourceful. He will also learn a lot by experience. But he should try to develop the qualities of tact, diplomacy and remaining alert all the time from the very beginning. He should also possess the quality of perseverance which will help him greatly in achieving success in his career. He should be mentally prepared to work for long hours and do hard and tedious work.

A person who wants to join the profession of journalism should also have a sound body. A good health is very necessary, for a person who gets tired after a little extra exertion or suffers from headaches and bodyaches, very often may not be able to remain long in this profession, because a journalist has to undergo the strain of long hours of arduous work. Thus, a journalist must have a sound mind and a sound body.

In this profession, he may have to travel a lot, in the city, in the interior areas and may be in different parts of his country. Sometimes, he may also have to travel to foreign lands as a foreign reporter to perform his journalistic assignments. He should be mentally and physically prepared for all this, because when one leaves one's home and goes to a foreign land, one becomes highly homesick. He may also have to travel day and night in strange places to meet all sorts of people. Sometimes, a journalist may be given a courteous welcome, whereas at other times he may have to face harsh treatment.

While covering the war news, a journalist may have to endanger his life for the sake of his profession. A person who wants to enter the profession of a journalist should have a lot of guts and courage. He should be bold and courageous in the moment of a crisis, especially when covering riots, communal disturbances, workers demonstrations etc. He may also have to be present at the scene of a lathi charge, police firing, or teargas. He should have the stamina to undergo all these physical strains, stresses and risks. Like a soldier, he cannot back out from such dangerous situations involving physical risks, once he has been assigned the duty to cover such events. Many a time you must have read in the newspapers how journalists have to suffer injuries while discharging their duties. They even lose their lives while covering a battle, a communal riot or some police firing.

There is a lot of competition in the profession of a journalist and the newcomer has to work hard especially in the first few years to learn the basic things of his profession. The life of a journalist has many compensations like high rewards—when a person has established himself as a famous journalist and writer—incessant change, a career full of adventure, meeting very important persons like big businessmen, famous industrialists, ministers, Prime Ministers, Kings, Presidents and other very important persons. A journalist goes everywhere and sees both the good and bad things of life behind the scenes, but his life is not a bed of roses. On the other hand, it is full of constant struggle, because a journalist works in a highly competitive profession where only the fittest and the ablest survive. An incapable and inefficient person cannot survive in this profession for a long time

Patience Required : A journalist may not earn a very handsome salary in the very beginning of his career. When he starts his career, he may even have to work as an apprentice or as a junior for a few years to learn the rudiments of his trade. During this period, he will have to content himself with an income which may not be very high. Of course, when he has proved his worth and knows his work thoroughly, he will have ample chances of progress and promotion in his career and earn a handsome salary.

As we have already seen, journalism is a very competitive profession. The progress and success of a journalist depends solely on his worth and merit. He may get many chances to rise in his career, but it depends upon him how he makes the most of these chances which come in his way. Once he has established himself as a good journalist, he will start earning a very comfortable and high salary according to his worth. The famous journalists in this profession draw higher salaries with many fringe benefits.

It is a profession where only the proficient and the best have a chance to reach the top. You can find many top journalists and editors of today who joined as juniors and learnt the art of journalism through their hard work. Even today, there are many chances for the brilliant youngmen and women who have the ambition to join this profession, provided they have a strong will power to undergo the hard life, especially in the beginning of their career. No doubt, once a new entrant establishes himself as a good journalist, then life becomes a smooth sailing for him to a great extent. Learning all the techniques of the profession of journalism by going through the mill is the only sure and certain road to success.

Practical Experience

Journalism like many other professions has also become quite organised now-a-days. In the foreign countries there are a large number of organisations and professional institutions which impart theoretical and practical training in journalism. In U.K. and U.S.A., there are very good arrangements for imparting training to those who want to join this profession

In India also many universities have started the course of journalism in their teaching curriculum. After completing this course the students are awarded the Diploma in Journalism. In the recent years, many professional institutions have also come into existence in India, which are running full time and part time evening courses in journalism. Some of these institutions are also running correspondence courses. These courses are becoming quite popular in our country.

In U.K. the training for journalism is organised by the National Council for the Training of the Journalists.

It was set up in 1952. The aims and purposes of the Council include the establishment of standards and qualifications for entry into journalism as well as the formation and administration of schemes for the training and education of journalists including press photographers. In 1956, an international centre for advanced training in journalism was also set up in Strasbourg under the auspices of UNESCO.

Although it can be said that there are certain men and women who are born journalists, yet in reality they are very few. Now-a-days all those desirous of joining this profession can be trained. If you read this booklet thoroughly, it will give you the basic knowledge regarding the profession of journalism. Of course, vast general knowledge, common sense, objectivity, logic, clear thinking and a flair for writing, are very important requirements for a successful journalist. These are the qualities which one must develop and acquire. Although methods and techniques of journalism media can be taught, yet it is necessary to have some practical experience.

Academic Background

There is no doubt that in the past there were no hard and fast rules regarding the educational or professional qualifications for a person who wanted to join the profession of journalism. In reality, journalism was an open profession for all. Anybody having the flair for writing and liking for this profession could join it, because ultimately his succeess depended upon his merit and capability. Even then, there were not many institutions in the past which imparted training in journalism.

In the opinion of certain authorities, journalism, like writing, should and will always remain an open profession for which no specific educational qualifications should be laid down. It is a fact that the famous writers of the world like Shakespeare and Rabindra Nath Tagore did not possess any university degree or for that matter any professional training in writing.

Similarly, many famous journalists and editors in the past did not possess very high educational or professional qualifications. Even some of the top journalists and editors of today neither possess very high educational qualifications nor any professional training. They have come to occupy the high positions in the journalistic profession due to their flair for writing and their hard work.

In fact, the two main qualifications of a journalist are that firstly he should be a good writer and secondly he, should have a 'nose for news'. Possession of academic educational qualifications like a B.A. or M.A. degree and professional training like a Diploma in Journalism are not a guarantee for a definite success in this profession. A university degree or a diploma in journalism may be desirable these days, but not absolutely necessary for achieving success in one's career.

However, some of the educational and other qualifications which a person who wants to join the profession of journalism should possess are mentioned below :

(i) A minimum basic educational qualification which may enable a person to express his ideas fluently in writing. Of course, now-a-days a minimum educational qualification of a B.A. degree is insisted upon by the management of most of the newspapers for the new entrants into the profession of journalism.

(ii) A Diploma in Journalism, which is desirable but not absolutely necessary. Some newspapers do insist on this qualification also.

(iii) Good knowledge of shorthand and typewriting.

(iv) A flair for writing.

(v) A good knowledge of grammar and the correct use of language.

(vi) An inquisitive mind and willingness to learn more and more concerning different fields of subjects.

(vii) A vast general knowledge about national and international affairs.

(viii) A person who wants to become a journalist should possess a vast vocabulary and love for learning new words, because the words are the tools with which he has to work.

(ix) Whatever may be your educational qualifications, if you are prepared to study hard, then there is no reason why you should not excel in the journalistic profession.

(x) You must develop the habit of reading, especially the important national and international newspapers and periodicals to increase your general knowledge.

(xi) You should try to possess some background knowledge of history, culture, civilization and other, interesting facts of life.

(xii) You should also try to pick up some of the basic knowledge of business, industry, commerce, banking etc. It will help you greatly in your profession.

(xiii) You must also have the curiosity to know about places, things and events happening around you. A knowledge of the political affairs of the country and the laws under which it is administered will also help you in your profession.

(xiv) You must possess the qualities of honesty, integrity and character. These are essential to win the faith of the people you come, across.

You should not be frightened by the long list of the qualifications mentioned above. Of course, the person who possesses all the above mentioned qualities, will be an ideal in any profession. Even if you possess the majority of the above qualities, the others you can develop by hard work and study. But you must have the basic qualifications like a minimum educational qualification, flair for writing accurately, spirit of learning and an aptitude for the profession of journalism.

There is no doubt that a young man or a woman who possesses a good educational qualification and a flair for writing, will not find it very difficult to become a good journalist, provided he has the liking for this profession. If you want to join this profession, start writing small articles or join some newspaper and try to learn the rudiments of this trade practically to become a successful journalist in due course of time. There is a lot of scope for the intelligent and hardworking young men and women in the field of journalism in our country.

4

Development and Growth

In India, Press has been closely associated with the freedom struggle. In the 19th century, the press fought for the freedom of information and the right to criticise. But in the early 20th century, the freedom struggle took a new turn and it was no longer petition-making. And thus, restrictions were imposed on it. The Hindu-Muslim disunity led to the division of the Indian Press into two categories-nationalist press and the Anglo-Indian Press. In all the national movement events-Jallainwala Bagh massacre, non-cooperation movement, Cripps mission, Quit India Movement the press was a direct participant. The nationalist press underwent the same kind of suffering as the freedom fighters.

Constant Change

Newspapers in India have undergone revolutionary changes. The number of publications has increased seven times and circulation by ten times as compared to that of 1950. In 1985 there were 3,000 publications, with a total circulation of over 26 million. Earlier, just 6 publications, namely The Time of India, Indian Express, Malayalam Manorama and Anand Bazar Patrika (dailies) and Malaya Manorama Mangalam and Kumudam (weeklies) have a combined circulation of five million, while 150 other publications have a total circulation of 25 million. The press is widely acknowledged as a watch-dog in a democratic country. Today the press is not merely informing, illuminating, investigating and exposing but even warning and biting, particularly when acting in the public's interest.

Effects of the Press—Newspaper readers, though numerically small in India, largely constitute the intelligentsia. The press has a 'multiplier effect' its message spreads far and wide. The impact of the press can be determined only in the perspectives of current development and pace of change in the country. The power of the press is mainly seen as responsible for the major political developments in India during the 1990s. The capacity of Indian press to generate a healthy debate on public issues has been partially realised. But with increasing literacy it holds out infinite possibilities in the future.

Impact of Radio—Radio is serving as an effective medium not only to inform and educate people, but also to provide healthy entertainment. It can justifiably be called the medium for the masses. Radio has the inherent advantage to overcome three major hurdles to meaningful communication such as-mass illiteracy, lack of efficient means to reach the remote places and poverty which prevents access to mass media.

Impact of Films—In India, with its cultural and linguistic diversities and the problems of illiteracy the film is the most powerful medium of mass-communication. It gives not merely information, but creates a demand for change and modernisation. It has earned universal acclaim and is a versatile means of communication.

Impact of Television—Television is considered one of the greatest inventions of man..It is a multi-media system predominated by the visual medium. It has the power to instil desired attitudes among the masses.

Effects of TV—TV can transport the viewers to the actual

scene of action to see things as they happen. Take the example of the Kargil war or the rescue of the people from under the debris due to earthquake in Gujarat on 26 Jan, 2001. But many have also come to hold TV responsible for inciting violence, corrupting the young and creating a make belief world of illusion.

Video, Cable T.V. and Satellite—Video burst on the Indian scene sometime in the mid 80s. It holds out infinite promises of entertainment and information. Its safe and easy facility for stop, go, forward, reverse viewing is invaluable for teaching and learning.

But with the advent of the cable TV and satellite TV the demand for video has reduced although not lost totally. And it was due to satellite TV only that one was able to experience all the horrors of Gulf war sitting in any corner of India. Cable TV has emerged as an important medium for advertisements as well.

Impact of Mass media*—Areas of Danger*—Mass Media has an intense impact on the Indian society. It is claimed that this proliferation of information and the swiftness of its distribution would certainly improve the human conditions. However, with positive values it has also created areas of danger.

Manipulation—Clever uses of electronic devices can alter the meaning of recorded visual and audio material, making it appear to be what it really isn't.

Privacy—The whole question of co-relating the right to privacy with public interest has become a vexed problem for policy planners and social scientists alike.

Security—Protection of secret government information, private transactions, and institutional records in computer systems has become a matter of concern.

Democratic Process—Democracy functions best when voters are widely informed on all problems and issues. But if given power to select the information they desire with the aid of new technologies and by choosing to see and hear only what interests them most, will they be able to vote intelligently.

Isolation—Although the communication revolution has the power to draw the global community closer together, it also isolates individuals and small groups. Both adults and children sit for hours, aware only of what appears on small screens often they seem visually drugged.

Significance of Journalism

The Print Media, like others, have power, and this power must be exercised with a sense of responsibility. The printed word, as a carrier of knowledge, information and news stories was in vogue in China, Korea and Japan, a thousand years ago. In India, printing came first to Goa in 1556 and penetrated into Calcutta and inland provinces through the coastal towns.

One of the chief characteristics of print media is that they offer extensive news coverage and in-depth treatment of themes. They provide a large variety of coverage, through different kinds of writings, than any other media in India. Understandably good newspapers are described as Readers, University. The main weakness of the print media is that they can be read only by the literates. Secondly 93% of the newspapers are concentrated in Urban areas. Thirdly, the increasing rise in the price of newspapers and magazines prevent a large number of our people from purchasing them.

The Development—The two notable developments are shift towards commercialisation and introduction of new printing technologies.

Commercialisation—The national newspapers, during the British period, functioned basically with a missionary zeal and acted as the voice of the freedom fighters and stimulated the monument through advocacy journalism. But after independence, the missionary zeal of the newspapers evaporated. It soon became a publishing industry. And the theory of delinking of the press from business houses engaged in other industries was not accepted by the newspaper magnates.

New Printing Technologies—The introduction of modern printing technologies has brought about a new climate of working in the print media organisations. Printing today has become a graphic art. The newspapers are elegantly printed, bearing creative typographical and layout designs.

Small Newspapers—A large number of our newspapers belong to the category of small or medium papers with status no better than that of a cottage industry. They can not tap adequate advertising support to become financially strong. The cooperative type of management has not gained ground. The bottom line of the Indian newspaper industry remains weak. And it is well known that some of the newspapers have been censured by the press council for having succumbed to temptations of different kinds, which is a serious problem.

Professional Discipline—Professional discipline is necessary for all media. The western press has evolved codes of ethics to ensure discipline. The first press commission had empowered the Press Council of India to evolve such a code. There is a code only on the coverages of communal riots. The Press Council finds it difficult to enact an enforceable formal code and thus just lays down certain guidelines in its decisions taken from time to time.

Role of Electronic Media

Radio and T.V. are called the electronic media and are today the supreme media of mass communication. In the 1930s, the television made its bow in the west. Its true development took place after the 2nd world war. In India, the new glamour medium came in 1959.

Characteristics of Radio—Radio is a sightless or a viewless medium. It is also called blind medium as the performer doesn't see his audience and the listeners can not see the performer. The main characteristics of radio are—

A Medium of Sound—It is an auditory medium, a medium of the ear. The three elements of a radio broadcast are the spoken work, music and sound effects. They are all sounds carried on the air waves to the listener. All these sounds must be pleasant and expressive for the ears of the listener.

A Medium of the Voice—Radio is the medium of the voice. The producer mixes his voice with music and sound effects. A radio listener has a highly developed ear and so the broadcaster shouldn't sound fake or untruthful. A truthful vocal expression will come only if the whole person's mind, soul, psyche and imagination and his body are all in the tune with one another.

A Link between Speaker and Listeners—Microphone is the only instrument through which a radio broadcaster speaks to his listeners. It is a hi-fi instrument that catches the softest sigh, the tiniest rustle of the paper. It exposes all vocal lies, and tell all, the truth from a lie.

An Intimate Medium—A broadcaster must imagine as if the listeners are sitting by his side and to the listeners, it should sound as if the broadcaster is speaking from within the sound box or the-transistor. The best subjects for radio broadcasts are those which intimately concern the listeners. The words and the manner of their expression must be intimate as the condition in which broadcasts are received are very informal.

A Mass Medium—Radio is a medium of mass communication. Its broadcasts reach hundreds of thousands in one go. The task of the performer is to find out the lowest common denominator to communicate well with the largest number of listeners. It is a much cheaper medium of mass communication. Thus, it is very relevant to developing countries like India.

Simple Language—Large number of people are illiterate or semi-literate in India and other developing countries. So, the language of the radio broadcasts must be simple and should be closer to the spoken language that the common people use.

A Mobile Medium—Radio is a mobile medium, and so it is a

most convenient medium for anybody. It doesn't respect units of time, place and action as prescribed by Aristotle.

A Cheap and Quick Medium—It is a medium of the 'here and now' as it can report the events almost instantly. Radio is a much cheaper and quicker medium than TV for production of programmes; thus, it can produce a wide variety of programmes.

No Shared Experience—Radio listeners are sitting alone or with one or two members of the family, and not like the stage where spectators are sitting in a crowd. Thus the psychology of reception for a radio broadcast is much more informal. The radio listener will not accept any untruth in a radio performance nor does he see any glamour personality to be impressed.

Characteristics of Television—Television is an audio-visual medium and its broadcast is uniquely telegenic. TV has both sound and sight.

An Audio-Visual Medium—A TV broadcast is conceived and produced and received in audio-visual terms. Thus, it directly affects two senses simultaneously, those of hearing and seeing. It is more effective than radio broadcast as radio is a unisense medium, affecting only one sense.

Features of other Media—TV has borrowed certain features from the other media of communication like the stage, the film and the radio. TV has integrated all these into a whole that makes TV a uniquely new medium, different from all other medium.

Wide Reach and High Credibility—TV is a supreme medium of mass communication. And with the help of satellite technology, today, it can reach all the concerns of the globe. TV has turned world into a global village. Thus, it has widened the mental horizons of man and has become the supreme educator of man.

TV is a credible, a believable medium. Seeing is believing. Things shown on TV become effectively truer than those that one reads in the print medium or listens to the radio.

A Glamourous Medium—One can watch on TV the glittering personalities and events, international conferences, sports, festivals, travel shows etc. The facility of watching almost round the clock enhances the glamour appeal still more. Because of its glamour, TV has been called the magic box. The tele-addiction has become the greatest addiction of our times. And thus, the reading habits are declining as people now get their news and information more from TV and earlier also.

A Medium of the Close-up—It is an ideal medium for expressing reaction and interaction between people for presenting an interview and a discussion etc. If something has happened or somebody has said something, the camera would slow the reaction of several people, one-by-one, in a close-up.

A Living Room Medium—TV is a medium of and for the family. TV brings theatre and cinema auditorium to the living-room and brings together the family increasingly. Earlier, people used to get dressed up specially to witness a stage drama or a film. It is the reverse process now. The film or the theatre comes in your drawing room under home conditions.

A Democratic Medium—It is available to all people. It deals with the problems of all sections of the society. It democratises information and informal education and also democratizes literature, by discussing it in broadcasts, or by telecasting it in a dramatic version. But it can not afford to be highly artistic like stage, as things might go over the heads of the common viewer.

A Medium of Immediacy—It captures the events even as they are happening, much before the newspaper comes out with information on events next morning. TV is a supreme reporter. TV operates in fixed time units. And the time unit must be respected.

Advertiser's Influence—TV is the great salesman of modern times. The businessman sells his products and services through TV. Advertisements can reach millions of people at the same time.

Characteristics of Films—Cinema is a highly mechanical

medium. It uses many mechanical devices like Cameras, Microphones, Dubbing machine, Editing machine etc. Film is a product of interaction between machines and artistic and technical people.

A Mass Medium—It is a medium of mass communication. Millions can watch the movie in a country and can be watched by a very large number of people in several other countries also. Today, a film can also be transferred from the celluloid to the video cassette and the cassette can be played at home also.

Mechanically Reproducible—Film can be preserved and can be seen again and again. It can be useful for research on a relevant subject.

A Collaborative Medium—So many people collaborate to make the film and to reach out the film to the people. No other medium depends so much on so many people. It is the director's medium. All artists and technical people have to work in a team spirit but the director is the boss. And every body must carry out his directions.

An Art Medium—In the beginning, it was considered as a medium of cheap entertainment but now it has come to be considered as art form. Intellectuals and serious thinkers have associated themselves with cinema.

Government's Role—Harsh rules and high taxes imposed by government give an impression that cinema is treated as an undesirable activity. Thus, the licensing rules for cinema must be relaxed. The setting up of some organisations for promoting cinema goes to the credit of the government.

A Medium for Development—Film is an effective medium for development. Development means the growth of the individual and the society in all aspects, which include political, social, economic and cultural aspects. Film can also promote national and emotional integration.

A Medium that Demands People's Concentration—The conditions under which a film is screened and is received by the cine-goers in a cinema house demand concentration of different sections of society, sitting together in the same hall and constituting the audience. All these people tend to be unified. Concentration is centred on the screen and the audience almost appears as a unified mass.

A Realistic but Expensive Medium—The film can be effective in hitting the consciousness, sometimes conscience of the audience with the camera. Film is a realistic medium. Camera and microphone can never be kind to any exaggeration. But it is an expensive medium. Although, film making is expensive but it is a cheap medium of entertainment. Because of the high cost our films tend to be cheap commercial cinema. By providing cheap entertainment, the producers think that, they can recover the cost and earn profits.

Role of Audiences

Information technology has advanced too much in the recent years that it is now possible for people, while sitting in the drawing rooms, to witness the events taking place in any part of the world or even in space. National boundaries hold no barrier for mass communication.

Meaning of Mass—The word mass is used to refer to common people, especially the lower classes. In general usage, the word mass refers to people in a large number. If it is said that masses are ignorant, we mean that a very large proportion of the population is ignorant. Similarly, if we say mass destruction, it means destruction on a very large scale. The most important feature of mass is its very large size in terms of the number of individuals and second is that masses are geographically distributed.

Emergence of the Theory of Mass Society—Society is a large and complex society with modernisation the complexity of the society further increases. Such a society which is very large in size but where members are isolated and relationships are contractual is called a mass society.

However, the concept of mass society is not to be equated with that of massive society. It is more than the massive society. There are many traditional societies-that are very large in numbers but are not necessarily mass societies. It will be useful to understand the concept of mass society using a set of contrasts with other kinds of units in social life, like groups, crowd and public.

In a small group, all members know each other. The members of a group interact with each other for a purpose.

The crowd is a spontaneous collection of individuals. It is temporary and never reappears with the same composition. Members of crowd share the same mood but there exists no order in the crowd. Crowd is physically present at a particular place. Unlike crowd, public is widely dispersed. Its size may be small or large. Public may be quite heterogeneous and members may not be aware of each other. Political parties treat us as public.

The Media Audience—The commonly used meaning of the term Media audience is the aggregate of persons forming readers, listeners, viewers of different media. That is, audience is a group of individuals with a common pattern of media consumption. There are four different ways of looking at media audiences. They are-

Media Reach—The owners and producers of mass media conceive the total population whom their communications can reach. It may be different for different means of communication.

Media Access—Mass media may be available but the capacity or willingness to use the media may not be there. A large section of the population doesn't have the radio or TV sets. But access may not overlap ownership. Group watching of television at a TV shop is a common sight. Many families don't buy newspapers but they may read at some other place.

Media Exposure—Everyone who has access to radio or television doesn't necessarily use them. In a family that subscribes to a newspaper, everyone doesn't read it. So only those individuals who actually expose themselves to the media are the media audiences.

Media Effects—Another way to think about audiences is in terms of individuals who have been exposed to mass communication products and have undergone a change in their knowledge, opinions, attitude or behaviour. A person may not recall anything of the information received after listening or watching a news programme. But the same person, after watching an advertisement, may immediately rush to buy that product.

Quality of Audience—The most interesting feature of a mass communication audience is its dual nature. Media audience is a collectivity formed in response to media content. Audiences, are both the cause as well as the response to the mass communication process.

Audience Types—The types of audiences can be distinguished on their demographic characteristic and mental make-up.

Elite Audience—They are composed of the people who are decision-makers and trend-setters in the society. They are economically well to do and are highly educated. Their number is small but their influence is strong.

General Audience—They are very large and highly diverse groups that represent the broad cross-section of the society. Majority of the people belong to this category.

Specialised Audiences—These are composed of individuals who possess similar characteristics. They are relatively small in number.

Nature of Experience—Audience is the single most important element in any conception of mass communication. If we observe the media audience relationship, we find that the audiences actually exercise their choice as to which medium is to be used and also which content they would like to be exposed to. But the question is why does an audience choose a particular medium or a specific content of the media? Wilbur Schramm proposed a formula for this.

$$\frac{\text{Promise of Reward}}{\text{Efforts required}} = \text{Probability of selection}$$

Rewards may be immediate or delayed but the focus is on the satisfaction of the audience needs. The effort required for attending to mass communication may be considered in terms of availability of the media.

Audience's Response

The producers of mass communication keep a hand on the pulse of their audiences in order to make their products more and more acceptable. AFS are the mechanisms through which information regarding audience reactions is taken back to the owners, controllers and producers of the media.

Marked-based Feedback—Mass Communication receive the following information through the M-BF System

(1) Audience Access to the media

(2) Audience Exposure to the media

These informations are received by three methods—

(i) Audience Decision Making

(ii) Direct Feedback

(iii) Media Review

ADM—Audience decision to subscribe to newspapers or magazine is a direct feedback about the popularity of the publication. Sales at box-office is a good feedback about the popularity of a film.

DFb—Newspapers and magazines have columns reserved for letters to the editor sent by the readers. Similar is the case with radio and television. It is rendered recently that the needs for direct feedback from the audiences is increasing.

MR—Media gives the greatest importance to the feedback received through the reviews. There are regularly reviews of films, audio and video cassettes published in newspapers and magazines. The role of media reviews is two fold—(1) The owners, producers, controllers of radio and television programmes take the comments very seriously (2) The reviews provide information to the audience.

Research Based Feedback—The market based feedback and the reviews are more or less passive systems feedback information gets generated without the producers making effort for it. Research based feedback systems are created to provide systematic information about audience responses to a particular mass communication products of services. Many media organization have their own audience research system.

Conveyance of Message

A message may be communicated through words, pictures, gestures, signs and symbols or even through silence. But if it is not understood properly by the audience concerned, it is an exercise in futility. The message to be effective must have certain attributes.

Clarity, Coherence and Consciousness—The message which is clear, lucid and concise is generally understandable. Coherence is another attribute of a good message it should be a narration of a story.

Simple Language—The path to good and effective communication is plainness, simplicity, orderlines and sincerity. There is a need for the communicators to take all precautions to ensure that messages are not misunderstood.

Credibility of the Source—"Who" is another mportant factor in communication? The credibility of a speaker in respect of a particular topic matters a lot.

Persuasion—The contents and appeals should have the power to influence the receiver's attitudes. Communicators today are acquainted with the package of techniques which can endow that thrust to the message.

Enchancing Impact—Even ordinary messages can be turned into interesting ones. They can become very convincing and credible if presented graphically and supported by statistics.

Pathetic Stories—One can narrate a pathetic story to evoke an effective human response. Human misery can be vividly illustrated by a small documentary.

Statistics in Support of Correctness—The use of statistics in an economic survey can lend support to the correctness of conclusions drawn from the survey.

Emotional Appeals—Emotional appeals, if used properly at an appropriate time, can stir imagination. Appeals and self-esteem or social status have made people buy costly goods which normally they wouldn't.

Perception Filter—Any message is called a stimulus, and a strong emotion-laden message is termed as a strong stimulus. However, before any stimulus or message can transfer knowledge, create an image or change an attitude or a behaviour. Perception is the process whereby an individual receives stimulus through the various senses and interprets them.

Hot and Cold Messages—Marshall McTuhan differentiates between hot and cold messages. By the former, he means the message with highly understandable specific contents. Such messages are good for disseminating specific information, e.g. announcement of a new product in the market. Cold messages are on the other hand more appropriate if the objective is to have people intervalise and retain the information. In such messages, there is more involvement of the people.

Creative AD Message—A print copy is described as "Salesmanship in print". Creativity in the ad format is required towards this end. The message must be concise, precise and eye-catching.

Radio and Copy—Radio copies, messages and jingles are very vigorous although they are oriented only to the ears of the listeners. Radio copywriting is an imaginative and professional job.

T.V. Commercial—This medium draws more ads than any other individual medium does as it is a combination of all the virtues, strengths and beauty that audio-visual technology can import. TV commercial must ensure that viewers grasp the entire story the first time they watch it.

Journalism in this Country—In general sense by press we mean "printing press" but in journalistic and mass communication terminology by "press" we mean print media-newspapers, journals, magazines, periodicals, leaflets, books etc. A newspaper means "any printed periodical work containing public news or comment on public news."

Origin of Press in India—The writings on the walls and on stones dating back to several centuries before Christ were the first signs of the origin of the press in India. The newsletters, later, were regularly issued during the Mughal period. It is the dissemination of these newsletters which perhaps inspired James Augustus Hicky to start his newspaper Bengal Gazette in 1780. The first printing press was established in Bombay in 1674, 2nd in Madras in 1772 and 3rd in Calcutta in 1779. Micky's newspaper Calcutta General Advertiser or Bengal Gazette was born on 29 January, 1780. Some other weeklies and monthly newspapers started in 19th cent in Bengal were Dig Darshan, Samachar Daipan, Friend of India and The Statesman.

Nationalism and the Indian Press—The growth of the press in India was facilitated by the nationalist movement for freedom. Press frequently took up the cudgels with the authorities and transmitted the messages of freedom to the masses of India.

Vernacular Press Act—Lord Lytton, worried over the increasing impact of the writing in the press enforced the Vernacular Press Act on March 1st, 1878, for controlling the Press. He also instituted the post of "Press Commissioner for India."

When the World War I broke out in 1914, British Government released nationalist leaders from jail with a view to soliciting their support in the conduct of war. But several newspapers took divergent steps and as a result 180 (approx.) newspapers were asked to pay security deposits and assure support to the government in 1914-15. During the World War II the press initially supported the stand of the British government in India. But soon a conflict arose on reporting the war news in the newspapers. It was around this time that All India Newspapers Editors Conference came into being.

Post Independence Press—After Independence in 1947, a new era began in India in which the role of the press changed slowly. It had to shoulder new responsibilities now. A thorough inquiry into the structure and functioning of our press was made by the Press Commission during 1952-54. Among the many recommendations of the commission, one was for the appointment of a Press Registrar and setting up of a Press Council.

The 2nd Press Commission in 1982 recommended the delinking of the press from its connections with other industries. One of its major recommendations was to set up a National Development Commission.

Now we have a large and well developed press. These is use of latest technologies and management by the press in India now and it has a bright future ahead.

Radio, Television and Cinema—In U.S.A. the beginning of Radio was made somewhere in 1909. But regular and systematic broadcasting began only in 1920.

In India, amateurs were the first to start broadcasting. The Radio Club of Bombay, broadcast its first programme in June, 1923. In November, 1923 the Calcutta Radio and on 31 st July, 1924 the Madras Radio club started broadcasting. But it soon closed down. However the Madras corporation restarted the broadcast service in 1930.

Organised broadcasting in India was started by the Indian Broadcasting company in 1927 but was closed down in March 1930. However, the government took over the Bombay and Calcutta station in April, 1930 and the Indian Broadcasting Service was formed. But due to the world wide depression, the IBS was closed down on October 10, 1931. However, later it was decided to start a radio station in Delhi and it actually went on air on January 7, 1936.

All India Radio—The BBC loaned the services of Lionel Fielden who became the Controller of Broadcasting. He got together a group of devoted young people. And he soon started short wave service in 1938, to cover the entire country. A new broadcasting house was built on Parliament Street, New Delhi. In the midnight of August 14-15, 1947, Nehru broadcast his famous speech "Tryst with Destiny".

After Partition 6 Radio Stations Cameup—Bombay, Calcutta, Delhi, Tiruchi, Lucknow and Madras. When the princely states became a part of India, five more station Hyderabad, Aurangabad, Baroda, Mysore, and Trivandrum, were taken over by AIR.

Chanda Committee—In 1964 a committee on Broadcasting and Information Media was set up under the Chairmanship of A.K. Chanda. It recommended in his report of 1966 separation of radio and television with two independent corporations. Although not accepted by the government then, later the separation ultimately came about in 1976, and TV set-up was called Doordarshan. Another recommendation was that of set-up of a commercial service, which was started from Vividh Bharati in 1967.

Verghese Committee—In 1977, Janta government appointed a working group under B.G. Verghese, to suggest an autonomous set up for AIR and Doordarshan. It recommended the creation of Akash Bharati in 1978 and thus abill was introduced in 1979 in this regard. But, with the fall of Janata government the bill lapsed.

Origin and Development of TV in India—TV came to India On September 15, 1959. It was feared that TV might alienate us from our cultural roots. The first rural programme "Krishi Darshan" was started from Delhi on the Republic Day, January 26,1967. On 3rd December, 1971, the first English news bulletin was introduced.

In 1975, the Satellite Instructional Television Equipment was conducted. The one-year SITE exercise proved to India itself that it was ready for the satellite television. Educational programmes were broadcast direct from a satellite to the TV sets for the first time.

National Broadcast Trust—On April 6, Doordarshan was separated from All India Radio or Akashvani. But both AIR and Doordarshan continued to be under the Information and Broadcasting Ministry.

The Verghese Committee recommended the National Broadcast Trust, to look after both AIR and Doordarshan. The trust would be responsible to the Parliament through its budget, annual reports, auditor's reports etc., by AIR and Doordarshan.

Joshi Committee—Joshi committee set up under the chairmanship of P.C. Joshi on Software for TV in its report of 1985 criticised Doordarshan for concentrating mostly on the North for its programme content. It also recommended the setting up of a National Doordarshan Council and the decentralisation of Doordarshan. However the committee didn't ask for an autonomous corporation for Doordarshan. But it asked the organization to find its roots in the rich Indian heritage and develop a strong Indian personality.

Effectiveness of Doordarshan—Our TV offers a wide variety of programmes. These programmes are generally divided into general audience and special audience broadcasts. First category includes programmes of general interest like news, films, current affairs etc. Second category include broadcasts for particular sections of the population.

Our TV has made some contribution no doubt but there is

much left to be desired. Although it has provided entertainment to the viewers, it has served the farmers by informing them of new methods and techniques of agriculture, it has made people aware of what is happening beyond India but it has not been impartial and fearless in reporting political developments. It has not been an effective medium for social change and development.

Origin and Development of Films in India—Indian cinema is almost a century old. It remains a cheap medium of entertainment for the masses. The films in India are made in several languages and regions. The first important step in the motion picture industry was the invention of kinetoscope by Edison. The first film to be ever shown in India was screened at Watson's Hotel, Bombay.

In 1902, J.F. Madan in Calcutta launched his "bioscope" showings in a tent. By 1905, it was possible to have a film of 30-40 minutes duration. The first attempt to make a film with a dramatic story and treatment was made by Torney, who made Pundalik released in 1912. Dada Saheb Phalke made Raja Harish Chandra in 1913.

From 1913 to 1931 was the era of the silent cinema in India. About 1300 films were made during this period. In 1930, came the first attempt to make an Indian talkie programme and the first talkie film which came in 1931 was Alam Ara.

The first attempt to produce a film in colour was made in 1932 by Madan Theatres. The film was Bilwa Mangal. And then started the trend of coloured films.

Folk Media—Traditional Folk Media is a term used to denote 'people's performances'. It describes folk dance, rural drama, and musical variety of the village people. This term speaks of those performing arts which are cultural symbols of people. Traditional folk media have been consciously persuaded to come out of their shell to give a personal touch to the otherwise impersonal mass media programmes. Traditional Folk Media are personal forms of communication, of entertainment.

Strength of Folk Media—Since these arts are woven into the social and cultural fabric of the rural society, their role in educating the non-school population assumes significance. They have lived and grown with the rural people and so the rural masses, without any inhibition, get involved in their game and emerge more relaxed and better informed.

There are many advantages of traditional folk media for the purpose of informing and educating the rural illiterate. They are rich in variety and readily available and economically viable. They command the confidence of the rural masses as they are LIVE. And above all they are in a 'face to face situation' between the communicator and the receiver of the message.

In India, traditional folk media have been reckoned as successful mass-motivators. They inspire the masses during the times of stress and strain. These forms of art are a part of the way of life of a community and provide acceptable means of bridging development issues into the community on its own terms. Mass media have extended the area of coverage of a folk performance, while traditional folk media with their aspiring colour and costume, dance and music, have enriched the content of the mass media channels.

Role of Traditional Folk Media—There is a tremendous wealth and variety in traditional folk media of India. Conventionally, the traditional folk performances have been theme-carriers, usually carrying themes of morality. The rural drama, with its stock characters, has also carried across modern messages, without, in any way hurting the community's traditional culture. During the past few years they have slowly acquired a functional dimension without losing their cultural roots.

Soon after achieving freedom the National Government started a full-fledged Song and Drama Division in 1954, with the objective of, training and utilising the service of traditional folk performers to inform the rural masses about the planning and development programmes of the country.

Flexibility is the most important factor which determines the viability of a folk medium for rural communication. Flexibility of a folk medium might reveal itself either in its form or theme or in both.

Various Categories—Depending on the nature and extent of flexibility, the traditional folk media reveal themselves in three categories-rigid, semi-rigid and non-rigid.

Rigid Media—It is those that reject the new message summarily. These are ritualistic or intensely religious in form and theme. Their content is hardcore and are unchangeable e.g., African and Indian ritual dances.

Semi-Rigid—They are those that provide limited scope for the new message. Even while dealing with a classical theme, the medium would have in-built characters or situations which hold out flexibility.

Non-Rigid—They are those that absorb new messages without any reservation to reflect them effectively in the field.

Increasing the Efficiency of Communication Strategy—For increasing the efficiency of communication strategy in order to obtain the intended results there are 4 methods.

Multi-media Approach—The multi-media approach holds glamour for the field, covers different aspects of the message and interacts with different sections of people simultaneously. It demands careful planning and faultless coordination. Folk media performances in-built into the multi-media package, would surely establish a two-way communication channel. The programme would also pave the way for smooth functioning of an extension service. The multi-media approach demands fool-proof planning and involves more expenditure.

The Package Plan—It is an integrated time-bound work programme which eliminates time-lags between communication, extension and service and brings to fruition the efforts of the communicator.

Utilising Rural Structure and Village Functionaries—Mass media channels of sound and sight do bring awareness to the people of a developed theme, and traditional folk media succeed in reinforcing it with information and education by a personal approach. However, motivation for action could be energised by change-agents who are inter-personal communicators and one should look for such change-agents in the rural situation itself. The service of the traditional folk artists will draw good results with village-based functionaries.

Objective Evaluation of the Strategy—A need for scientific research on the role of folk media in communication is essential. With the feedback collected it should be possible for the communicator to identify attitudes 'that need to be changed in order to create the necessary social and psychological climate' in the field for people to receive the needed message. The programme package should then be suitably altered to incorporate the required messages.

Evaluation studies may tend to become quantitative rather than qualitative in terms of achievement. They may prove to be general assessments of the impact of all types of media and not of folk media in particular. It is therefore, time that specific studies were developed in folk media 'in an effort to acquire some reliable measurements for further guidance'.

Role of Agencies

News agencies form a major part of the print media, without which many newspapers would find it difficult to function.

What is a News Agency? A news agency is an organization which collects or gathers news and supplies it to different newspapers, magazines, radio stations and television stations. News gathered/reported by reporters/correspondents is sent to newspapers via electronic teleprinters or computers and these newspapers, in turn, pay a monthly subscription to use news agencies for the news they receive. The news agency works round the clock.

How is it Different from a Newspaper? News agency works in a completely different fashion from a newspaper-

(1) The news agency doesn't publish any newspaper of its own. All the reports are transmitted to the newspapers and radio and television stations. And then it is upto the newspaper to use the news item sent by one news agency or that sent by another. In fact, at times a newspaper may even prepare an item quoting some paragraphs from one agency and some from another agency.

(2) Every news agency report has to be attributed to a source, unlike a newspaper story, i.e., every news item has to be quoted from someone.

(3) There will be no comments, editorializing or interpretation in a news agency report and it will be purely a factual report.

(4) For the news agencies, it is a deadline every minute. Since a newspaper goes to the press after midnight, a reporter knows that he has plenty of time to file his report. But a news agency reporter must file his report immediately.

(5) Accuracy and speed being very essential for a news agency, it becomes important that a news agency report should be crisp, precise, and to-the-point.

(6) Since there is no time for a news agency reporter to confirm or re-confirm facts, it is important that there is an eye on accuracy. The newspaper reporter has a whole day to correct any mistake but a news agency will not get another chance.

(7) A news agency is not serving the city in which it works, but the whole nation and beyond. Therefore, its news will not be purely from a local perspective, whereas, newspaper devotes lots of space to local stories, reporting the events in great detail.

(8) A news agency generally avoids publicity of commercial

units. A newspaper on the other hand may not mind publishing an individual.

(9) A news agency always gives its news without any comment or personal opinion. This is unlike a newspaper which may be permitted not only to give a news item without a source, but also to put in reasonable comments.

Ownership Pattern—Both the main agencies-Press Trust of India (PTI) and United News of India (UNI) are owned by groups of newspapers who have bought shares to run them.

These newspapers have established Boards of Directors, each headed by a chairman to make the policies of the respective news agencies. There is a constant professional competition between the two agencies. But these boards do not interfere in the day-to-day working of the agencies.

Financial Structure—Various newspapers and the electronic media, apart from government departments and private entrepreneurs, buy the news from the agencies. The newspapers and other subscribers pay a monthly subscription fee, plus rental charges for the computer, teleprinter, apart from the installation charges paid when the subscription was first taken. Government don't own these agencies but is the largest subscriber.

The Organizational Structure—The agency is run by a General Manager-cum-Chief Editor, who is assisted by Deputy General Managers. The Editorial Desk is under the charge of a News Editor and reporting section is under the Chief of Bureau. The reporting staff is divided into-two sections-the reporters who deal with the day-to-day reporting are under a chief reporter and correspondents who deal with Ministerial and Legislative reporting are under the Chief of Bureau. Thus, the Chief Reporter is answerable to the Chief of Bureau.

The news agencies are the first to get wind of a news break. The agencies have offices in all the state capitals, many world capitals and at the United Nations.

The Growth—When India attained its independence on 15 August, 1947, some vestiges of the British remained behind. The news agencies operating in the country at that time were either foreign agencies with offices in India or British-owned Indian agencies. The foreign agencies operating in India then, which are still reporting from India, include Reuter, the United Press International, the Agence France Presse etc.

However, with the help of the government, some major newspapers joined together to form a trust, and then came the Press Trust of India in 1949. It took over the business of the Associated Press of India.

Although both PTI and UNI are professional rivals, the UNI owes its birth to PTI. UNI was formed in 1961 and registered under the Societies Act. The PTI had headquarters in Bombay, while UNI had its head office in Delhi.

In 1948, a Hindi news agency had come into being, called the Hindustan Samachar. In 1966, came up another Hindi news agency called the Samachar Bharti. The Asia News International (ANI) came up in the eighties.

The National Emergency of 1975 imposed Press Censorship in the entire country. A censor office was established in the Press Information Bureau. From time to time, the government issued certain directives about what to report and what not to report. The government, in a surprise action, decided to merge the news agencies into a single unit so that it would be easier to control. On February 16, 1976 orders were received by the agencies that all of them had ceased to exist and a new news agency called Samachar had been created and that UNI and the two Hindi agencies would be sent down. The topmost posts were given to the staff of the PTI. The Hindi Agencies not doing well financially, welcomed this merger. However, UNI staff felt let down. But the situation was accepted and the agency continued to work as one. But after the defeat of Mrs. Gandhi in 1977 elections, large sections of the staff of Samachar, mostly belonging to the former UTI, demonstrated with the Janta Party government. And in April

1978, the government announced that Samachar would cease to exist from September 1978 and the former four news agencies would be brought to life again.

Services Provided by News Agencies—As the agencies grew in size in terms of subscribers, both the agencies felt the need to diversify. Now, both the news agencies are providing several other services, some of them aimed at specialised business interests.

Services Provided by PTI—News Scan, Comscan, Features (sent as mailer service weekly in English and Hindi on various subjects), Economic Service, Science Service, Stockscan, Photo service, PTI, T,V, NITEL, some of the other additional services of UNI are-Stock Exchange Service, Financial Service, UNICON, UNEN, Agriculture Service, Feature Service, Backgrounder Service, UNICAN, Photo service, Unidarshan (TV), Videotex, UNI Graphics.

Role of News Agencies in Non-Aligned Countries—In the late seventies, the non-aligned countries, at one of their summits, discussed how the international news agencies and visual media, were damaging the understanding amongst people by misrepresenting facts. And so it was commonly adopted by all, that the non-aligned countries should have their own news agency. It was also agreed that before such an agency could be set up, one national news agency would coordinate on behalf of each member country to present and disseminate news on behalf of a non-aligned newspool. In India, this task is being performed on by the PTI on behalf of the government.

Foreign News Agencies—Indian newspapers get news transmitted by AP or D P through UNI, and that transmitted by AFP, Reuters, or UPI through PTI. Similarly, while they do have their own bureaus here, they depend mostly on the Indian agency they subscribe to and then add their own background before transmitting any news abroad. However, some news agencies have now sought permission to operate directly. Some of the foreign news agencies operating in India are-Reuter-British news agency founded in 1851 by Paul Julius Von Reuter; Associated Press (AP) established in New York in 1848; Agence France Presse (AFP) established in Paris in 1944; United Press International (UPI) founded in U.S.A. in 1907.

Syndicated Columnist—A syndicated columnist is a senior journalist whose much sought opinions, views and analyses are distributed by feature agencies. The feature agencies undertake to sell such articles to one or more newspapers. A feature agency depend solely on freelance writers. The feature agencies working in India are Indian News & Feature Alliance, which is the oldest and the best, Indian Press Agency, Gemini Features, Compass Features.

5

Constant Evolution

With extending impact of media of mass communication on individuals and groups, the Indian society overall is reacting swiftly. The pervasive effects of the various media on the varied spheres of the Indian life-economic, social, cultural, intellectual, religious and even moral values are transforming rapidly.

As a result of this change, what is emerging in the Indian situation is, in DeFleur and Rokeach's words, "a conception of the media audience as a set of individuals who now encounter the media as social beings connected to their social environments." In fact, some two decades before this would not have possible or practicable at all.

India, as is well known, is a nation of diverse and divergent cultures and sub-cultures, languages and dialects that run into several hundreds, varied religions and faiths. An ancient country with civilization some 4,000-year-old, India, now a land of teeming millions, is abounding with challenging themes and problems of development. The 640 million people are waiting for a revolution in all aspects of human endeavour, a rich field for mass media to exert the influence and cast their impact.

It is unfortunate that prior to 1947, when India formed a part of the British rulers acted only in those directions which either aided in extending their influence or perpetuating their power.

With the consequences that no consistent attitudes or patterns of behaviour could be formed or inculcated among the masses. Newspapers were not permitted freedom of writing, radio was under the control of the government, television had not even been conceived, although Britain had a well-established television and radio networks at home, black and white cinema was unaware of developments in colour techniques in the west and other media of mass communication did not progress in any systematic, planned direction to assist the country in any way.

The advent of independence in August 1947 removed the shackles of the colonial era and a new horizon breathed in all aspects of the country's life. The media of mass communication also rose to the occasion. There was a tremendous progress in the fields of print and the broadcast media, the rate of literacy rose, more cinemas came into being, more and more people came in contact with one another in the countryside and the urban areas. The impact of the wide world was beginning to be felt at large.

Most of the laws restriction or controlling the activities of the journalists and writers were either withdrawn or suspended. Freedom of speech and expression (including thereby the freedom of the press) was guaranteed by the Constitution as a fundamental right (Article 19 A). The Constitution also granted freedom of movement, right to profession and property and also to hold meetings and cultural gatherings. All this added to the momentum of growth of mass media immensely. Since the Indian Constitution recognizes 16 provincial and regional languages, equal opportunities were available to all of them for instituting newspapers and periodicals in their respective regions for their proliferation and development. Radio though remained under the control of the Central Government, but several new stations were planned to give coverage to all national and regional languages including several dialects.

In 1976, twenty-nine years after independence, India had 13,320 newspapers in 65 languages. Of which, 10,947 or

78 per cent were started after independence. The largest number of newspapers was in Hindi—a language spoken by about 40 percent of the country's population, followed by English. The number in Hindi was 3,289 and in English 2,765 next probably only to the USSR. The total circulation of all the newspapers, though not very large as compared to the Western standards, amounted to over 34 million copies. Weekly and other journals in the Indian and regional languages numbered 12,445. The progress has continued unabated, despite several hurdles of low advertising and shortage of newsprint, specially in the field of regional and provincial languages.

Started with only six broadcasting stations in 1947, All India Radio (AIR) has also greatly extended ts services and progressively created its impact on the masses. In 1977, 155 radio stations including relay station, were functioning and these stations were broadcasting in several foreign, national and regional languages. A regular feedback was in existence in most languages wherein listeners could have a say in programming and broadcasting scheduled in these languages. AIR went commercial in 1967.

Television arrived in India in 1959, though pretty late and on a rather too restricted scale. The United Nations Educational, Scientific and Cultural Organisation (UNESCO), the USA, West Germany, Yugoslavia and Japan helped India in establishing, extending and programming of the television network in India.

In 1975, the US-loaned satellite enabled India to initiate the SITE (Satellite Instructional Television Experiment) programme. It was the first experiment of its kind ever made in the world. Some 3,000 villages in the six Indian states were brought under the focus of the television programs for four hours every day. This was the greatest achievement for the country's mass media. Although the NASA (National Aeronautics Space Administration of the USA) has now withdrawn the satellite, the Indian Government is determined to establish the television link to the 70 per cent of the 3,000 villages to the television stations to be started in the near by states to these villages. This is being done expeditiously with a view to keeping these villages further exposed to the new medium the "magic box."

Besides the seventeen television stations set up in various towns of the country are now covering 15 per cent of the population, as per the UNESCO figures published in the publication entitled "World Communication."

The Indian cinema has also taken rapid strides: some 619 films in 15 Indian regional languages were produced in 1978 and there were over 8,000 cinemas in the country's various states.

Right now, the Indian mass media are actively involved in the different aspects of national development. After the national emergency declared in India in June 1975, the mass media, especially the press, came under stress. But it should be stated to the credit of the media that in spite of severe restraints, they gave increasingly contributed to improvement of the situation and assisted the government and the masses in social, economic and political endeavour. People are being systematically educated in the new and modern means of production. Much more needs to be done however.

The coming of huge industry and large-scale construction works in India after independence have brought problem: complex working groups human resources mobilisation for national development, which have in turn changed the skill, training and attitudes which usually go side by side. As "the mobilising of human resources requires a great deal of attention of what the population knows and thinks of national development, and especially to the encouragement of the attitudes and social customs and the provision of knowledge, which will be favourable to the development", the mass media have undertaken the job quite competently.

This task of creating and encouraging attitudes and providing adequate information is being increasingly entrusted to the mass media. For, unless, according to Wilbur Schraemm, there is enough information designed to encourage productive attitudes, social patterns and customs, the development process is bound to suffer and be blocked. The individual differences perspective, the social categories perspective and the social relations perspective theories as enunciated by Melvin' De Fleur and Sandra Ball-Rokeach find a fair amount of application in the present Indian situation, if we assess the economic, social and political perspectives in the country in the last three decades or so since the dawn of independence. Terrific changes have taken place in the entire range of human activity in the country.

Schramm notices change in social, cultural, religious and personal attitudes which subsequently have helped change and shape a society completely differently. The Indian society has by and large reacted almost in an identical manner. This has been amply established by some well known studies conducted by Indian mass communication scholars such as Rao, Damle and several others. These researches have proved that mass media have immensely aided and assisted the rate and score of development and the pace of people in absorbing the new media which has completely revolutionised the style of people.

In bringing about these changes in which the various media are fully participating and getting involved include political consciousness, urbanisation, professional mobility, adult literacy, media consumption, and a broad general participation in the nation's reconstruction and similar activities. This has given a new dimension to the media's role in a developing situation and this is media in action in a country well on a road to progress which India presents today in the last quarter of the twentieth century.

Considering its size, swelling population and a fairly developing economy and a comparatively stable political system, India is the largest country in Asia today, second only to China. A great task of building up the country and developing its various latent human and natural resources lies on the head of the people in numerous fields. For its economic recovery and raising a complex infrastructure, India has already executed its four five-year development plans; the fifth commenced from April 1976 and will cost the country about $1,000 billion (Rs. 70,000 crores) on its completion and full execution in 1981. It is a colossal task requiring close cooperation and thorough coordination of the various factors including the mass media.

The Indian people "raised in different social environments" are therefore passing through a series of changes in "attitudes, values and beliefs that constitute their personal-psychological make-up." No system of mass media are "poorly developed." They have not been put to work "for economic development nor have they been used to bring about common anxieties, common concerns, and common emotions for India as a whole."

But it must be recognised that "it is through communication that people can learn about new ideas, can be stimulated by change which is conveyed to them or be cognizant of change and what it means, and can understand what is going around them." Mass media are essentially agents of social change, and the "specific kind of social change they are expected to help accomplish in the transition to new customs and practices, and in some cases to different social relationships. Behind such changes in behaviour must necessarily present substantial alterations in attitudes, beliefs, skills and social norms."

Thus the carious people would take the perspective that media present to them not in the same uniform way but in varying manners suiting their personal and psychological viewpoints which the media would possibly focus on resulting in individual differences in perspective on the mass communication process.

In fact, the initial stages, as Rokeach and DeFleur point out in their Dependency Model, the cognitive effects of mass media may be creation and resolution of ambiguity which "can occur because people lack enough information to understand the meaning of an event, or because they lack adequate information to determine which of several possible interpretations of an event is correct one." Besides, in such a situation "attitude formation", "agenda-setting," "the expansion of people's beliefs" and "the values" of a society are also affected in a changing situation.

Since the most media messages at present are closely linked to the Indian audience dependence, perceptible influence on their activities, attitudes, values, aspirations and endeavours have been keenly noticed. The active media message reception of the people has been effectively instrumental in changing individual needs, psychological and social characteristics. And in some cases they flow back to alter the nature of social system itself. These factors play an overriding role in shaping the developmental attitudes of a people and which changes the developmental strategy of a nation.

As India is passing through an era of economic transition, people's attitudes and values are changing fast; media use by the people is also going through quick shifts. Although communication facilities prevalent in the urban areas are much more than in the rural areas, villagers are becoming increasingly conscious of the power of knowledge. There has been quite a spurt in the rural press in the recent times in almost all regional dialects and national languages.

This has led in rural families now have one or two members who either subscribe to the newspapers, borrow from others or read in the village reading rooms. More villagers now visit cities, there is more interpersonal communication. The rural people now get more opportunities to see films as cinema houses have been brought to the villages. Actually, the shows are always full to the capacity now than ever.

With transistor revolution, more radios are used by the rural people; there were some 150 million licences issued until December 1973 by the various radio stations in the country. A farmer with a radio transistor tucked on his shoulder working in the fields is a common sight now. As the portable television set has already been manufactured in India itself, the radio transistor would, it is hoped to be replaced by the portable television.

The commercialisation of radio and television in India has brought the whole world of advertising to his door steps. As the messages about the new goods and products reach the rural homes and " if they (the messages) relate to their (people's) interests, consistent with their attitudes, congruent with their beliefs, and supportive to their values", as De Fleur and Rokeach point out, these are quickly acted upon and "hotly" pursued.

The proof of this, if one were required, lies in the improved living standards of the farmers, their better dressed and well-fed families, their awakening to health and family planning methods, their awareness of modern agricultural techniques and latest innovations. In fact, they are deriving the maximum use of media messages concern directly individually and jointly.

But it is true that majority of people are not gaining or are not able to benefit so much from the media messages. "Since there are individual differences in personality characteristics among such members, it is natural to assume that there will be variations in effect which correspond to these individual differences."

Another aspect of the Indian life, an altogether different and novel, is in the urban areas. The journals and periodicals published in most regional and national languages have fairly good circulations; majority of the people have seen television at some place or the other and a good number have them in their drawing rooms. They watch all that this "magic box" has to offer day in and day out.

The programme presented by the SITE offered a year-long contact with the modern information science and technology in kaleidoscopic forms and fashion. People have learnt from media and acquired ability to cope with new ideas and innovative techniques. Most people are acquainted with the human machines called the computers; they are familiar with A-bomb; they try to keep themselves abreast with what is happening in the most important parts of the world through radio, newspapers, journals and television. When they learnt about the murder of John Kennedy, many people stopped work and mourned; news about the forthcoming change in the American administration and Carter's victory were widely acclaimed all over.

Awareness of the media message even among the old people, who were markedly passive to political, social, economic and cultural developments, is also rising. Even a 70-year-old illiterate woman in a middle-class Delhi home knows how to switch on/off radio and television, air-cooler and fan, often enjoys the radio and television programmes that concern her and interest her.

More and more people are being exposed to technical subjects which one can use in everyday life. Some of these include things such as the DDT powder, chemical fertilizers, pesticides automatic machines and the intricate electronic gadgets. This is also raising their general level of understanding and information. The level of knowledge on abstract subjects like the local and national politics, diplomacy, air-carriers, pollution, ecology, elections, dictatorship, democracy, etc. expanding steadily.

The elites are still feetter off: It is, however, interesting and significant that the sense of change separates the elite from the masses most dramatically. Some 30 percent of the Indian people belong to the elite class and these people are as Westernised as could be conceived. They have completely shrugged off old traditional ways, attitudes and customs. And the Western media, newspapers, magazines films and television show have drastically transformed them into entirely new personalities. Living in the urban areas also means frequent mixing with the people from other advanced nations who come there as tourists or on business or in international gatherings and conferences (which are now a common feature). These intercourses have brought them nearer to the people in the United States, the U.K., West Germany, Canada, Australia and the USSR. And this has taken them away from superstitions, obsolete habits and beliefs of the yore. There is a great desire for change in life styles, values, economic status, social position and overall thinking.

Media have immensely contributed to this change and this development taking place in the Indian society. Like a wild magic media have placed the Indian society "up to hill higher than we can see on the horizon and let him look beyond." Media are like magic because "they can let a man see and hear where he has never been and know people has never met."

This indeed is a tremendous achievement for the Indian media and their yeoman's service in concrete terms to the national development and the common man.

Societal Forces

It has been prominently borne out by several research studies conducted in the various developing countries that modern communication media have immeasurable potency for improving and changing the face of a traditional society like that of India.

The studies conducted by Lerner, Schramm, Rao, and Doop, etc., have amply demonstrated that the interaction between the media and the society from development point of view is "constant and cumulative." The prominent reason, according to De Fleur and Rokeach, is that "people located at similar positions in a similar social structure would be similar in personality because of similarity of their immediate social environment." And they would naturally react and are most likely to grasp identically the gains in the form of knowledge of new techniques and new ideas have to offer.

Thus with constant communication flow, people will have a great deal in common in setting before them their developmental goals, deciding when and how they should change and what they want their society to be changing when such a communication is available and established in a society, the job of arriving at social consensus, designing a policy and directing action is entrusted to the government, but social and political organisations and the mass media become the most powerful instruments of change and development. The communication is fundamental to all social and development processes.

Development in India has been more or less on these very lines. Media, print and electronic, have played their role in framing economic and development attitudes for the five-year plans, directing and helping action by the government with people's participation, as far as practicable under the existing limitations of literacy and access. Of course, success has been slow and tardy.

Huge economic and development five-year plans for overall economic emancipation, giant industrial establishments and mammoth power works, enormous network of state undertakings, elaborately spread health and family welfare programmes and well-developed telecommunications, air and rail transportation networks and primary and higher education systems would not have been possible without a responsible and responsive mass media asserting their influence. These projects may only have come about slowly in the ordinary course of history by continuing contact with other economic systems through mass media.

It seems to be a simple and straight procedure, but actually it is a long drawn-out programme. To work this out would not have been easy and the process not so smooth. But the media helped expedite it and manoeuvre it through engineering human cooperation, consent and skill.

It is indeed a great task, which media could assist in bringing about in most amiable way. In its drain, change is also introduced in cultural fields and group relationship by participation, decision making and action. India has organised and successfully held six general elections for the 520 seat Parliament and several for the 22 state legislatures, wherein thousands of candidates and millions of electorates had complete liberty of "formulating voting decisions and actually going to the polls" where mass communication media barring radio and television had a full free-play of their potentialities, where people had not only "direction of exposure to mass communicated campaign material, but also the kind of effects that such material would have upon them." The mass media effects on the Indian situation have been indeed invaluable, of late specially.

We therefore, see "communication is a two-way process", as Dube says, "it involves giving as well as receiving information and direction. While this fact has been recognised in defining the role of community development projects (in the rural areas) as agents of communication and change, in actual practice the projects have tended to assume the role of the giver and the village people have mostly been at the receiving end."

In fact, India's swift agricultural progress, commonly termed as the "green revolution" in the late sixties and the early seventies.

It is a living tribute to the power of mass communication which has carried the results of the university laboratories to the farmer in the field and has made India almost self-sufficient in feeding its 630 million people.

As social relations perspectives of the Indian people are being progressively altered by the all-pervasive force of the mass media, family system, relations between parents and children, old and young, clothing habits and fashions, dressing and eating, and cultural and moral values are being assessed and reassessed. Large families, arranged marriages, women confining to kitchen drudgery and bearing children, etc. are becoming things of the past. Diehards are losing ground and mass-communicated youngsters with modern ideals are rapidly taking over even in the tradition-ridden homes and changing the society tremendously.

Although the government in India is very powerful in the field of mass communication and has complete monopoly of radio and television, and its films division produces a heavy proportion of the films made in the country, the government also publishes a large number of journals and periodicals-states and the central governments together are certainly the largest publishers in the country-nevertheless other mass communication media too have a heavy impact in the total situation of the nation.

That the mass media are trying to involve themselves and participate in the overall national development process is apparent from glancing through any issue of a newspaper or magazine. There has been an active realisation to the fact that there cannot be and significant economic development without the use of mass media. You cannot increase agricultural yields, convince people about family welfare, persuade them to hold off from buying or to bring their crops to the market, or teach them the value of sending their daughters to schools, without reaching them through radio, television, films or newspapers. Nor can one hope, without better mass communications, to weld together a vast country with many languages; bring about a concern for the same thing, see to it, that the citizens talk about the same national problems and, further take positions about them which are not primarily dictated by regional or other narrow considerations. For this we need, of course, the expansion of media.

Mass media in India are therefore striving to perform three developmental tasks (as outlined by Schramm): the populace must have information about national development: their attention must be focussed on the need to change, the opportunities inviting change, the methods and means of change; and if possible their aspiration for themselves and their country must be raised and highlighted.

In the second place, there must be opportunity to participate intelligently in the decision process, and thirdly, the needed skills must be taught: adults must be taught to read, children must be educated, farmers must learn the methods of modern farming, teachers, doctors, engineers must be trained, workers must master technical skills, people in general must learn more about how to keep themselves healthy and strong. The end result of this process in the situation as it develops would ultimately play a very vital role and would lead to the emergence of informal social relationships which would be helpful in "modifying the manner in which given individuals will act upon a message that comes to their attention via the mass media."

As De Fleur and Rokeach have underlined, "conceptually speaking, considerable similarity exists between the case of a farmer being advised to adopt a new form of weed spray via a radio programme devoted to farm problems and the case of a person being advised to adopt a new household detergent (or family planning method as in India) via a radio commercial designed to sell soap (or the family planning device)."

Media in India by and large in the near future would be able to assist in decision-making process which must accompany the country's overall developments and allround progress. The result indeed would be much better if the media get more and more opportunities and their activities have a free, unfettered flow.

There are, however, serious hurdles indeed: financial,

technological, political, and social. But these would certainly be overcome as the nation moves further in the realms of development and progresses with the impact of its media of mass communication.

Elements at Work

Of late, the concept of development itself is undergoing vast changes, and mass media's role in this process is being redefined and reassessed. Everette Rogers of Stanford University has recently tried to improve upon Schramm's concept of development. He states, ".....equality of distribution of information, socio-economic benefits; popular participation in self-development planning and execution usually accompanied by the decentralisation of certain of these activities to the village level; self-reliance and independence in development, within an emphasis upon the potential of local resources; integration of traditional with modern system, so that modernisation is a syncretisation of old and new ideas, with the exact mixture somewhat different in each locale form the essential elements in the new concept of development."

There has already been immense realisation in India of the type of development envisaged by Rogers. With mass communication media constantly "bombarding" these concepts, the rural and urban poor are receiving keen attention, and getting priority audience in development programmes so that the gap between the rich and the poor is being bridged as ably and quickly as possible.

Media have already started giving ample space and time to the villages, which they were earlier either doing casually or not doing at all. And with stimulus and incentives being promised, villagers and people of the lowest rung of the society are themselves being induced to develop themselves. Radio, television and cinema are persistently focussing on the plight of the downtrodden, the underprivileged and the unprivileged. Some old habits and customs are being yoked to reinforce new ideals on development so that every village, township or city may develop in their own way. Newspapers are adopting villages and with their influence, colleges and universities are following suit. As the news media report about the changes taking place in these villages at regular intervals and the spotlight works as a catalyst agent for the development of the entire community, a pattern suited to a particular environment is being worked out. This would also be determined by local and personal behaviour, style of living or community patterns. Thus Indian mass media are striking to focus development as a widely participatory process of social change in a society, intended to bring about both social and material advancement (including greater equality, freedom, and other valued qualities) for the majority of the people through their gaining greater control over their environment. This is Rogers' definition of development given in 1975 which exactly fits the Indian panorama and the mass media's emphasis.

But there are still huge problems awaiting solutions. Agriculture, health and family welfare, education, and adult literacy, obscure habits and outdated customs yet untouched and unearthed. These need media's urgent attention. There is lot to be done to accomplish these problems. This will immensely stimulate the people in their self-development patterns and would provoke them to outline their own achievements and successes in the various fields.

At political plane, masses still need to be educated about the necessity of stable political environments, they require to be enlightened about the importance of a pliable democratic process, and the role of a common citizen in the over-all administration of the country.

As Y.V.L. Rao points out in his study on the role of communication in the growth and development of the various aspects of the village life, the mass media should help the Indian people to raise their economic status, bring about greater respect for human dignity and greater equality among the masses, make cultural, social, political and economic chances a perpetuating process.

It is, therefore, clear that mass media have an eminently significant role in the total development and is "tied inseparably" in the entire process in India. However, as De Fleur and Rokeach underline that there is need to recognise and establish that "the effects of a given mass-communicated message sent out on a given channel will depend 'upon a large number of psychological characteristics and social categories similarities which audience members bring to their encounters with the quickly gaining momentum of the mass communication function. The method is to involve in the innumerable fields of activity. Communication specialists and researchers over the world are looking at the outcome of media's this involvement in India development with interest, and perhaps with an amount of concern.

Communication, as it is known today, has originated and evolved in the West, particularly in the United States of America. With the development of technologies, the communication methods also developed. The methods became complex and sophisticated. But the concept of 'communication' has been with us since the creation of man. The methods and the process is differ from region to region, country to country. Even now, with the idea of 'global village' becoming a reality, we differ as far as methods and process of communication are concerned.

You must be aware of various seminars and workshops being conducted to formulate a policy regarding satellite communication. Some experts say as a result of exposures to foreign television programmes, our values and culture may be damaged beyond repair. The negative influence of such telecasts may prove detrimental to the development of the nation.

Some scholars say that the Indian tradition has hardly any thoughts on communications. Those who grant such thoughts have negative vies on the issue. 'Communication' is a word coined in the recent past to explain a particular area of study. Therefore, in our ancient literature this view was not dealt with separately. But, a lot has been said on the process and methods of communication is an integral part of our socio-political and cultural life. It was as important then as it is now. It worked according to the social and cultural norms. At present, we must ensure that it works as per the socio-cultural ethos of our nation. Otherwise the fabric of the nation may be disturbed.

Our way of life is influenced by religion and various philosophical teachings. As a God fearing people, we have found various ways to worship. Mysticism is one such way.

Mysticism has given birth to a new method of communicating one's deep realisation and understanding of God and the Universe. Mysticism is centered on oneself. It is a process by which one plunges into the deepest core of one's heart of self. A profound communication takes place in one's innermost core. This communication process can be termed as interpersonal communication-communication with oneself. Mira Bai and Kabir communicated so much in a very easy way because their realisation was clear. We have not explored this mystical process. This mystical approach possibly can help us to communicate with our people more effectively. Interpersonal Communication enriched interpersonal communication. This area of communication has not been sufficiently explored. Some enthusiastic communication professionals take a parochial view and try desperately to invent a communication theory or a model which existed in the ancient times. Having discussed the importance of interpersonal and interpersonal communication, we shall discuss the importance of Indian philosophy in Communication. We come to know about the process of communication in ancient India through treatises on arts, religion, and mysticism. We can also go through Sanskrit, Persian, Urdu and Hindi sources.

Accounts of Vedanta, Bhakti, Vaishnavism and Sufism speak volumes on communication. To be effective in our communication we should be able to establish their relevance to the people of modern India. This Indian orientation will help us to recast and reframe the whole outlook towards communication concepts norms, and beliefs.

We ought to turn to the Indian philosophical tradition which has tremendous intellectual and spiritual resources and can easily supply us with basic framework for a creative and relevant communication process. The impact of this heritage has been felt through the ages and its richness and university has been acknowledged by the world. Since the present communication concept and discipline has developed in the west, we do get carried away by its Western perception and hence become ineffective in the Indian situation. It is necessary, therefore that we ground ourselves firmly in our culture, beliefs and ethos. We need not copy the western models blindly. And thus consequently suffer the loss of inspiration.

The Legacy

In India, communication is inextricably linked with philosophy and religion. Sarvapalli Radhakrishnan says, "the pursuit of philosophy is deemed a religious vocation. Therefore, in order to come to terms with the cultural ideal that animates Indian society, we need to examine, brief though they may be, the outlines of Indian philosophy."

The Upanishads call attention to the value of the knowledge of ultimate truth as a means of liberation. The Upanishads, greatly emphasise the need to look inward for a clearer understanding of reality. The basic tenet of the Upanishads is the need to acquire self-knowledge and thereby liberate oneself from worldly bondages.

With the passage to time, a number of non-Vedic philosophical traditions sprang up. The Charvakas placed heavy emphasis on the material world on the material world and discarded all notions of transcendentality. Jainism was another tradition of philosophy which was non-Vedic in character. In maintained that both the animate and the inanimate world were eternal and independent. Therefore one has to be tolerant to all that exists on earth. Buddhism, another non-vedic philosophy constituted a powerful reaction against the ritualism that characterized the Vedas and the transcendentalism that was associated with the Upanishads. The individual, according to Buddhism, should diligently work out his salvation, from pain and suffering.

Later, Indian Philosophy began to move further and further away from the original ways of thinking and, indeed, split into different and competing systems. Although these systems do not by any means constitute mutually exclusive categories, they display sufficient variation for each to warrant on autonomous conceptual status. Of these, there are six that deserve close attention. They are the Nyaya; Vaishesika; Samkhya; Yoga; Mimamsa; Vedanta and Advaita. These schools, too, contributed to the formation of the Indian tradition.

The Indian schools philosophy originated from the Vedas; two schools are Vedic—the Mimamsa and the Vedanta; the four-Samkhya, Yoga, Vaishesika, and Nyaya-have their base in the Vedas. Therefore, these six schools are classed as Vedic or Astika. The two schools of Buddhism and Jainism are called Nastika as they do not accept Vedic authority. These eight schools are products of the great thought that characterised the post-Vedic age. Each school of philosophy is called a Darshana, meaning a view or a vision of the truth. The aims and aspirations of life are not only the pursuit of material gains and pleasure but also virtue and morality which chasten life and spiritual enlightenment and freedom.

Each school is associated with a sage as its first promulgator—Samkhya with Kapila, Yoga with Patanjali, Vaishesika with Kanada, Nyaya with Gautama, Mimamsa with Jaimini and Vedanta with Badarayana-Vyasa. Because of their mutual relationship, these six schools fall into three groups of allied systems. Samkhya is accepted by Yoga, with the addition of God as the omniscient first Teacher. The speciality of Yoga is the practical aspect of the methods of mental control by which the philosophical ideal of the Samkhya, namely, the isolation of the Spirit from Matter is achieved. But Yoga as a Sadhana or preparatory discipline and means came to be accepted by all schools.

Today, it has, with the help of science, grown in strength and gained a world-wide vogue. The vaishesika doctrines form the basis of Nyaya, both being schools of realism and pluralism. The Mimamsa and Vedanta go together because of their common Vedic basis but otherwise they differ fundamentally. The former is concerned with Karma and Dharma, the performance of ordained duty, but the latter to the opposite of Karma, namely, renunciation from activity; according to Vedanta, knowledge is the means of salvation. Mimamsa is thus related to the Karma-kanda, and Vedanta to the Upanishads. The Mimamsa also made a valuable contribution to the science of interpreting texts; it came to be known therefore as Vakya Shastra.

But what do all these mean to us today. Our tradition, philosophy, culture, and religion are not dead. We still practice our ancient religion. We do study our ancient philosophy and theology. Our beliefs are largely based on Karma and Dharma.

Therefore, these things have meaning in our day to day life. The words coined in various philosophical and theological books are still being used by us to convey the same meaning. Thus, to communicate meaningfully, we must be well grounded in this rich heritage. But a little caution-we must not be so heavily grounded in these, so as not to be able to fly and explore the richness of clear blue sky.

What implication does this survey of Indian philosophy have for communication theory? On the basis of these philosophical tenets, we can construct a workable model of communication for the Indian situation. This may differ substantially from models found in the Western countries. Each culture may have models of communication of its own. What is essential is that any communication model must be based on a cultural context. Otherwise the meaning conveyed may differ from the intended meaning to be conveying in a communication. Many times, we may fail to communicate if we do not take this cultural context into consideration.

In India generally the primary focus of interest in communication is how does the receiver make sense of the stimuli that he receives so as to deepen his self-awareness. In the Western model, the basic question that present themselves are how does the Communicator affect/influence/manipulate the receiver and how does the communicator and receiver share information and enter into a two-way relationship. According to traditional Indian views, meaning should necessarily lead to self-awareness. Hence the Indian definition of communication would be that it is an inward search for meaning—a process of intra-personal communication.

In the West, communication is seen as the transference of meaning with the intention of influencing the receiver. But in Indian meaning brings enlightenment. Meaning, according to traditional Indian thought, was seen as process which leads to self-awareness, then to freedom, and finally to truth. Here, by freedom we mean the liberation of persons from ignorance, from illusion of the world, and the web of the artificial categories constructed all around us. Indian and the Western ways is that the Indian way focuses attention on the intra-personal dimension as opposed to the inter-personal dimension.

The Western way is expression-oriented but the Indian way is interpretation oriented. The Indian way seems to suggest that what is important in human communication is to find out how a receiver makes sense of the verbal stimuli that are received by him and engages in a search for meaning. This search is an inward one. The traditional authorities maintain that the reality is indeed within man. To know it is to be. In other words, distinction between the knower and the known narrows down considerably. The realization of truth is facilitated neither by language nor by logic and rationality. To know is to be; to know is to become aware of the artificial categorization imposed on the world by language and logic. It is only through an intuitive process that man will be able to lift himself out of the illusory world, which according to the Indian viewpoint, is indeed the aim of communication. People may differ with this view. But we all must agree that in India realisation dawns when we internalise the communication. It needs to be pointed out that one may not understand the current development in communication solely in the light of this model. We are living in a world where the border lines between countries are disappearing very fast. We do know and feel at one with the happenings in other parts of the globe. We are passing though a phase of civilization which could be termed, at best, the transition, and 'chaotic' at worst.

Indian communication centres on the word Sadharanikaran. It is derived from the Sanskrit world Sadharan meaning simple, common or ordinary. Sadharanikaran would thus imply simplification. The word has a familiar ring and is equivalent to the Latin word "communs" that is communication, meaning commonness of experience.

Sadharanikaran has been vividly described in Bharata's Natya Shastra, which though discovered in the 10th century A.D. by Bhattanayak, has now been established to have its authorship in a period as early as 500 BC. It is also known as the fifth Veda, as in it Bharata Muni had condensed the essence of the four Vedas for the benefit of the common man.

How does Sadharanikaran take place? Bharata describes Sadharanikaran as that point in the climax of a drama when the audience becomes one with the actor who lives an experience through his acting on stage and starts simultaneously reliving the same experience. The process has been described as rasa swadan. When Sadharanikaran happens, universalisation or commonness of experience takes place in full form. According Bhattanayak, the essence of communication is to achieve commonness or oneness among the people. Later, this word was extensively used in literacy circles for explaining poetics, aesthetics and drama.

But today, Sadharanikaran is often employed to convey the idea of commonness and simplification. The entire superstructure of Indian aesthetic centres on the act of Sadharanikaran through rasa swadan.

Rasa has been explained thus: man in his essential characteristics is a bundle of bhawa that constitute his being and form part of his total consciousness. These have been categorised as 50 in number. Of these nine are described as Sthai bhawa 33 as Vyabhichari bhawa and the remaining as Satwik bhawa. Bharata, after an intensive study of these moods, has grouped them under one all encompassing expression bhawa for purposes of establishing Sadharanikaran.

Coomaraswamy describes 'bhawa' as springing from aesthetic emotion of person who derives its existence from sensory experience. Each mood is capable of arousing a relevant state of feeling/quality of response.

Bharat Muni also postulated that for Sadharanikaran to take place, Sthai Bhava, that is, permanent moods in the audience, have to be aroused which will result in the unleashing of the attendant Rasas, feeling or aesthetic pleasures, thereby completing the process of communication.

A Bhava is the first reaction or sensation caused in the sympathetic mind by a stimulus called Vibhavas sone, a bird, a picture. A sustained Bhava that leads to Rasa is the Sthayee Bhava.

An Anubhava is the physical manifestation that takes place immediately as Bhava registers itself in the mind.

The Sthayee Bhava is stimulated by the Vibhava in the mind and is heightened by Anubhavas and Sanchari Bhavas. In this state, the mind will be highly receptive to the Rasa experience.

When a person experiences the intensity of the Bhavas of the Vaibhavas he overcomes his own personality and completely identifies himself with actual state of the Vibhava: This is state of universalisation. The universalisation leads to identification and involvement. Whatever is communicated leaves deep impact. Rasa can be understood only by the Sahridaya the person who alone is capable of rasaswadan. Who is Sahridaya? He/she is person in state of emotional intensity i.e. a quality of emotional dimension coequal to that of the sender of the message of communicator. Both must be sahridayas.

In India, communication lays great stress on the communicator and the one who receives communication belonging to the same cultural group. The same cultural context will help the communicator and the receiver to communicate effectively. The sender and receiver of a communication belonging to same culture, would be able to communicate more effectively. In other world, it is emphasised that communication may be ineffective between an individuals or groups, not belonging to the same culture as total grasp of symbols, signs and meanings are essential for effective communication. The relevance of the message, the code and the experience that the code stands for, to the group with which communication is sought to be established, is an important factor in communication.

In Western societies sources and receivers, at least in principle, communicate as equals, but in Indian society, it is not the case. The source is viewed as higher and the receiver as lower in status. The relationship is a hierarchical one of dominance and subordination. The source is held in high esteem by the receiver of communication, a relationship idealized in the gurushishya relationship. Even though the source and receiver are unequal, they are Sahridayas, having a common cultural orientation. This makes the communication is their unequal relationship satisfying.

The hierarchical aspect of Sadharanikaran contributed to the blossoming of Indian civilization through efficient communication. This was, however, later taken to the level of absurdity, resulting in highly rigid and hierarchical society. To some extent, it made Indian society into a more or less closed system and thereby contributed towards its stagnancy and decay. It is true Natyashastra was written by Bharat Muni to simplify the complex Vedas for the benefit of the common man and thereby bridge the gap between the elites, the priests, the nobles and Sudras. However, with the passage of time, Sadharanikaran resulted in divisions within society. Later, with institutionalization of difference the society became stagnant.

Sadharanikaran, through communication, between unequals over a period of time, contributed toward the development of more or less permanent and rigid hierarchical social relationships, as reflected in the caste system. Not only that, it seems that the values supporting the hierarchical nature of social arousal of permanent mood and particular aesthetic pleasure made them natural and acceptable as well as satisfying. Acceptance of this type of communication pattern by the people belonging to different castes, made the system stronger and permanent.

Today, to a great extent, the caste system influences communication patterns, particularly in Indian villages. Within a village community, far more communication takes place among the members of a caste than between castes because of the highly stratified and hierarchical nature of the caste system. People of high and low castes accept their position as natural. The asymmetrical relationship between high and low caste members is hereditary and is accepted by those who are in a disadvantageous position.

It may be pointed out here that in Indian many sages and saints, in different times, launched reform movements against social inequalities. They attempted to further simplify and reinterpret Indian philosophy for the benefit of the common people and thereby bridge the gap between elites and commoners.

However, the question arises: apart from the academic exercise, is there any use of studying of the Indian view on communication? In think, it is necessary and the need is urgent. Some the reasons are as follow:

(a) The Indian view of communication takes into consideration the man and his environment as healthy unit as against the mechanical and quantitative view of man.

(b) The use of technology has added a new dimension to use of world as a tool of communication. The printing press, radio TV and satellite have multiplied words and their use to an immeasurable extent. The knowledge of Indian view of communication may help in minimising the use of words to create a greater effect with aid of visuals.

(c) The emergence and use of large number of words has resulted in the distortion of the meaning or words. Words, however, would continue to occupy primacy in human communication in future despite the expansion of electronic media. "Better than a collection of thousand meaningless words is one word full of meaning on hearing which one becomes peaceful", says the Dhammapada.

(d) The Sadharanikaran theory underlines the role of communication. It is total communication and communication at its best. It is more integrated approach to communication because it seeks to affect the behaviour of human beings by arousing emotional and physical response simultaneously.

Impact on Life

Indian society is often characterised as one of "unity in diversity" and its villages as "independent republics." These characterizations have important implications for the patterns of human communication in India.

In ancient India, cultures blossomed in different parts of the subcontinent. These were unique and independent of each other. These cultures derived strength and inspirations from each other. The merits of cultures were communicated through the long established oral tradition.

The roving saints and sufies performed the task of communicating messages. They propagated the gospels of truth enshrined in the Vedas and Puranas, epic stories like Ramayana and Mahabharata and other scriptures. They reinterpreted these messages as per the realities prevailing in the society. In the process, they succeeded in communicating the norms values proper for decent social living.

At the communicating level, known as a class of knowledgeable people, Brahmins enjoyed the highest social status. They played an effective role as "link persons" between the common man of their own community and persons from outside the community.

Village communities were mostly self-sufficient. Each community had strong and extensive cultural links with other communities beyond the neighbouring villages and towns. Administrative contract were minimal, largely confined to revenue collection. Even this task was performed through intermediaries such as the Nawabs Zamindars and Lambardars. Thus, in ancient or traditional India, there existed effective systems of communication which were both local and pan-Indian in character. Such communication provided meaning and justification for the social order. It inculcated the spirit of devotion, love and faith.

Indian society was highly stratified and hierarchical. Communication tended to flow from persons of higher status to persons of lower status. In any communication situation, the relationship between the source and the receiver was that of dominance and subordination. In spite of this there as some dialogue between the two. Both shared a common frame of reference which made communication smooth and effective.

New Order

With the advent of British rule in India, there was an increase in administrative links, and physical mobility was encouraged through rails and roads. A new philosophy and culture spread by Macaulay's education system started making inroads into traditional Indian society and culture. The two were incompatible in many ways. However, the communication of foreign concepts, ideas and philosophies was successful as a lot of Indians accepted them. At the same time the conflict between the Indian and British ways of life became evident. As a consequence, there were upheavals, and turmoils, which ultimately led to the birth of independent India.

Free India has adopted democracy based on universal adult franchise as form of government. As welfare state it has opted for planned development. The technological growth and developments, huge development in communication and increases in the scale of economic activities have enlarged the range of choices. The philosophy of equality, irrespective of caste, creed and religion and the compulsions of democratic elections at all levels—village panchayats to the Parliament help to minimise the disadvantages of the traditional social and political relationships.

Communication is not confined only through to religion and practice of social norms. Its task is much more than maintaining the order and stability in society. Though the speaker is till viewed as an authority figure, particularly in rural areas and the listener as subordinate, such a relationship does not go unchallenged in many parts of our country to day. Tensions centred on such relationship do exit and report of social tensions from different parts of the country are frequently published. At the same time, there are situations where communication patterns are more on a basis of equality. Communication is no longer viewed only as a means to stability and harmony but for change as well. Thus communication in India has become a complex subject.

We are well aware of societal conditions that have given rise to various mass media. It is normally assumed that technology has been necessary for the reproduction of communications for mass audiences. Industrialisation, with the division of labour and urbanization, has created mass and heterogenous audiences. The proponents of this idea also hold that in the pre-industrial period, the communication system was restricted to direct face-to-face communication between individuals.

These assumptions, as far as India is concerned, are not wholly true. First, despite passing from the First Information and Communication Revolution, the Indian society has largely retained the traditions of oral and interpersonal communication. Therefore, when we consider the distinguishing features of modern society, it is not the 'mass' of people that constitutes 'a mass society', but the relationships between the members. The western concept of mass society explains its heterogenous nature due to its being alienated by technology, socially differentiated due to occupation and physically separated through expansion of urbanisation. Thus the need to reach out to this highly "impersonalized" mass society, requires various "mass media" not only to bring together its members into mainstream, but also to seek their consent for social action.

Does this portrayal of the "mass" of people provide an accurate picture of present-day Indian society? Clearly it does not. Yes, we have undergone industrialization, urbanisation and modernisation. Yet life in contemporary Indian society is very different, because of these changes. But when we look at the villages in India, we see large "masses" of people living together as homogenized blocks, linked together by their myriad languages, dialects, common culture, traditions and so on. So, what we have today are groups of "masses" linked together by oral tradition, culture and language, giving a picture of homogeneity.

However, in recent years, even among communication scholars, there has been tendency to transplant communication models from the West to developing countries. They have transplanted the idea that rational independent messages beamed at "individuals" will lead to motivation and attitude change. This basically the advertising and marketing model of a society believing in perfect competition.

We are now beginning to realise that there is another model of society in which the indivi-dual derives his legitimacy from the system. In such a society the role of "communication" is quite different. Therefore, attempts to inform, educate and motivate the individual in many a times do not succeed. However, messages with symbols appealing to the "collective" consciousness many times do succeed. The Indian society, with its unique concept of the "collective" nature of interpersonal networks, affirms that while we keep our windows open to the world, our feet are rooted in the innate wisdom that has come down to us over the last 5000 years. It is within these parameters, that India's transition from the oral to the modern mass media-based society, has to perceive.

In India, the print media took roots first in the major provincial capitals of British Indian—Calcutta and Madras and later Bombay. These cities with their surrounding areas accounted for the bulk of their newspaper circulations. Advertising also developed in these metropolitan centres. As the freedom struggle gained momentum, newspapers were published from main centres of the agitation like Delhi, Lahore, Lucknow and Kanpur. Other newspaper centres were concentrated in the princely states of Mysore, Hyderabad, Bhopal and Baroda. These cities also had their own radio stations.

Newspaper readership continued to remain in urban areas.

After independence the print medium emerged from its pre-colonial past and spread into the semi urban and rural areas. Advanced technology, better roads and transport helped the press to move into semi urban centres, but they were still rotted in the cities. A new class emerged—the information rich who were already modernised, literate and economically well off. With development and growth of newspaper technology and sharp competition the costs of publishing a newspaper also rose. The advertising world—the backbone of newspaper—hitched its wagon to the highly-circulated newspaper and magazines, fuelling the growing difference between big and small newspapers and magazines. The power of the print media attracted bit industrialists to invest in the newspaper industry. Monopolies and chain newspapers became the order of the day. Suddenly, the missionary zeal of pre-independence days gave away to a competitive frenzy in commerce. Today we have chain-newspapers controlled by business tycoons who run them purely on commercial lines.

What has been the impact of newspapers on Indian society? A difficult question to answer. But a few pointers would give us somewhat clear picture. Newspapers have become a class medium, catering only to the rich and the powerful. However, the language newspapers do cater to the lower levels of society. But their reach and access are linked to literacy and capacity to purchase. According to present estimates, newspapers are purchased and read by less than 20 per cent of India's 900 million population. A wide gulf has been created between the "information-rich" and "information-poor." Instead of a democratising and bringing equity the newspapers have helped to perpetuate a class structure in society.

The broadcasting media though government control, have the capacity to reach out to the people in every nook and corner of the country. While both are highly capital-intensive, it is their capacity to reach out to millions that makes them a people's medium. The development of Akashvani and Doordarshan in India has had its ups and downs, but today we have about 545

TV stations covering about 90 per cent of area and catering to about 60 per cent of the population. Radio has much wider reach and access. But in case of the two media, it is not the development of infrastructure that we need to look into, but their programme content and how it is being received by the people. It is in this area that both AIR and Doordarshan have not been found wanting. While "news" has been accepted as the important segment in their programme content, other aspects lime development and education have been given adequate attention. However, entertainment has become synonymous with these two corporations.

AIR has opened various channels for entertainment; but has failed to evoke the same kind of audience response to other development-oriented programmes as to entertainment. Even its educational programmes have restricted listenership. Researchers have pointed out to the lack of quality programmes over AIR.

Doordarshan has fared no better. The criticism levelled against AIR also applies to Doordarshan. The criticism levelled against Doordarshan is sometimes more severe as the policy formulated for it says that it should serve the developmental aspirations of the majority. The Doordarshan has ended up with more entertainment than any other type of programmes. Except for news and few current affairs programmes. DD largely depends on films and film-based programmes to fill in its telecast time. Criticism about lack of professionalism, creativity and production skills, have been levelled against DD. What has been its impact on society?

People do say that TV is an "idiot box" and has harmful effects on children. But TV is a tool of learning also and so far, has been well-received. Further, information on health, family planning and eradication of social evils like drugs, smoking, alcoholism and dowry, have all been successfully projected over Doordarshan.

Let us take another important mass medium—films. Films can be produced on almost all subjects of human interest and include, broadly speaking, feature films, documentaries and newsreels. The themes may encompass such diverse subjects as industry, agriculture development, education, environment and vital national issues like family welfare, national integration and untouchability. In fact, a large number of films are not commercial in the usual sense.

Contemporary film making more than ever before, is a big financial venture. It is usually controlled by commercial consideration rather than the demands of the art. The star system, lavish promotion and publicity and huge budgets for formula pictures are all frantic attempts to minimise the financial risk involve in film making. No wonder such films aim to please the audience by creating a synthetic world of unreal emotions. They make no demands on the power of thinking and ignores are for the sake of commerce. Films seeks to attract the audience by providing rather glib and naive entertainment in order to covert people's childishness into cash. For the majority of the viewers, a film is day-dreaming device in which they forget their worries and get lost in world of fantasy—full of melodramatic sentiments, songs and dance, violence and sex. In fact, with only a few honourable exceptions cinema in India has been overwhelmingly entertainment-oriented almost since its beginning. The Indian film stars have exerted such a hypnotic hold on the masses that they have made a place for themselves in public life, politics and even influenced the living style of the people. Exceptional Indian Films, with their intense realism and abiding concern for the common man, have found their way to international acclaim. The emergence of the new cinema as a movement, presenting a modern humanistic approach, offered a refreshing contrast to the commercial cinema.

Video has grown to be a very popular mass medium within a remarkably short times. It has endless possibilities for entertainment and education. Video in India in India is largely perceived as an alternative source of entertainment. However, video news magazine has caught the popular fancy and many leading newspapers have come forward to launch news magazines in audio-visual form. Public sector companies have utilised the video medium for bringing out house journals. But video has also come to occupy an important place in political and poll campaigns in India.

A communication satellite is a man-made platform launched into space; it remains relatively stationary over the earth. It serves as a platform for radio relay stations which receive radio signals beamed to it from the earth and relays those signals back to other locations on earth. Satellite communication greatly benefited the newspaper industry. It made possible facsimiles of newspaper pages to be sent electronically via satellite to receiving station anywhere in the world where printing facilities may be located.

The satellite distribution systems give the newspapers a flexibility hitherto not possible. Satellites now link news bureaus all over the country and can instantly transmit news reports to any station. Computers can automatically set the stories in type and start the process rolling. The cable TV system can receive programmes through satellite and deliver them by cable to subscribers' sets. In another form of transmission, called Direct Broadcast Satellite, television programmes are directly received by the dish antenna at home, totally bypassing the cable system.

But the strongest impact of TV comes through the Hong Kong-based STAR-TV, CNN, the BBC and Pakistan TV, using satellites to beam programmes right into our homes. There has been a furore over the role of these foreign satellite broadcasts, referred to as post-colonial cultural imperialism. They have made serious inroads into DD viewership. Innumerable dish antennae dot the horizon of Delhi, Mumbai, Kolkata, Chennai, Bangalore and Ahmedabad and a large number of smaller cities in the country. DD replied to this "invasion from the sky" by opening the 5 Metro channels to Indian viewers from August 15, 1993. It also hopes to use the terrestial links to further upgrade the coverage geographically. Multiplicity of channels has increased the choice for the viewers. The question always is as to which channel will win the audience—ratings race. It has been observed that a large majority of TV viewers seem to be convinced that the foreign-based TV channels, thought better produced, are not culturally conducive to a large number of viewers.

It should be obvious by now that for an Indian approach to communication a sound knowledge of its philosophical, cultural and linguistic traditions is necessary. It is also necessary to go to Sanskrit, as it may provide us with a lot of materials on communication which could be of use to communicate to our people properly and effectively. It is only by undertaking such kind of studies and by relating these to the demands of modern life that we will be able to re-cast and reframe our whole outlook toward communication concepts, norms and beliefs.

In this connection, we have to look at the trends in characteristic of the highly industrialised west and particularly of the USA. There the science of communication have been mastered, but because of a highly materialistic focus, who are losing the true purpose of communication is lost sight of in their eagerness to consume more and provide themselves with more free time and leisure, the listener has unleashed a Frankensteinian unstoppable momentum to the growth of sophisticated technology. The wisdom of the East, from India and China, may help them to reframe their communication priorities.

It is a matter of concern, that the lure of technology is creating a wide gap among various communities and classes in Indian society. We require to prioritize our use of technology, particularly those needs related to the socio-cultural and linguistic demands. According to many scholars, catering to this large number of people with diverse needs has become a problem. Faced with spectre of proliferating communication technology, India is on the threshold of a giant leap forward. Just acquisition of communication technology may not help the Indian society. India has used a lot of communication technology in almost five decades since Independence. But the increase in the use of modern technology for development did not make our communication better. Analysis reveals that during this process of modernisation, very powerful political and economic forces have gained control over the communication system. This in turn had led to either distortion, discrimination of even total obstruction of the communication flow from and to the grassroot level. This has not only resulted in cultural erosion, but at the same time has pushed large masses of people below the poverty line of information. This needs to be guarded against India with its teeming millions cannot afford to sustain an imbalanced system of communication. We have communicated with our people for so long through the oral tradition, now, let us not destroy this tradition.

Long before the mass media were invented, Plato may have provided the opening round in the controversy over the social costs and benefits of mass culture. In his commentary on the training of the children who were to become the leaders of his ideal Republic, he saw the mass culture of his day as posing a threat to the minds of the young.

Then shall we simply allow our children to listen to any stories that anyone happens to make up, and so receive into their minds ideas often the very opposite of those we shall think they ought to have when they are grown up?

No, certainly not [replies, Glaucon].

It seems, then, our first business will be to supervise the making of fables and legends, rejecting all which are unsatisfactory; and we shall induce nurses and mothers to tell their children only those which we have approved...

Most of the stories now in use must be discarded.

This theme-popular entertainment is harmful to the minds of the young has been a consistent one from the beginnings of mass communication. It has been claimed from time to time that such charges can be validated by scientific evidence, but repeatedly this evidence has turned out to be difficult to interpret and therefore controversial. Social sciences insist that any important conclusions about the effects of the media be supported by solid evidence. Because of such insistence upon data rather than emotion, they sometimes find themselves in the awkward position of seeming to defend the media when actually they are simply refusing to accept the inadequately supported claims of critics.

Nevertheless, the insistence that conclusions be based on adequate evidence has never deterred the literacy critic from charging the media with a deep responsibility for society's problems. Most nineteenth century's American writers at some point in their careers took time to criticize and condemn the newspaper for superficiality and distortion.

Practical Aspects

The tenacity and stability of the mass media generally in the face of such a long history of criticism by powerful voices needs explanation. The problem at first seems deceptively simple: the media appeal to the masses and the masses want the kind of content they get and so the media continue to give it to them.

Many social scientists, such as Skornia, have exposed the inadequacy of this explanation by nothing the old chicken-and-egg problem. It is difficult at best to know if the public taste determines the media fare or if the media fare determines public taste. The answer probably lies somewhere in between with public taste being both a cause and effect of media fare. The relationship between public taste and media fare thus becomes a circular one which, in terms of the chicken-egg analogy, is an ongoing process of chickens producing eggs and eggs producing chickens.

The structural functional analysis of social systems (or "functional analysis" for short) concerns itself with the patterns of action exhibited by individuals or subgroups who relate themselves to one another within such systems. A social system is, for this reason, an abstraction—but one not too far removed from the observable and empirically verifiable behaviours of the persons who are doing the acting. The social system, then, is a complex of stable, repetitive, and patterned action that is in part a manifestation of the culture shared by the actors, and in part a manifestation of the psychological orientations of the actors (which are in turn derived from that culture). The cultural system, the social system, and the personality systems (of the individual actors), therefore, are different kinds of abstractions made from the same basic data, namely, the overt and symbolic behaviours of individual human beings. They are equally legitimate abstractions, each providing in its own right a basis for various kinds of explanations and predictions. Generally speaking, it may be difficult or nearly impossible to analyse or understand fully one such abstraction without some reference to the others.

But, granted that the term "social system" is a legitimate scientific abstraction, how does this general conceptual strategy help in understanding; the mass media of communication? To answer this question, we need to set forth in greater detail exactly what is meant by the term social system, and what type of analysis it provides. To aid in providing such an explanation we turn briefly to several ideas that are important aspects of the study of social systems. One of the most important of these ideas is the concept of the "function" of some particular repetitive phenomenon (set of actions) within such a system. The fact that such content has long survived the jibes of influential critics was said to require explanation. One form of explanation will be provided by noting the function of such a repetitive phenomenon within some stable system of action. The term "function" in the present context means little more than "consequence." To illustrate briefly, we might hypothesize that the repetitive practice of wearing wedding rings on the part of a given married couple has the function (consequence) of reminding, them as well as others that the two are bound together by the obligations and ties that matrimony implies. This practice thereby contributes indirectly to maintaining the permanence of the marriage—the stability of that particular social system. The practice is in a sense "explained" by noting its contribution to the context within which it occurs. A comparison of a number of such systems with and without this particular item (but in other respects matched) would test the assertion.

In the above example, the social system is a relatively simple one. There are only two "components," and each of these happen to be the behaviour pattern of an individual. Their patterns are derived both from the individual psychological makeup of the partners and from the cultural norms concerning marriage prevailing in their community, social class, and society. It is a miniature system whose stability is dependent upon satisfaction of its "needs." For example, such a system requires that the partners perform roles that meet the expectations each has of the other and the expectations the community has of married couples. This can be thought of as a "need" for adequate role performance, without which the stability of the system would be endangered. Other "needs," related to economic matters and emotional satisfactions, could be cited.

More complex illustrations of social systems can easily be pointed to, where the "components" of the system are not the actions of individual persons but subsystems. A department store, for example, is a complex social system consisting of the actions of managerial personnel, buyers, salespersons, the clerical staff, customers, transportation workers, a janitorial team, and security employees. Each of these components is a smaller system of action within the broader system of the store itself, and it in turn is a complex system of action carried out within the context of the external social conditions of the community. In spite of the complexity, any given set of repetitive actions might be analysed in terms of their contribution to maintaining or undermining the system's stability. Granting to employees the right to buy merchandise at cost could have the function (consequence) of maintaining their morale and loyalty, and thus would contribute fairly directly to the maintenance of the system. Rigid insistence on the observance of petty rules, such as docking the pay of an employee who on rare occasions was late for work, might be disruptive of morale and loyalty, and by contributing to labour turnover it could be dysfunctional. Instead of contributing to the maintenance of the system, it could cause disruptions and instability. Such inductively derived conclusions would be subject to testing for validity, of course, but the functional analysis would have generated the hypothesis to be tested an important role of theory.

The Organisation

A "functional analysis," then, focuses on some specific phenomenon occurring within a social system. It then attempts to show how this phenomenon has consequences that contribute to the stability and permanence of the system as a whole. The phenomenon may, of course, have a negative influence, and if so, it would be said to have "dysfunctions" rather than "functions." The analysis is a strategy for inducing or locating hypotheses that can be tested empirically by comparative studies or other appropriate research methods.

The analysis of social system is extremely difficult, no infallible rules specify precisely how to locate and define the exact boundaries of a given social system, particularly if it is relatively complex. As yet, no completely agreed upon criteria exist for establishing linkages between the components of a system, and no standard formulas can uncover the precise contribution that a given repetitive form of action makes to the stability of a system. A functional analysis of the contribution of some item to the stability of a system, then, is a procedure that is somewhat less than rigorous. But in spite of this source of potential criticism, this strategy has proved useful in our attempts to understand complex social phenomena, such as the mass media.

How can this type of analysis be applied to the mass media? First, we can identify that portion of the content of the mass media that is in "low" cultural taste or provides gratifications to the mass audience in such a manner that it is widely held to be potentially debasing as the "relatively persistent trait or disposition" of the mass media we seek to explain. It would be difficult in practice to construct a set of categories under which to analyse the content of the media so that material of "low" cultural taste can be identified readily. It would be difficult, but actually it would not be impossible. Excessive violence, the portrayal of criminal techniques, horror and monster themes, open pornography, suggestive music, and dreary formula melodramas are typical categories of content that arouse the ire of critics. Considerable disagreement would probably occur as to the exact content that should be included in any given category. There would also be debates over the number of categories used.
There would also be debates over the number of categories used.

Nevertheless, it is theoretically possible to identify the content of any given medium that is most objected to by the largest number of critics. We will assume that given sufficient time and resources, and using survey techniques, preference scales, attitude measuring instruments, and other research procedures now available that the content of any given medium could be divided roughly into something like the following three categories:

Low-taste Content: This would be media content widely distributed and attended to by the mass audience, but which has consistently aroused the ire of critics. Examples would be crime dramas on television that emphasize violence, openly pornographic motion pictures, day time, confession magazines, crime comics, suggestive music, or other content that has been widely held to contribute to a lowering of taste, disruption of morals, or stimulation toward socially unacceptable conduct. Whether or not such charges are true.

Non-debated Content: This would be media content, widely distributed and attended to, about which media critics have said very little. It is not an issue in the debate over the impact of the media on the masses. Examples would be television weather reports, some news content, music that is neither symphonic nor popular, magazines devoted to specialized interests, motion pictures using "wholesome" themes, and many others. Such content is not believed either to elevate or lower taste, and it is not seen as a threat to moral standards.

High-taste Content: This would be media content sometimes widely distributed but not necessarily widely attended to. It is content that media critics feel is in better taste, morally uplifting, educational, or in some way inspiring. Examples would be serious music, sophisticated drama, political discussions, art films, or magazines devoted to political commentary. Such content is championed by critics as the opposite of the low-taste material, which they see as distinctly objectionable.

Of course, the first of the above categories is the one to which we wish to direct most of our attention. It is the repetitive phenomenon whose contribution to the media (as a social system) needs analysis. Nevertheless, it would also be possible to study the other two categories with somewhat parallel perspectives, but this will receive relatively little attention in the present discussion.

We need now to begin to identify the components and boundaries of the social system within which low-taste content occurs so that eventually the contribution it makes to the system can be inductively hypothesized.

Rather than develop a purely descriptively scheme that will apply only to a single medium, it will be more fruitful to attempt to develop a general conceptual scheme into which any or all media could be placed, with suitable minor modifications in details. Such a general scheme will emphasize the similarities between media, particularly in terms of relationships between the components in the system.

Audiences: The first major component of the social system of mass communication is the audience. This is an exceedingly complex component. The audience is stratified, differentiated, and interrelated in the many ways that social scientists have studied for years. Some of the major variables that play a part in determining how this component will operate within the system are the major needs and interests of audience members, the various social categories represented in an audience, and the nature of the social relationships between audience members. These variables point to behavioural mechanisms that determine the patterns of attention, interpretation, and response of an audience with respect to content of a given type.

Research Organisations: The rough typology of content suggested is in some degree related to the characteristics of the audience. Organizations devoted to research, to measuring the performances of media audiences, or to various forms of market research provide information to those responsible for selecting the categories of content that will be distributed to the audience. There is a link, then, between the audience as a component in the system and the market research-rating service organizations as a second component. In purely theoretical terms, both components are role system themselves and are thus actually subsystems.

This is in a sense a one-way link. For very minor (or usually no) personal reward, audience members selected for study provide data about themselves to such an agency, but very little flows back. This linkage between components is by comparison relatively simple.

Distributors: The content itself, of whatever type, flows from some distributor to the audience. The role system of the distributor component varies in detail from one medium to another. In addition, several somewhat distinct subsystems exist within this general component. First, there are local outlets, which are likely to be in the most immediate contact with the audience. The local newspaper, the local theatre, the local broadcasting station play the most immediate part in placing messages before their respective audiences. But inseparably tied to them are other subsystems of this general component. Newspaper syndicates, broadcasting networks, or chains of movie theatres pass content on to their local outlets. The link between these two subsystems is a two-way one. The local outlet provides money, and the larger distributor supplies content. Or the link age may be that the local outlet provides a service, and the distributor (who is paid elsewhere) provides money.

The relationship between audience and distributor seems at first to be mostly a one-way link. The distributor provides entertainment content (and often advertising), but the audience provides little back in a direct sense. However, it does provide its attention. In fact, it is precisely the attention of the audience that distributors are attempting to solicit. They sell this "commodity" directly to their financial backer or sponsor. In addition, the audience supplies information to the research component and this is indirectly supplied to distributors in the form of feedback so that they may gauge the amount of attention they are eliciting. The linkages between components grow more complex as we seek the boundaries of the system.

Producers and their Sponsors: To the audience, the research, and the distributing component, we may add the role system of the producer of content. This component's primary link is with the financial backer (or sponsor) component and with the distributor, from whom money is obtained and for whom various forms of entertainment content are manufactured. A host of subsystems are included in this producer component, depending upon the particular medium. Examples are actors, directors, television producers, technicians, foreign correspondents, wire-service editors, film producers, labour union leaders, publishers, copyeditors, clerical staff, and many many more.

Advertising Agencies: Linking the sponsor, distributor, producer, and research organization are the advertising agencies. Paid primarily by the sponsor, this component provides (in return) certain ideas and services. For the most part, it provides the distributor with advertising messages. It may have links with the research component as well.

Subsystems of Control: Over this complex set of interrelated components, there are other subsystems that exert control. The legislative bodies, at both the state and national level, which enact regulative statutes concerning the media, constitute an important part of such a control component. Another important part of this role subsystem is the official regulative agencies, which implement the policies that have been legislated. The link between the legislative body (control component) and the audience is, course, one of votes and public opinion, to which the component is presumably sensitive and dependent. Information lines between audience, legislative bodies, and regulatory agencies are more or less open. To the regulatory components whose role definitions are found in legal statute can be added the private voluntary associations that develop "codes" and to some degree serve as a control over the distributors. Such distributors provide them with money, and they in turn provide surveillance and other services.

The regulatory subsystems draw definitions of permissible and non-permissible content from the general set of external conditions within which this extremely complicated system operates. Surrounding the entire structure as an external condition are our society's general norms concerning morality, and the expressions that these find in formal law. Similar, although less likely to be incorporated into law, are our general cultural norms and beliefs regarding what will be likely to entertain or otherwise gratify Americans. Thus, we seldom see traditional Chinese opera but frequently see western horse opera. We seldom hear the strains of Hindu temple music but frequently hear the "strains" and other noises of the latest singer whom teenagers admire. If our interests run to more serious fare, we are likely to hear the music of a relatively small list of European or American composers who created their works within a span of about three centuries. Or we are likely to view ballet, opera, drama, and so on, of a fairly limited of artists whose products are defined by our society as classics or as innovative new approaches.

Each of the several media will fit into this general model of a social system in slightly different ways. A complete description of each of the media separately would be tedious. Indeed, each could well occupy the contents of an entire book. Two decades ago, Opotowsky attempted just such a detailed analysis of the television industry, although he did not use the social system concept.

To add to the complexity of this conceptual scheme, it must be remembered that although each medium constitutes a somewhat separate social system in itself, the media are also related to one another in systematic ways. Thus, we may speak of the entire set of communication media, including those which have not been specifically analysed in the present volume, as the mass communication system of the United States.

The structure of this mass communication system has been heavily influenced by the general social, political, economic, and cultural conditions that were current during the period when our mass media were developing and remain as important socio-cultural forces in the society within which they operate. Because of their importance for understanding our mass media as they are today. Our free enterprise beliefs, our views of the legitimacy of the profit motive, the virtues of controlled capitalism, and our general values concerning freedom of speech constitute further external conditions (in addition to those related to moral limits and cultural tastes) within which the American mass communication system operates.

The Strength

Within the system itself, the principal internal condition is, of course, a financial one. Most of the components in the system are occupational role structures, which motivate their incumbent personnel primarily through money. To obtain money, they are all ultimately dependent upon the most central component of all the audience. Unless its decisions to give attention, to purchase, to vote, and the like, are made in favourable ways, the system would undergo service strain and would eventually collapse.

Almost any dramatic change in the behaviour of the audience would cause the most severe disruption in the system for any given medium. The consequences of attention loss to the motion picture theatre as a mass medium was shown to be severe.

Such disruptions are infrequent, buy they do occur. The key to heading off dramatic changes in audience behaviour, of course, is to provide entertainment content that will satisfy and motivate the largest possible number of audience members to carry out their roles in accord with the needs of the system. Such content will, in other words, maintain the stability of the system. The ideal, from the standpoint of the system, is content that will capture audience members' attention, persuade them to purchase goods, and at the same time be sufficiently within the bounds of moral norms and standards are not provoked.

The entertainment content that seems most capable of eliciting the attention of the largest number of audience members is the more dramatic, low-taste content. Since the most central media system goal is economic profit, sex and violence or any other attention-getting and attention-maintaining content is functional in the sense that even though it may be of low-taste, it maximizes the size of the audience exposed to advertisements. In general, the larger the audience, the more the distributor and producer can charge for advertising. For example, ads in prime-time television periods cost substantially more than those aired during relatively low-audience-size periods, such as early in the morning.

The assumption made by many media personnel and advertisers that low-taste content appeals primarily to the relatively uneducated, who still constitute a majority of the potential audience, may be false. In an early study Wilensky found that educated people said that they preferred and exposed themselves to high-taste content more often than did the relatively uneducated. But when observations were made of what the educated and educated actually aid, there was little difference between their levels of exposure to low-taste media content.

There is a great deal of evidence to show that the relatively uneducated spend more time than the educated being exposed to the mass media. It may be misleading to conclude that they do so only because the uneducated relish low-taste content. The relatively uneducated majority also have relatively low incomes, which probably means they have less choice than their more educated and wealthier counterparts in how they spend their non-working hours. The mass media may be more appealing to the relatively uneducated and poor in large part because the media are relatively inexpensive forms of leisure. Moreover, as Baker and Ball point out, it is probably superficial to think that the only reason people in general spend time with the media is because of the inherent appeal of their content. Any number of need-fulfilments and gratifications, over and above those related to entertainment or staying informed, are provided by the media. Babysitting and companionship (even when it is electronic companionship) are examples.

When all is said and done, however, it is still true that low-taste content sells and sells big. This fact establishes it as the key element in the social system of the media. It keeps the entire complex together by maintaining the financial stability of the system. Critics who provoke public attention by denouncing media content or by proclaiming that a casual connection exists between media content and socially undesirable behaviour may temporarily receive some recognition, they may also achieve some temporary disturbance in the system, or if they are persistent enough, they may ultimately even displace some specific from of low-taste content from a given medium altogether. Examples from the past are quiz shows that were found to be "rigged," and popular disc jockeys who were receiving "payola" (a fee for repeatedly playing a song to make it popular). In such cases the audience may be temporarily disaffected, low-taste content comes in such a variety of forms that the temporary or even permanent absence of one minor form does not alter the major picture. Critics have been complaining about newspaper concentration on crime news for a century, yet there has been no noticeable abatement in the reporting of such stories. Critics of the soap opera may have breathed a sigh of relief several years ago when these programs at last disappeared from radio. Their joy must have been short-lived when such daytime serials turned out to be quite popular with television viewers, so popular in fact that soap operas now appear during prime evening hours. Analyses of the level of violent television content show that it goes down slightly after federal government investigations on the effects of television violence or widespread campaigns by voluntary associations (e.g., the P.T.A.), only to return shortly after the public outcry has subsided.

When a formula is discovered for eliciting attention and influencing purchasing decisions from any large segment of the audience, it will be abandoned by the media only with great reluctance, if at all. The broadcast ballgame, the war movie, the star comedian, the family situation comedy, the western thriller, the detective story, the adventures of the secret agent, the drama of the courtroom-all are beginning to rank with such time-honoured formulas as the sob story, the funnies, the sex-murder account, the sports page, and disclosure of corruption in high places as attention-getting devices that can bring the eye or ear of the consumer nearer to the advertising message.

In short, the social system of the mass media in the United States is becoming more and more deeply established. Some future change can be expected in the kind of content it will produce to maintain its own stability. At present, however, the function of what we have called low-taste content is to maintain the financial stability of a deeply institutionalized social system that is tightly integrated with the whole of the American economic institution. The probability that our system of mass communication in this respect can be drastically altered by the occasional outbursts of critics seems small indeed.

Far more likely than media system change brought about by periodic attacks on low-taste media content is media system change brought about by trends in the economic system such as the emergence of a "post-industrial" society. Because the media system is also a subsystem in the larger economic system, it will have to adapt to such changes if it is to survive. If Bell's forecast that systems in the business of producing, processing, and transmitting information will become increasingly involved in key economic sectors of our society is valid, then we would expect significant changes in the nature of the mass media system. One change would surely be a marked increase in the knowledge and technical information of "non-debated" media content will rise sharply with a corresponding decline in low-taste media content.

But as is usually the case when talking about changes in social systems, such future developments in the nature of the mass media are not likely to by that simple. Recall Durkheim's basic principle that as organisms or systems grow, they are likely to become more differentiated or complex. Taking this assumption and combining it with the enormous technological advances in electronic communications technology witnessed in recent years, it may be hypothesized that media systems will become more specialized. Some media organizations, for example, might specialize in low-taste content, others in knowledge and technical information, others in news content, and still others in high-taste content. Such technological developments as closed-circuit and cable television already are making such specialization possible.

6

Journalism in India

Anglo-Indian Newspapers

English newspapers were published in India to convey news from Britain and Europe to those reading here. The Christian missionaries were the first to start newspapers in English. James Augustus Hicky started the first, English newspaper in British India in 1780, called the Bengal Gazette. He attacked the East India Company vigorously through his paper. James Silk Buckingham was another pioneer of English newspapers in India. He started the Calcutta Journal. Bengal Harkaru, Friend of India and Bengal Herald were other newspapers that were quite popular in the beginning of the 19th C. Bombay Herald was started in 1789. Madras Courier was the first newspaper to be published from Madras in 1785. Reformer was started by Prasanna Coowar Tagore and Bholanath Sen in 1831. The first Indian-owned English newspaper appeared in 1816 called Bengal Gazette after Hicky's venture and was owned by Gangadhar Bhattacharya.

Contribution to Independence—In the 19th century when just a few Indians were acquainted with the English language, some educated leaders ventured-to publish English newspapers. Their efforts were twice successful, as these publications put across the majority viewpoint to the British rulers and also initiated British-influenced into the freedom struggle. Soon restrictions were imposed on the freedom of information and the registration was made compulsory in 1835. Licensing was introduced by an Act in 1857. Leading members of the elite in society enthusiastically contributed to their views to Indian-owned English newspapers. While the government clamped restrictions on the English and Vernacular Press, those papers which were owned by Anglo-Indians were exempted since they were not too critical of the British government.

M.K. Gandhi regularly published Indian Opinion, when he was in South Africa-and also started Harijan to support the struggle for freedom. The Indian-owned newspapers were cheaper than the British-owned ones.

Post-independence Role—The role of the English press in the 1950s was necessarily shaped in response to the immediate needs of development and modernization. In a newly democratised country, the Indian Press had the responsibility of educating the masses about the intricacies of the functioning of the administrative, legal and other departments of the government.

As the government emphasized planned economy, the volume of economic news that the English papers carried, multiplied. The press stressed the importance of economic progress and interpreted the government's goals for the people. When India was at war with Pakistan and China the English Press did a commendable job of defending the country's sovereignty. The English Press also covered the front of population boom. During the Emergency of 1975 there were severe restrictions on the freedom of the press. The English Press was muzzled.

In the early years of 1990's, the government's economic measures of liberalisation and integration of the country in the global economy are issues thai have been receiving ample coverage in our English dailies.

There are quite a handful of English papers which are truly

national in character, they carry news of national importance to households spread across the country. The Times of India, Indian Express, The Hindu are national multi-edition newspapers that are published from various cities situated in different parts of the country.

As for content, newspapers have contributed a great deal towards making the people, more conscious politically. Also, no newspaper can claim to be neutral or apolitical. The general trend which is apparent is one of increasing sophistication in the packaging and presentation of news. The news is segregated on the basis of the topic referred to. It is then printed on separate pages such as foreign, national, regional, local, sports, economy, edit page etc. Some newspapers bring out supplemen's on different days of the week.

In some newspapers there is a tendency to sensationalize negative events. There is also a lack of adequate effort on the part of newspapers to provide any constructive solutions to the many social problems that are plaguing our society. However, it can be laid that the English newspapers measure well against the time-tested standards of objectivity, credibility, balance and accuracy. However, the style of writing in English newspapers has changed over the years. News reports are short and there is more stress on interpretative and investigative reporting. Analytical writings on many important issues are now available. They are also giving a boost to the government's schemes to bring about planned economic development.

Recommendations of Second Press Commission—The commission recommended to delink the press from industry. The commission viewed journalism not merely as an industry but as a public service and profession and observed that public interest should be the criterion to regulate the news and views of the newspaper and not ownership. The 2nd press commission desired the setting up of National Development Commission to promote the entire Indian Press. NDC was to set up advisory councils for each language. It was also to help provide common distribution arrangements for newspapers, published in hilly and remote areas.

It also recommended to specify a price-page schedule and a news-to-advertisement ratio, in order to promote competition and prevent monopoly of a few newspapers. The NDC was also to extend financial assistance to small and medium newspapers.

Indian Newspapers

India has officially recognised many languages. The 1961 & 1971 census had listed 1652 languages as mother tongues spoken in India. The Indo-Aryan Branch of the Indo-European family came into India with the Aryans. It is the biggest of the language groups in India. The Dravidian family, is the 2nd largest group in India and it was present in India centuries before the Indo-Aryan. But with independence, the question of a common language naturally came up. It was put to vote and Hindi won by the margin of a single vote.

The constitution, however, recognised Hindi as the official language of the Union and the regional languages as the official languages of the states concerned. English was recognised as the authoritative legislative and judicial language. Article 343 of the constitution provided that for a period of 15 years from the commencement of the constitution, the English language shall continue to be used for all official purposes of the Union. And that after the expiry of the stipulated period (after 1965) Hindi would displace English as the official language of the Union. But it was found favourable to continue English as an additional official language.

Language Newspapers—The mass media, particularly print medium, radio and TV, were the first to be affected by the "language wave". The regional language press soon overtook the English newspapers and periodicals both in number of publications and in circulation. Malayalam Press tops all the language dailies and weeklies. Following it are Bengali newspapers and Tamil and Gujarati press. There are more newspapers in Indian languages.

Assamese—The Assamese daily Dainik Assamiya ceased publication in 1951 and Natun Assamiya was launched.

'Assamiya' is the oldest weekly of the state followed by Deka Asom, Asom Sevak, Sramik and Janmabhumi.

Bengali—Bengal may well claim credit for pioneering Indian journalism. In 1937, when Anand Bazar Patrika started the English Hindustan Standard, the Amrita Bazar Patrika brought out the Bengali Jugantar. The Amirta Bazar Patrika was started in English from Allahabad (1943) and since 1950 it has added the Hindi daily Amrita Patrika from the same place. In 1941 was started Navajug and 5 years later came Swaraj.

Gujarati—The first Gujarati newspaper, Bombay Samachar began its long career in 1822. A Gujarati weekly Jam-e-Jamshed started in 1831. Surat has two leading dailies, Samachar, started in 1922 and Gujarati (1921).

Kannada—Journalism in Kannada started almost around 1870, but didn't prosper because of political and administrative reasons. Between 1880 and 1908, a number of newspapers in Kannada made their appearance, prominent among them was Desabhimani. In 1947, two daily papers, Vishal Karnataka and Navyug were started at Hubli and are still being published.

Malayalam—Malayala Manorama, the leading daily of Kerala was founded 85 years ago by Kandathi Verghese. This is the largest circulated multiple edition daily in the country. Kayana Kaumudi started in 1905, which published news, is now published as a literary magazine. The struggle for independence brought into being a number of dailies, most important being Mathrubhumi (1923) (tri-weekly) and is now published as a daily and a weekly.

Marathi—Bal Shastri started the first Anglo-Marathi paper, the Bombay Durpan, in 1832 as a fortnightly, and a few months later it was converted into a weekly. He also brought out a monthly Marathi magazine Dig Durshan. In February 1849 was started Dhyan Prakash, started as a weekly, was converted into a daily in 1904 and rose to great heights. In 1923, Khadilkar started Navkal which is today the oldest Marathi daily. Loksatta is the first Marathi daily to be published from Bombay after independence.

Oriya—Asha and Samaj are the earliest Oriya newspapers. Asha closed down in 1951 but is now again published as a weekly. Today Samaj and Praja Tantra are major Oriya newspapers.

Punjabi—In the beginning of the 20th century, the use of Gurmukhi type was well established and Punjabi prose began to make good progress. In 1920 started the first Akali paper. Ajit, Akali Patrika, Khalsa Sevak, Prakash, Nawan Zaman are the major Punjabi newspapers. Preeth Lari is the largest circulated monthly magazine.

Tamil—Tamil is one of the oldest, richest and the most highly cultivated of Dravidian languages of South India. Tamil Patrika, started in 1831 was the first Tamil monthly. Tamil daily, Dina Thanthi, was started in 1940 and it overtook the Swadesmitran and Dinamani, and became immensely popular. Ananda Vikatan, Kalki and Kumuduin, are the major Tamil weeklies.

Telugu—The first newspaper in Telugu was Satyadoota, started in 1835. In the beginning of the 20th cent. Samadarshini, a Telugu daily was started. In 1914, Andhra Patrika, shifted from Bombay to Madras, came to be issued as a daily newspaper, and was acclaimed Andhra's first successful daily paper. In 1974 came up Eenadu, which picked up circulation within no time.

Hindi—Hindi phase was concerned almost solely with social and religious questions and there was not much involvement in political affairs. The earliest Hindi newspaper was started in Calcutta in 1826. The first daily, Samachar Subha Varshan came out in 1854. In 1920, was started Aaj, which played a very notable part in the freedom struggle. The Nav Bharat Times of the Times of India started in 1950 and is the largest circulated Hindi daily. Amrita Patrika is another daily.

Urdu—The Urdu press today is the 4th largest group numerically. Fawaid-ul-Nazarin and Kiran-us-Sadai (1852) are the earliest Urdu newspapers. By 1880 there were more than 12 newspapers. Maulana Azad's Al-Hilal came out from Calcutta in 1912, and achieved unprecedented popularity within a short time. Milap, a daily was started in 1923 by the Arya Samaj. Today, Urdu journalism has assumed an All-India character coming next to English and Hindi. The leading Urdu daily of India, 'Inquilab' was launched in 1926.

Contribution—Vernacular newspapers which were isolated during the freedom struggle are now wielding a lot of influence and are potent instruments of moulding public opinion. Initially, they were organs of individual opinion. Now, they are preoccupied with political, economic and social issues of general interest. They are providing adequate coverage on all aspects of life. They have built up circulations by giving more attention to news coverage and by catering lo the entertainment needs of readers. There is more diversity in the contents of the Indian language newspapers and they show greater responsibility in the collection and presentation of all reading material. The role of the press has certainly undergone a change after 1947 but the press has not wavered from its fundamental role of a critical social educator.

However, the Indian language newspapers will continue to expand and advertising revenue and political excitement will determine their contents and character. In the present situation, there seems little doubt that capitalism and consumerism will continue to grow. Indian language newspapers will play a key part in spreading consumerist messages in the various regions. The diversity and competition which characterise the language press at present may be obliterated in the next 10 years.

The Magazines

In India we intermingle the terms magazines, journals and periodicals, although they have different connotations. "Magazine" indicates a stitched paperback of writing by different authors and traditionally a medium of light entertainment. It includes articles or stories or both and it is published at regular intervals. The word magazine is derived from the Arabic word 'Makhasin'.

"Journal" means a daily record and covers all periodicals publications providing such information. These also carry serious or scholarly articles with or without illustrations and advertisements. The word 'periodical' simply means a publication other than a daily, which comes out with a fixed periodicity.

Whatever be the term employed, these periodical publications contain some built-in merits. They provide a wide variety of information, opinion and entertainment and are designed to be kept by the readers for a much longer time than daily newspapers. They provide reading material of enduring interest and contain different shades of opinion. Besides visual appeals, titaliting covers, pretty graphics and typographical variety, the topics covered by the magazines vary from science to fiction, from current affairs to fine arts, and from social sciences to religion and philosophy.

Magazine Boom—Since independence, the periodical press in our country has been expanding and exploding, diversifying and professionalising and thus becoming enriched in contents, looks and impact. The sudden growth during the 1970-80 is called the 'Magazine Boom'. Even otherwise, during the last 45 years, magazines of all categories and periodicity, expanded nearly six times.

A Good Magazine—A good or bad periodical is basically a matter of opinion and individual taste. A good magazine must be the 'readers' forum. It should satisfy their needs and fancies, and should also fulfil the aspirations of each segment. Apart from being imaginative and creative in the treatment to topics, a better quality periodical should reflect a sense of advancement and excitement about life in general and about events, issues, values and literature in particular. Most of the magazines, as critics point out, seek to lure the readers by providing juicy and spicy materials and stories, gossip columns, morbid sensationalism and exposures of the private life of the VIPs or stars.

The Hindi magazines and journals which are the largest in number, carrying the highest circulation, cover a variety of subjects and are widely recognised as potent in reach, and influence in certain areas. However, one eminent journalist observes in a professional journal that "news value that Hindi periodicals adopt are dubious."

Accomplishments of Magazines—Magazines fulfil the need for a medium of information, instruction and entertainment. They also interpret issues and policies.

(1) During India's freedom struggle, opinion magazines like Gandhiji's Harijan played a vital role in moulding public opinion and mobilizing it against the foreign rule.

(2) Magazines have helped strengthen social, religious and national bonds.

(3) They provide excellent entertainment.

(4) They act as an effective medium of education and instruction by interpreting issues, events and developments and putting them in proper focus.

(5) They help in bringing about social, cultural and political reforms on rational lines.

Categories of Periodicals—In India the Registrar of Newspaper's Report categorised periodicals into 21 groups. The 2nd Press Commission report, on the other hand, preferred to classify them into 10 categories-

(1) News and current affairs journals (e.g. India Today, Sunday, The Week, Frontline)

(2) Opinion Journals (Mangalam, Malayala Manorama, Aajkal)

(3) Farm Journals-Dealing with agricultural and other allied activities e.g., Shetkari, Gramsevak

(4) Economic and Financial Journals e.g., Business India, Business World, Business Today, Vyapar Udyog.

(5) Science Journals e.g., Vigyan Pragati and Science Today.

(6) Literary and Cultural Journals.

(7) Women Journals e.g., Vanitha and Femina.

(8) Sports Journals e.g., Sports Star.

(9) Children Journals e.g., Chandamama, Irajal, Bal Bharati.

Giants and Dwarfs Co-exist—Among the Indian periodicals, both giants and dwarfs coexist. The giants are well managed and are in sound financial health. They have well-known columnists to contribute. By comparison, the small and medium magazines have not been able to maintain professional standards. They lack trained journalists and adequate number of reporters. Most of them lean heavily on fiction, gossip columns, detective stories, cheap humour etc.

Advertising revenue is another crucial part for the periodical press. So, a mad struggle is on to get a larger and larger piece of the cake. The sudden increase in advertisement revenue, especially on consumer goods, motivated the leading periodicals to improve their production standards and editorial contents. However, the government has pursued a liberal advertising policy of offering special rates to Indian language newspapers and small newspapers. Lack of adequate newsprint, however, continues to be one of the main problems for the small periodicals.

Promotional Devices—With literacy increasing steadily and the country making economic progress, both in rural and urban areas, there is a tremendous readership potential in India. Publishers can adopt ingenious promotion techniques. They need not make loud claims, but resort to persuasive and credulous pleadings or appeals tied to the needs of the target, readers. Here are some promotional devices which would be employed profitably-

- Promotion of sales on news-stalls, sales depots of other public places
- Soliciting advance subscriptions by issuing appropriate direct mail literature
- Simulation of the sale of advertising space
- Building up of goodwill or corporate image

- Promoting understanding of the contents of the publications
- Making editorial contents more effective and problem solving
- Seeking wider involvement of readers
- Making advertisements more attractive and creative.

Challenges from Electronic Media—Periodicals are exposed to competition from video magazines, satellite TV and Cable TV. These media are captivating the mind and time of the people. To play its due role, the magazine publishers must make their magazines still more attractive, vibrant and satisfying. The soaring prices are no doubt a great hindrance and makes it all the more necessary for the magazines to step up their efforts to improve their quality and ensure adequate circulation and advertising support, cater to the needs of diverse readership and should woo their readers by satisfying their curiosity and by giving them the type of detailed information and entertainment which they wish to have.

Structure and Setup

Changing Nature of Newspaper Management—James Augustus Micky's Bengal Gazette, the first newspaper in India, was a one man show. James Augustus was himself the founder-editor, printer and promoter of his newspaper. But today's newspapers and magazines are giant enterprises. The owners and managers have, over a period of time, adopted certain unique practices to make the newspaper enterprise economically viable and profitable. The development of newspaper ownership patterns has passed through numerous stages, and all through it has been influenced by business environment in India.

Newspaper Ownership Patterns in India—In case of newspaper ownership, concentrations of two kinds are evident. Firstly, newspapers are concentrated in urban areas and secondly the ownership of these newspapers is concentrated in a few big business houses.

Types of Ownership Patterns—In India, the newspapers concentrated in the individual ownership is the largest, followed by societies/ associations. Although, the ownership is important, but more significant is the influence that a newspaper unit commands.

Distinctive Features of Ownership Patterns—It would be appropriate to understand that what a particular type of ownership stands for.

— A single individual owner means one who generally owns 100 percent of the newspaper company's stock and runs it as a private enterprise e.g., The Hindustan Times, owned by K. K. Birla and the Telegraph owned by Avik Sarkar.

— There can be partnership of a small group of individuals holding stock in the company e.g., The Hindu (Madras).

— A joint stock company is a big commercial organisation such as Bennett Coleman and Company, publishers of The Times of India and other publications.

— A trust is a non-profit organization which runs a newspaper such as the Tribune of Chandigarh or the Lok Sevak of Kolkatta.

— In case of Central and State Governments' publications, the ownership is generally vested in the departments of information, publication, publicity, public relations etc.

Organisational Structure—In a modern newspaper unit of medium size, the organizational structure is divided into 5 strict sections Editorial department, Printing & Production department, Business department, Computers, Engineering and Equipment, Personnel, Sales promotion and Public Relations. However, in some organizations engineering and equipment sections are merged with printing and production departments. These are discussed below-

The Editorial Department—This department of a newspaper organization is its heart and soul. Infact, the entire business of a successful newspaper depends on the effective, efficient and prompt operations in this department. This department collects, receives, processes and finalises the news and all other writing related to news for publication in the newspaper or magazines. It is the life sustaining force and be-all and end-all of a newspaper establishment. The three main operations of this department are-

(1) Editing and processing the news on the editing desk.

(2) Making arrangements for gathering news from the city where the paper is located, other parts of the country and other countries.

(3) Every newspaper or magazine has one or more editorial pages which reflect the policy of the organization. Thus, every newspaper has its own opinion on all serious national and international issues.

The Business Department—The business department looks after the sale of space, that is, advertising, and the sale of printed copies, that is, circulation. The collection of advertising revenue is the job of the advertising section in the business department. Similarly, the circulation section is concerned with organizing the network of hawkers/selling agents at the station where the newspaper/magazine is published and at other places, where its copies can be sold.

Other Departments—Other departments have their own respective jobs to perform. The general structure of these departments is briefly discussed here. However, the structure of these departments is not fully identical in any two newspaper organizations.

Printing & Production

— Press manager,

— Composing Supervisor,

— Press Supervisor,

— Paste-up Supervisor,

— Process Photographers,

— Platemakers,

— Press Operators

Engineering, Equipment, Stores

- — Manager Computer operation,
- — Computer Engineer,
- — Data Processing Supervisor,
- — Computer Operators,
- — Programming Managers,
- — Systems Manager,
- — Store Manager,
- — Purchase Manager,
- — Store Supervisor

Development and Growth

- — Manager (Personnel),
- — Administrative Officers,
- — Establishment Supervisor,
- — Sales Promotion Staff,
- — Public Relations Officer,
- — Sales Representative,
- — Agents, Hawkers.

7

Media's Relevance

The main function of the press is to communicate news along-with the editorial opinion. As a media of information, we can even call the press as an important adjunct to the school as an educational institution. In fact, now more and more opinion is veering round to the point that journalism should be considered as a medium of education and mass communication.

Every newspaper has a point of view which is reflected both in its news columns, on the editorial page and, to some extent, in the columns of its syndicated writers. Although, the fiercely partisan press of the past has more or less disappeared, it is still difficult to discover a newspaper which is completely neutral. Every newspaper as a free medium should have a point of view and should interpret the news in depth. There is no doubt that it must maintain a balance and an integrity in which the news is not slanted or tilted completely.

The Position

Similarly, the editorial while taking a position should not be false or misleading. Some degree of partisanship is always there, but it should not be done at the cost of dissemination of truth.

There is always a point where espousal should stop, so that accuracy of information can be maintained. A newspaper which becomes too much involved in the advocacy of its partisan views, loses its audience, because it compromises its main function of the communication of information. In fact, just like other professions there should be a code of ethics or code of conduct even for the journalists.

In every country, the press has to function within the framework of the laws of that country. Generally, under a democratic government a newspaper is not prohibited from printing any information, provided it is not libellous, slanderous or obscene. No doubt, in times of war or during some national emergency the newspapers should impose some self-censorship, because the press is also responsible for what it prints. It is also susceptible to the laws of libel. The press as an institution suffers from the same limitations and restrictions as any other media or social institution.

Freedom of the press is also subject to a continuing struggle, a continuing appraisal and a constant effort by pressure groups to erode it.

Freedom of the press does not imply a license to print anything and everything. It is always subject to legal review as well as to the pressure of public opinion. Generally, the rule of reason prevails over the press and it stops short of engaging in activities which are contrary both to the laws and public interest.

In fact, it is not the democratic society alone which has made freedom possible for the press. The press and other media are also equally responsible for the successful functioning of democracy. The press and other mass media are the most powerful sources in the society for creating an informed public opinion. There is no doubt that the relations between the press and the government have always been delicate and full of troubles. It is due to the lack of trust between the government and the press that the 'credibility gap' comes into existence between the government and the people.

It is necessary for the government that it should allow free access to the reporters to perform their functions regarding the collection of news. The newspapers have always argued vigorously to preserve their right to receive and report the news freely. Sometimes, the newspapers and other media are accused of misreporting the news. Certain reporters of newspapers have also been accused of giving a tilt to their stories in favour of certain parties or certain personalities. Sometimes, the owners of the newspapers have been criticised for harassing certain reporters for their objective and true reports criticising a particular point of view. Fortunately, these cases are not very many and public opinion is always against such misdemeanour either on the part of the journalist or the press.

Against all Odds

There is no doubt that conscientious journalists would always resist the pressure either from the editors or the owners to slant their news. Even the self-respecting editors would not like to use any pressure on their reporters to give coloured news. But sometimes, the owners of the press who have certain other industrial interests also, use certain pressures on the reporters to safeguard their own selfish interests.

It is also sometimes alleged that the government exerts pressures on the press overtly or covertly which is a big danger to the existence of a free press. The attitude of the government of the day is very important for the existence of a free press. Every government must remember that the more the difficulties it places in the path of the reporter in gaining access to the news, the greater will be the credibility gap between it and the press. It is the duty of the press to make all efforts to get the news and report it to the public impartially. Maintenance of a healthy interaction between the press and the society and between the newspaper and its readers is the basis of a truly democratic society.

Professional Honours

There has been a great change in the newspapers as mass medium over the past thirty years. The press has now become a vast institution and a medium of mass communication. Advertising has become an essential part of newspaper publishing and large circulation has become necessary for attracting the advertisers successfully. The press today has become not only a national institution but it has been completely institutionalized. Newspapers have become a part of large business enterprises. Of course, journalism has now also become more newsworthy and more informative. Now-a-days editorials are written more cogently and objectively rather than out of sheer partiality. The twentieth century has seen the appearance of journalistic empires.

Total Concerns

Journalism has not only been institutionalized but concentration and consolidation of journalism has taken place all over the world. There has been a trend towards the merger of newspapers in order to survive. Modern journalism is an impersonal corporate type enterprise. Many newspapers depend on wire copies from newspaper agencies. Printing of pictures by tele-photo has also speeded up both the transmission and printing enormously. Now-a-days, newspapers are circulating with dispatch due to the development of the linotype machine which has replaced setting of type by hand.

This change has also brought about stereotype and standardisation in journalism, which has resulted in loss of independence and enterprise to some extent. The big news agencies have tended to standardize the news printed in the press. These agencies have also made it possible to print national and international news quickly. In this manner, these news agencies supply the news to their client papers quickly and accurately. Of course, there are still newspapers having their own sources of news, especially the weekly and the small town newspapers.

Collective Efforts

So many news agencies and syndicates have come into existence which supply news, readymade features, serials etc. to their clients all over the world. Today, journalism depends heavily on advertising and circulation to keep it viable financially. Although the press is an institution, yet it is also a business. Therefore, it must function with economic success, if it has to remain in business. There is no doubt that the costs of producing and distributing newspapers have risen too much during the recent years. Still the owners of the newspapers are also entitled to expect a fair return on their investment.

In many advanced countries of the world, most mass media are corporately owned. They are also financed by the sale of stock in the market. No newspaper can be run in the present day only on the profit of circulation. Hence, there is heavy reliance on the source of advertising. Due to economic problems many big newspapers in the world had either to go out of business or merge with others in the recent past. Even in advanced countries, a lot of caution is observed in newspaper journalism. Newspapers that do not function with economic success, are frequently absorbed in mergers where success prevails.

Sometimes, this continued merger of newspapers has resulted in the monopolistic ownership. The press today, as a medium of mass communication, has become a huge and powerful institution with an enormously delicate and complex involvement on national and international scale. In the present times, newspapers do not suffer from a lack of news but from an overflow of news. In this way, by reporting and interpreting the news the press has become a very important source of education and information.

On the one side, being a private enterprise, the press is an institution, but on the other side it is also clearly a public service. The news is selected on the basis of a certain value judgement. With the widening scope of newspapers and other media, this media must assume a greater degree of social responsibility. These medias are accountable not only to the public but also to other social institutions for their behaviour as means of communication. Because of its vast readership and the consequent influence, the press needs to maintain a high standard of moral responsibility. Good journalism should not only give the public what the public wants, but it should also give them what it thinks is good for the public. In this way, the press should enjoy its freedom with responsibility and balanced reporting of news and views.

Liberty of Expression

Freedom of the press is very essential if the press has to play a significant and constructive role in the life of a nation, especially in a democratic society. Unless the press itself enjoys freedom, how can it become the defender and protector of the rights and liberties of the citizens ? A free press signifies an open society where decisions are made according to democratic traditions and not according to the dictates of one person. The press can only perform its sacred duties of the fourth estate if it is free and independent in reporting its views and news.

But like all other freedoms, freedom of the press should also not be used as a licence. It should not be misused to create a situation of the law of the jungle. The press should observe certain self imposed limitations on itself, so that instead of publishing views detrimental to the interests of the nation, it strengthens the national unity, upholds the laws of the land and contributes towards the emotional integration of the country. For example, howsoever free the press may be, it cannot be allowed the freedom to call in question the integrity of the judges of the High Courts and the Supreme Court or to defame them. It cannot be allowed the licence to incite communal riots in the country. No state can grant such unlimited freedom to the press by which law and order in the country is endangered.

On the other hand, the press should also not be afraid of upholding and supporting a just and righteous cause, because it may antagonise the governmental machinery or some influential interests. The press has to be eternally vigilant to protect the rights, of the workers, backward people and the suppressed sections of the society. It should also give a balanced view of the things and happenings, so that the people can be helped in the formation of a healthy public opinion and correct perspective of the events. The press can play havocs by suppressing a news, or giving it an importance out of all proportions. Our constitution under Article 19, has recognised the freedom of expression and speech of the citizens, which is the basis of the freedom of the press.

In India, since our independence the press has been enjoying more or less complete freedom in its working. The press in India has on many occasions crossed swords with the government and has done a good service in protecting the democratic traditions. But during the nineteen months following the imposition of internal emergency, which was declared on 25th June, 1975, the freedom of the press in India was curtailed by the government. Strict censorship was imposed upon the press and it was not at all allowed to publish any report against the government. This censorship was removed only after the sixth General Election in March 1977, when the above emergency was revoked.

In reality, freedom of the press is very essential for the free flow of information and success of democracy everywhere. There has been a demand in our country that an appropriate amendment should be made in the Constitution, so that in future no government is able to clamp censorship on the press. Even there has been a demand that the freedom of the press should be included in the Chapter on Fundamental Rights and made an essential feature of the Constitution, subject to reasonable restrictions.

There is no doubt that censorship on the press violates the freedom of speech and expression of the citizens. It also violates the citizens' right to free flow of information. Censorship cannot be justified except in times of war or internal insurrection. Freedom of the press is, in fact, the symbol of dignity and freedom of man. However, as already stated, like other freedoms, freedom of the Press should also not be used as a licence.

Sense of Authority

The press plays a very important role in the modern age. Inspite of the heavy impact of television news coverage on the public, newspapers still continue to serve as the basic news medium for a majority of the population. Although the newspapers lack the speed and visual quality of television news, yet they provide greater depth and variety in reporting. People today depend greatly on the press for local, national, and international news. They cannot be kept well informed about these in the absence of newspapers. A newspaper reader can obtain a lot of information regarding local, national and international affairs from a single issue of a newspaper. A newspaper caters to the needs of different readers by publishing various types of news such as political, economic, social, scientific, developmental etc.

Although there is more mental effort in reading a newspaper than watching a television news programme, yet the effort is worthwhile. In a way, we can say that the newspapers are the written record of our contemporary civilization. The increasing literacy in the developing countries and the suburban spread of cosmopolitan cities have led to the creation of many new daily newspapers. There are different sizes of newspapers, some are small and some are big. A small newspaper may be employing only a few persons, whereas a big newspaper may be employing hundreds of persons with a daily circulation of several lakh copies.

Whether newspapers are large sized or small sized, all of them are printed by type and ink on newsprint. The main purpose of the press is to inform and influence the people who read it. Into the pages of every newspaper goes an essential but intangible extra ingredient, the minds and the spirits of the men who produce it. Journalism work is like an adventure which is full of fresh experiences and unexpected developments take place everday. No doubt, there is a firm discipline involved in the bringing out of a newspaper, because every issue of a newspaper should be printed in time so that it can reach its subscribers and the news stands at the fixed time. The regularity and punctuality in printing a newspaper or a journal can only be maintained if a definite work pattern is followed in all departments.

There are innumerable exciting things that can happen in the production of a newspaper. The reporters feel the stimulation of being on the inside of big developments, of watching history being made. They also have the thrill of meeting important and interesting persons. Similarly in those persons who work on the advertising and circulation side, there is the satisfaction that in conceiving and executing ideas they bring in money and influence the people through their skill with the word. By working in a newspaper a person has a lot of opportunities to create ideas and put them to work. The successful newspapermen handle the necessary routine connected with the production of a newspaper meticulously. These people always try to bring to their jobs an extra element of creative thinking. Such persons cannot remain in the newspaper business for a long period, for whom there is no excitement in the atmosphere of journalistic activities.

The press performs a very important role as a means of mass communication media in the modern world. The press tries to inform its readers objectively about what is happening in their community, country, and the world at large. To bring certain developments into focus, editorial comments on the news are also given. Now-a-days the newspapers also provide the means whereby persons with goods and services can sell and advertise their goods. The newspapers also play a very important role in eliminating the undesirable conditions prevailing in the society. Sometimes the newspapers carry on campaigns for some highly desirable civic projects for the service of the society.

For the entertainment of their readers the newspapers publish comic strips, special features, interesting columns written by famous columnists etc. Sometimes, certain newspapers also act as friendly counsellors for their readers. And they give them information regarding specific matters through question and answer columns. The newspapers also act as the champions of the rights of the citizens. Whenever the rights of the individuals are infringed they come to their rescue. Sometimes the newspapers also expose the corruption prevailing in the ruling circle or the high society. For example, the Watergate scandal was brought to light by two young reporters of Washington Post, Bob Woodward and Carl Bernstein.

Significant Jobs

When the press plays such an important role, in the society, it becomes integral part of it. The newspaper has become so much a part and parcel of our life that we cannot do without it. A strike in the daily newspapers creates an all round confusion in the economic, social and political activities of the community. A regular subscriber of a newspaper feels very lonely if he does not receive his, newspaper even for a single day. Without his daily newspaper a person feels as if he has missed something or lost something. There is no doubt that the printed word has a permanent and lasting impression whereas a spoken word or a visual image has only a transitory effect. In the case of a printed world a reader can refer to it time and again. Newspaper clippings of important news, comments, stories and happenings can be preserved in a reference file for future consultation. In this way, we see that newspapers play a very important role in the modern society.

Tasks Ahead

In the past, the press mainly concentrated on two important functions, that is information and influence. But now-a-days, it performs four major functions. In addition to the above two functions the press now also performs the functions of entertainment and paid advertising.

Information : This function includes all reports, news and happenings concerning the daily life. It does not include any information involving or concerning the pursuit of leisure. But it does cover all news, regarding government, politics, foreign affairs, weather, accident, business, labour, education etc. This function consists of most of the matter which is given in news-broadcast on the radio and T.V. as well as the news-columns of the newspapers and magazines. It does not include information regarding sports, hobby columns, theatre reviews, films, short stories etc.

Influence : It means influencing the opinion of the readers through editorials, articles, or certain special features. It also includes editorials, cartoons and comments made on the news and events by the journalists or the editors. But it does not include the slanted news or any other form of indirect influence, accidental or otherwise. In this, we should include only attempts which are made directly to influence the readers and listeners. It also excludes the space which is sold to the advertisers.

Entertainment : The next important function of the press is entertainment of the readers. Under this function can be included all types of fiction like comic strips, stories etc. It also includes the factual material, sports news, theatre reviews and hobby columns which deal with leisure. The entertainment function of the press is very important. This function not only competes for space and time with other functions, but it can also exert indirect influence and impart information incidentally.

Advertising : This function of the press can very easily be recognised, because it is commercially oriented. Sometimes, the advertisements also have some public service messages under the prestige advertisements regarding family planning, driving safely, child care, health care etc. The commercially oriented advertising seeks to promote the sale of their goods.

Generally, people have to depend upon the press for the major share of their total news information, because even television newscasts cannot carry that much bulk, nor could the television viewers assimilate it, if they did. Of course, information can be written and edited in such a slanted fashion that it exerts more influence than the printed editorial. Entertainment is the most important function of journalism, because it is like a magnet which attracts and holds large audiences. It plays a vital role in selling newspapers and magazines by the millions. The sports pages, comic strips, astrology columns, advice to the lovelorn and cross-words are essential to the average newspaper's survival as a mass media.

The entertainment function's greatest threat to good journalism is its competition against information and influence for media space and time and consumer attention. Addition of an extra page of comic strips may add to circulation and accompanying advertising revenues, thus enabling the newspaper to add editorial material, or it may simply oust a few columns of news and commentary. Similarly, a second lovelorn column not only steals space from significant offerings, but also tempts more readers away from the remaining substance.

The Strength

There is no doubt that information and influence play a very important role in the success of the largest general interest magazines. For example, much space of Reader's Digest is devoted to articles and opinion pieces, about government, foreign affairs, current morality issues, and education-Advertising also plays a very important role in the success of running a mass media. Advertising provides the largest part of the revenue to finance the most elaborate technically sophisticated press system. In fact all sorts of daily newspapers, magazines, publications depend on advertising revenue. Advertising also supplies essential marketing information to the public and helps inform the businessmen of changes within their fields.

8

Professional Journalism

An ongoing media information service is very much the backbone of any media relations programme. It supports the publicity for important activities and launches and provides the day-to-day contact which is so essential in ensuring that the organization and its activities, services and products receive a steady stream of coverage throughout the year.

Unfortunately this is the least glamorous of any of the activities of a busy public relations office and it tends to receive the least attention. Everyone is happy to jump-to and work hard on a new factory opening or a big product launch, but they are not so eager to rush off and fulfil the everyday requests which come in from the media. Yet service given to the media at this level can determine the outcome of much more important media decisions in the future.

Most editors and journalists are perfectly honest about the fact that when they need help they tend to go to those PROs who have been helpful in the past. A transparency sent round by cab or a special piece of artwork produced at short notice can be just as valuable as an exciting launch or a slap-up launch. Indeed it will contribute to a better relationship.

Nor is the role of an efficient information service purely a passive one. An imaginative PRO or press officer will be thinking up new and useful angles for in-depth feature material suitable for specific programmes or publications and will be spending a good proportion of his or her time selling them. Unfortunately, not enough thought is put into this area and many editors complain about the lack of creativity displayed in the ideas put to them.

Infrastructure

The degree of formal organization given to the media information service depends to some extent on the size of your organization or, for a consultancy, on the size of the fee paid by the client. Some large organizations have specially designated press officers working within a press office which, though coming under the surveillance of the public relations department, is separate from it. Other organizations designate a press officer within the PR office and others simply expect all the PR staff to act as press officers as the need arises.

It probably does not matter what title is held by the people who will be dealing with media enquiries, but what does matter is that they should be reasonably au fait with the company and its products. The lack of even basic knowledge is probably a fault encountered more when dealing with a consultancy than with in-house PROs. If the query is of a complicated or technical nature it is quite acceptable to pass it on to the expert. And you really should have price lists and stockists handy.

As well as having a good working knowledge of the subject with which you are dealing, you, as an efficient PRO, should also have at your fingertips the names and telephone numbers of people within the organization who are competent to speak to the media on specialist subjects, and this list should include others apart from the brand managers and marketing department personnel. It is annoying to a journalist who is working on a story to be told that the PRO will ring back with the relevant numbers and then not to get them for another two or three days.

If the queries coming into the public relations or press office are short questions they can usually be answered on the spot, but quite often they will be in the form of a general request for information on a specific topic and it could be that your organization has in its files material which could be sent out. Do make sure that all this material is filed in such a way that it is easy to find and is related to any photographic or other reference. Some information services are organized in such detail that they have a grandiose title such as 'The Barbed Wire Information Bureau', information sheets and a direct telephone line. However, such a detailed service is usually organized primarily for the consumer rather than for the media, though answering press queries will be part of its function.

If you do have a fairly sophisticated information service it is easy to think that you have all the answers to hand, but this may not be the case. So when taking down details of media enquiries don't just record them: listen, be constructive and ask questions. If you know what the story or feature is to be about and the angle from which the producer or journalist is approaching it you will be able to be more helpful. There may be a booklet on the subject, a special expert in the technical department who has sat on the relevant government fact-finding commission or a market research survey giving the latest market trends, any of which would help the journalists far more than the standard handouts.

System at Work

Most journalists agree that the telephone manners of some PR departments leave much to be desired. Some of them leave the impression that they are really too busy to deal with media enquiries and unless the journalist can use the name of a welt-known programme or a national daily the service is grudging to say the least.

However, there are other PROs who are extremely friendly and helpful on the phone. This immediately puts their organization in a good light and the journalist is disposed to feel that this outfit may be a useful source of information in the future.

If this friendly attitude is followed up with prompt service the good impression is stamped even deeper. Too often the executive forgets to phone back until the next day. Or even worse, the material promised does not arrive until the end of the following week. It has even been known for a company to respond to a request for information six weeks after the initial query and then to complain that their product had been left out! There also sometimes seems to be a feeling that the media could have got themselves better organized and asked for the material earlier. There is occasionally some truth in this, but very often the journalist's deadline is looming close, and the PRO is supposed to be providing a service not a favour.

Checklist for an Efficient Enquiries Procedure

1. Be friendly and helpful throughout; do not give the impression that it is all too much trouble.
2. Record the details of the request and ask for further details about the proposed story so that you can dig out the most useful in-depth material. Indicate that this is the reason for your questions.
3. Drop everything and treat the request as extremely urgent Even if you know that the answer can wait until the next day it is far better to deal with it at once. It may be forgotten later on.
4. If you need to phone back, do so as soon as possible. Phone back within hours to report progress even if you do not yet have the answer.
5. If you leave a message for someone else to phone the journalist back, check to see that they have not missed the message or forgotten to fulfil it.
6. If the request is for an expensive sample use tact in discovering whether it has a genuine background. You may not have heard of the journalist or author concerned but that does not mean that they are not engaged on a bona fide testing programme or working on a first-class magazine feature.

7. Where necessary send material by cab or messenger.
8 Check to see that both postal or hand-delivered material has arrived and whether the journalist needs any more material.

The Routine

Getting the enquiries procedure right is only the first stage in setting up a good media relations programme. The second stage is the much more active one of going out and securing a steady stream of coverage for the company and its products or services. Start by making a list of the areas in which you think you might be able to generate coverage over a three-month period. Such a list of objectives for the PR department of a food manufacturer might look something like this:

1. Feature material on cooking with a variety of the products in women's magazines and in regional media.
2. A series of radio interviews on local radio.
3. A feature on the use of some of the products in pubs for a catering trade magazine.
4. An in-depth feature on the new soup production line in a leading food production magazine.
5. An in-depth feature on the work of the new product development team in a food technology publication.
6. A visit to the Peterborough factory-where new jobs are coming on-line-by the industrial editor of one of the national newspapers.
7. A feature on the activities of the Skelmersdale factory social club in the local media and a possible visit by the local radio station disc jockey to a social evening.

A Similar List for a Heavy Goods Vehicle Manufacturer might Look Something Like This

1. A release on the year's export success for both the heavy goods vehicle publications and all the publications covering the industries to which the goods were sold.

2. Local radio sponsorship of a motoring and good driving show.
3. An in-depth feature on the conversion of a stand ard line for use in a mountainous area for a leading magazine in the field of civil engineering and for publication in the country concerned.
4. An on-site demonstration of the current range of earth-diggers for publications covering public works and civil engineering generally.
5. A feature on the new managing director for the heavy freight publications.
6. A feature on safety aspects of carrying chemicals and other dangerous substances for a lorry drivers' magazine.

To achieve the list of objectives set you will need to be in constant contact with the leading media in your field and in occasional contact with all the other publications which might be useful. This contact may be by post, by telephone or by personal meetings. Some enterprising PRs have also used humorous tapes and promotional videos to put their ideas over. The choice will depend on how important you are to a magazine or radio and the magazine or radio to you and thus how often you are likely to be working with this particular publication, how physically near you are to each other and indeed how well you get on at a social level.

However, if you have creative ideas and good material, face-to-face contact is by no means necessary. Unfortunately many editors feel that this kind of creativity is absent from the activities of a number of PROs. The only material they receive is the syndicated material which is sent out to everyone on the mailing list, and there is little attempt at placing original and exclusive material.

Syndication of material can work quite well at a regional level, though even here blanket coverage can be a real waste. If for example, you are running a recipe or a beauty information service you will be able, over time, to build up a list of regional dailies and weeklies who use the material regularly. Some sophisticated services send out portfolios of material to selected users and these are updated from time to time. If the subject is one which is likely to be covered fairly regularly the expense of such an operation will be recouped. But for most products and services this sort of exercise would be too expensive. Others run food and cookery programmes on their local radio stations or even sponsor national radio slots. The success rate for syndicated material can also be increased by sending out material with themes which are relevant to the local area or which are topical.

For national media the approach must be rather different. Monthly mailings are no use at all, and ideas are needed in the first instance rather than completed material. Once you have sold an idea to an editor you can then discuss how much material you will supply and how much the newspaper or magazine will want to write or photograph for itself. Some magazines are pleased if you can produce an illustrated feature to an agreed plan. Others have a large enough budget to be able to retain their independence, and these publications will probably ask for background material only or will send a journalist to cover the story on the spot.

However, if you are to write the feature remember to check on the editor's requirements as to length, the number of illustrations, the date of issue of the article and the copy deadline. Sometimes it is worth thinking about getting a well-known person in the field to write features for you or at least to suggest his or her name to the publication. This will be a more expensive way of producing feature material but it may also make it more acceptable.

If your work is mainly in the trade and industrial area it is even more important to keep in constant touch with the leading publications in the field. An editor will appreciate it if you supply him or her regularly with information about the company, giving advance warning of changes and additions to the product range, the factory or indeed any aspect of the company's activities. A good relationship in this area can mean extra coverage since the editor will be more inclined to ring your company for quotes or for filler items. Editors have also been known to remind PROs that their exhibition details have not yet been received. Nor should you forget the media local to your offices and factories. Community relations can be extremely important but they are often relegated to the bottom of the list of PR activities.

Checklist for Active Day-to-day Contact

List areas which are likely to generate coverage during a set period. Look at this list in terms of the relevant media and make a list of objectives to achieve within the period.

Send out syndicated material to specially selected regionals and place specific features ideas with nationals and specialist magazines. Be as original and creative as possible by letter or phone.

Once features have been placed take care to fulfil the editor's requirements.

The Handouts

Some PROs like to put together a newsletter to send to the media, outlining all the things that have happened to their company over the previous three or four months. These are often quite stylishly produced with a scanner and desk-top publishing packages. The idea is that journalists will pick up just those stories which are of particular interest to their publications.

The problem is that these newsletters are often so well produced that they look far too much like sales promotion material and they may indeed be of use in selling-in to the trade. Journalists are likely to bin this type of material before they even read it, assuming that it will be full of puffs and exaggerated claims.

Far better to forget the clever design and pretty colours and stick to the news. Write up the facts following the Who? What? Why? Where? When? If possible include some information on forthcoming events as well as past history and make sure that the latter is not too out of date.

It is quite permissible to include ideas for features, but it is a waste of time to write the whole piece. It is better to negotiate the placing of the complete material into those sections of the media that are likely to use it.

Other Aspects

Though entertaining is not an essential part of the media relations programme it can help to smooth the way. Discriminate in your entertaining. If you are taking a journalist to lunch you should know exactly why you are doing it and what you expect to achieve from it. Even more important, you should know what you have to offer. Journalists will not appreciate your wasting their time, however good the lunch. Indeed 'launching' in the old-fashioned sense is on the decline. So do not be surprised if a journalist simply cannot find the time to join you.

Reasons for individual entertaining might include any of the following:

- Briefing editors or journalists on changes and developments within your organization which could affect the industry as a whole.
- Briefing a newly-appointed editor or specialist writer on your company and its activities and the service you have to offer.
- A 'thank you' for successful cooperation throughout the year, usually coupled with a briefing on the coming year.
- An introduction for yourself to editors or specialist writers in an area of the media which is new to you.
- A general briefing for editors or journalists with whom you are not often in contact, usually coupled withideas for specific features.
- To introduce new senior members of your organization to key journalists.

The question of where to entertain is a function both of your budget and the inclination of your guest. It might be a pleasant gesture to ask your guest where he or she would like to go. On the other hand, if you have reasonable in-house facilities this might be a better venue as it will be free from distraction.

It is sometimes even more valuable to entertain a group of journalists together. This can serve both as a briefing meeting and as a discussion group. It is a good idea, for example, to gather together representatives of your immediate trade or industrial publications, together with specialist writers from the national media, at a briefing lunch on the forthcoming year. Such an event enables the senior personnel within your company to meet the leading journalists in the field and to tell them first hand of the company's plans for the coming year. The journalists can ask their questions direct and can also air any grievances or problems in an informal atmosphere.

It is important that the senior management is briefed to be as open as possible at such meetings, otherwise the value of them tends to be diminished. The representatives of the media should see the meeting as a constructive activity and not just a propaganda exercise.

Another example of extremely useful group entertaining is illustrated by a luncheon arranged by an organization which was moving into sports sponsorship for the first time. Leading journalists covering the particular sport were invited to attend the lunch and to give their views on how the sponsorship could best benefit the sport and on how they would like to be kept in the picture. The lunch also served the purpose of introducing the company's executives to this particular section of the media, and much was learnt about how to get the most out of the sponsorship.

Some companies operating in the consumer field have also seen the value of group luncheons in generating special features around products which are not very exciting and which do not really merit a series of individual lunches. Journalists must be told that this is a speculative lunch with only a small information content and that the genera! intent is to discuss the subject in broad terms with the injection of a few ideas from the PROs. The discussion around the table often generates even better feature ideas which can be taken up by one of the journalists present. The trick is to ensure that there are no magazines represented which compete directly with each other. A luncheon to talk about nail care and nail care products might take in one representative of each of the following types of publication: general women's interest magazines, teenage publications magazines, holiday magazines, regional newspaper, London office women's editors, retirement publications and secretarial magazines. There is very little clash of interests here and it will be quite obvious which magazine will be interested in which idea.

Checklist for Informal Entertainment

1. Entertain only if you have a good reason for doing so and only if you have something of value to impart to the guest.
2. Decide whether it will serve your purpose better to entertain individually or in a group.
3. Make sure that colleagues who are to be present from sections other than the PR department are fully briefed on their role and on what can and cannot be said.
4. Have a variety of ideas ready to throw into the conversation and listen carefully to the resulting discussion. Make a note of all requests made for further information and of any interest expressed in ideas for features.

Whatever the means of communication has been, it is important to follow up properly. If a specific idea has been discussed over the phone confirm the details in writing. If an outline idea has been discussed over the lunch table ring up to carry it further, and if you have floated an idea by post and heard nothing phone up to see if it has fallen on stony ground. And when an idea has been fully agreed make sure that you deliver on time. But whatever you do, do not send out a general mailing and then ring up and ask whether the recipient is going to use it or not. If they are, your phone call will merely be a slight irritant, but if there is no appropriate slot at that particular time your call could cause enough irritation to prevent the material ever seeing the light of day.

It is worth mentioning here that the PRO's job should be a two-way one. So far we have been talking about the flow of information from the company, but it can be equally important for management to receive information on how the world is thinking about the company and its activities, about rival companies and about the industry in which it operates. Thus a press monitoring service becomes even more important. If your organization is involved in foreign markets then reaction in these countries would also be important.

The Media Relations department may also be called upon to act as a general information service, in addition to media directories you may need to keep company and financial directories-*Who's Who* and the like. These may be physical or electronic.

The choice of electronic reference works includes CD-ROMs such as *Microsoft Encarta*. This is a kind of electronic encyclopaedia which you can use to find all kinds of facts and figures. Your electronic database might also include the *Oxford English Dictionary, Grolier's Academic Encyclopaedia* (US) or *Microsoft Bookshelf* (half a dozen standard US reference books).

Alternatively you can subscribe to a variety of services such as CompuServe which provides access to large commercial databases such as Reuters News, Associated Press On-Line and Dun and Bradstreet. Others include the Financial Times 'Profile', British Telecom's 'Gold', 'Prestel' (which will also get you into the French 'Mintel') or 'Gateway' the international airways guide, all of which offer a variety of services. 'Profile', for example, holds every word published since the early 1980s in every national newspaper save a couple of tabloids and a few of the more important regional newspapers. BBC Enterprises have also made their database available.

The Internet is another vast source of information and it is growing all the time. Whole newspapers and magazines, complete books, hotel and restaurant guides, tourist information, weather forecasts-the list is endless-can all be downloaded from the Internet. A useful book which will give you some idea of what is available on the Internet is *The New Rider's Official Internet Yellow Pages* published by New Riders Publishing.

The choice of which kind of electronic reference base to use will depend upon the time taken to access it and the cost. The

Internet is often the cheaper option but it can take a long time to find the information you need.

Fundamental Values

In essence, the mass media are the tools or technologies that facilitate dissemination of information and entertainment to a vast number of consumers. They are the tools of large-scale manufacture and distribution of information and related messages. These tools 'mediate' the messages; they are not the messages themselves. However, Marshall McLuhan, the media prophet, liked to proclaim that 'the medium is the message', though the title of one of his books suggests rather that 'the medium is the massage.' The media are technologies; they are also messages and massages. They can also be looked at as industries, as cultural or entertainment industries. While cinema, radio, television, cable, and the press can easily be recognised as 'mass media', it requires some stretching of the established meaning of the term to include recent technologies (sometimes termed the 'new media') such as pagers, cellular phones, satellites, computers, electronic mail and the internet as 'mass media'. More correctly, these new media may be termed 'interactive media' for they are not as much transmission technologies from one source to many receivers, as interactive technologies, which involve feedback, exchange and participation.

'A mass medium' says Wilbur Schramm, 'is essentially a working group organised round some device for circulating the same message, at about the same time, to large numbers of people.' Such a definition excludes the folk media, group media, and interpersonal communication such as rumour, education and preaching, where communication is not 'mediated' by a 'device'. Further, the pejorative term 'mass' (a way of looking down at people as 'masses') suggests that the modern media are 'experienced' not by individuals and groups in terms of their own cultures but as part of the 'mass' and as 'mass culture.' The term 'mass' also suggests that people's interaction with media is homogeneous, inactive and unquestioning. In communication studies today, however, the term 'mass media' has come to be a useful collective phrase, though it slurs over the distinctions among the various media.

As generally interpreted the 'mass' media are the press, cinema, radio and television. But books, magazines, pamphlets and direct mail literature and posters also need to be included in the label. They are so termed because their reach extends to vast heterogeneous masses of the population living in a wide and extensive area of a country. The means they employ to communicate messages to the masses are technological—printing machines, records, cameras, cable, modems, computers and satellites. Their communications are thus interposed and mediated; they are not as direct or face-to-face as in interpersonal exchanges.

The organs of the mass media are technological means of transmitting messages to large numbers of people. Indeed, they are much more than that. As they are very expensive media, (particularly the cinema, radio, television, video, cable, computers, and satellites) they have to be run by institutions like the Government or well financed private commercial bodies. They require a group of people to organise and administer, to produce, distribute and constantly maintain in working order the whole set up of, say, a studio, a transmitting centre, or a publishing house.

Yet another feature of the mass media is that they are founded on the idea of mass production and mass distribution-the marks of an industrial society. Copies of newspapers and magazines, for instance, are printed in thousands (some national and regional dailies in India have a circulation of over half a million) and are circulated over a vast area. But to enjoy a mass audience, the media have to cater to a taste that is not very 'cultured' or sophisticated. What the mass media therefore reflect and propagate is a popular culture. The culture made popular by Hindi films in our cities is a case in point. With the rapid expansion of television and video in cities and towns, popular culture is likely to take on new forms; the 'myths' of our culture will find expression in ever-new ways.

But the mass media in India are in fact a minority media as

access to them is still restricted because of poverty, low literacy levels, and familiarity with Hindi and English, the major languages used in the various media; moreover, reach is limited to populations living in metros and large cities. The folk media, in contrast, have a wide audience; they are media close to the hearts and minds of the people, suited to a poor country, and help facilitate identification and participation.

Modern mass media serve functions very similar to those fulfilled by traditional media in some ancient societies, and in some developing countries today. Western media theorists generally identify three major functions; surveillance of the environment, interpretation of the information and prescription for conduct, and the transmission of heritage. The developmental and liberation or empowerment functions, or even the ritualistic or celebratory functions of the media rarely find mention in Euro-American media theory. South American media theorists have contributed to our understanding of media for 'liberation' while African and Asian scholars have explored the relevance of media to 'national development.'

Other Values

Surveillance of the environment relates to information or 'news' about happenings in society. The mass media carry out this function by keeping us posted about the latest news in our own region and around the world. In rural societies, however, the word-of-mouth method is still the most credible means of spreading news.

Consensus—But the mass media cannot or should not stop at watching the horizon for us, through news bulletins or through advertisements of documentaries. They need, and often do help us to correlate our response to the challenges and opportunities which appear on the horizon and to reach consensus on social actions.

In rural India, the panchayat meetings help the village elders to decide on the challenges and the opportunities.

The mass media help us to keep the culture and heritage of

our society alive, and to transmit it to others. This is what the media should ideally do, but often don't. Folk media serve a similar purpose in developing countries.

A fourth function is the vital function of entertainment. Entertainment has been a legitimate function of the traditional folk media, but the mass media provide it with a vengeance. They help to pass the time, and to relax with family and friends.

Symbolic Function—Anthropologists of culture and communication discern a symbolic function of the media: the media provide a 'shared symbolic environment.' George Gerbner, for instance, sees television as the central symbol of American culture today. Horace Newcomb and other 'culturalists' (such as James Carey and Robert White) perceive the media as providing a ritualistic and 'liminal' experience.

An equally vital function is that of the mass media helping to sell goods and services through sponsorships and commercials. The commercial function has indeed been served well, perhaps too well, especially in the United States, where the networks would have to close down if the support from commercials were to dry up. At the same time, it would be suicidal to let this function dominate the mass media at the expense of the other four functions. India too promotes the commercial function, and though it has not allowed its representatives to take over the programming of radio and television, the influence is still strong. This is equally true of the press and its dependence on advertising.

Developing Values—In the developing countries of Asia, Africa and Latin America, the mass media, which include traditional media have a different function to perform. In a word, development communication i.e., communication that focuses on the information needs of the poor and the oppressed, and their socio-economic and cultural interests.

While these may be the five functions of the mass media, it does not necessarily follow that audiences go to them for the same reasons. In his book The Play Theory of Mass Communication, William Stephenson argues that fun is both the greatest impact and the greatest public service of the mass media.

Audiences use them as a form of play, or lila. Victor Turner, the anthropologist, believes that the media provide a 'liminal' ritualistic experience. James Carey, Horace Newcomb and others of the 'culturalist' school have developed this approach further by analysing the television experience in terms of 'ritual.'

So, for a good number of the audience, the mass media may be marvellous time-fillers, like listening to the radio while cooking or while driving, or reading during a long train journey. Further, some people use the media to fulfil psychological and social needs. They perhaps get vicarious enjoyment out of sex and violence in the media, and use the media to get topics for conversation at work, or to solve their own problems.

Still others might seek information, merely to be well informed, or perhaps to learn how higher-status people dress and live. Or, they might watch advertisements on TV not so much to know more about a product as to assure themselves that they have bought the best product. These are the 'uses and gratifications' of the media.

So whatever functions the media pundits say the mass media have, the people will continue to use them in the way they (the people, not the pundits) like. It is in this sense that audiences are 'active' rather than 'passive' receivers.

Journalistic Ethics

Western theories of the mass media (particularly of the news media) were first propounded by Fred Siebert, Theodore Peterson and Wilbur Schramm in their book Four Theories of the Press.

These theories have now come to be termed 'normative' in the sense that they 'mainly express ideas of how the media ought to, or can be expected to, operate under a prevailing set of conditions and values.' So, strictly speaking they are hypotheses rather than theories. These 'theories' were first enunciated in the United States during the height of the 'cold-war' against communism and the Soviet Union. They were thus part of American propaganda and only loosely based on actual practices in the media. They idealise the American practices, which are touted as being democratic and socially responsible, and deride 'Soviet' and 'Communist', practices as being 'dictatorial' and 'authoritarian.' They do not take into account the 'public service' models of print and electronic media widely accepted in Western Europe, and in many countries of Asia and Africa.

The 'original' four theories of the press/media are authoritarian theory, libertarian theory, social responsibility theory, and Soviet media theory. Each of them suits particular political and economic circumstances, and focuses not so much on the relationship between the press and readers as on the relationships between the press and Government. The major concern is with ownership and control rather than with different perspectives of Journalism or the people's right to information. Siebert, Peterson and Schramm limit their analysis to 'four' theories; three more need to be added to the original four to take account of circumstances in the developing countries of Asia, Africa and Latin America. The last three could be termed 'Developmental or Alternative Theories' of the media.

Authoritarian Theory—According to this theory, the mass media, though not under the direct control of the State and the ruling classes, must do their bidding. The press and other media are expected to respect authority, to be always subordinate to established power and authority, and therefore should avoid offending the majority or dominant moral, political and economic values. Journalists lack independence and freedom; their reports have to be submitted for advance censorship. This censorship is justified on the ground that the State must always take precedence over an individual's right to freedom of expression. Such censorship is more rigidly enforced in times of war and during 'internal' and 'external' emergencies. It needs to be noted that both dictatorial and democratic regimes resort to such authoritarian control of the media. The strictness with which the Official Secrets Act is enforced in Britain and in India is a case in point.

Libertarian Theory—The basis of this 'free press' theory goes back to 17th century England when the printing press made it possible to print several copies of a book or pamphlet at a comparatively low price. In contrast with the authoritarian theory, libertarianism is founded on the fundamental right of an individual to freedom of expression. Western liberal democracies swear by this belief. The First Amendment in the American constitution is an embodiment of this theory; it flows from the individual's right to life, liberty and the pursuit of happiness. The individual, not the State or society, is supreme, and popular will (vox populi) is granted precedence over the power of the State. The argument is that 'truth' can be arrived at only through the free expression of diverse points of view, no matter how erroneous. The great apologists of this theory were John Milton, the epic poet (in his Aeropagitica) and John Stuart Mill (in his essay, On Liberty). A free press is seen as essential to a free society and the dignity of the individual. Moreover, the freedom to publish is often linked to the right to property, and the free market system.

In practice, however, the theory provides the prerogative of free speech only to the rich and the powerful elites of a society. The marginalized groups do not have access to, and indeed, cannot afford the means or the tools of free expression. What happens on the ground is that media merchants and media monopolies (e.g. the big newspaper chains, the television companies) exploit that freedom to expand their empires. Market forces rather than public good mould the kind of information to be purveyed. The theory thus protects media owners rather than the rights of editors and journalists, or of the public. What the theory offers, in sum, is 'power without social responsibility'.

Social Responsibility Theory—This theory can be said to have been derived from the Hutchins Report (entitled 'A Free and Responsible Press: A General Report on Mass Communication: Newspapers, Radio, Motion Magazines and Books'). The Hutchins Commission on Freedom of the Press (1947) was established and financed by Henry Luce of Time Magazine at a time in the history of American Journalism when press barons like Luce sensed that government regulations on 'yellow journalism' were round the corner. Moreover, the years following the Second World War witnessed the rise of the Democratic Party in the United States, the restraints on business under the New Deal, and the strengthening of the trade union movement. The American press (which was known to be largely pro-Republican) feared that the federal Government would issue legislation to regulate the 'freedom of the press', despite the First Amendment.

Robert Hutchins, the Chairman of the Commission, was the Chancellor of the Chicago University at the time, and he was assisted by twelve others who were experts in different fields. The Report appeared in two volumes: the first on newspapers, the second on the other media.

The Commission found that the free market approach to press freedom had not met the informational and social needs of the less well off classes; in fact, it had increased the power of a single class. There was little expression of diverse views; the emergence of radio, film and television also suggested that some public control and some means of accountability had become necessary.

Thus, the theory had its roots in the view that the media had certain obligations to society-to serve its needs, rather than that of the free market. Hence the need for high professional standards; of truth, accuracy, objectivity and balance. Self-regulation and also state regulations were imperative. Public interest was a greater value than unregulated freedom of expression. So news offensive to religious and ethnic minorities, or news likely to lead to social violence needed to be underplayed. The Hutchins Report led to the establishment of Press Councils, the drawing up of codes of ethics, anti-monopoly legislation, and to press subsidies to small newspapers. State and public intervention in the exercise of free expression was therefore considered legitimate under certain circumstances.

Soviet Media Theory—This theory is derived from Lenin's application of Marx and Engel's dictum in The German Ideology that, 'the ideas of the ruling class are in every epoch the ruling ideas.' The media are thus a means of 'mental production' of the ideology. Hence the need for their control by the working class, that is, through the Communist Party, so that the interests of the working class rather than those of the ruling or elite class are projected. In a Socialist society, therefore, the media should be used as tools to 'socialize' the people; the primary functions of the media are to educate, inform, motivate and mobilize citizens, and to support 'progressive' movements everywhere. What is expected is 'objective' (or 'scientific') presentation of society. Censorship and restriction on the media are legitimate for the media are accountable to the State, to the public and to the Party. The public is encouraged to provide feedback, as it is only in this way that the media will be able to serve the public interest.

Development Communication Theory—The 'four theories of the press' are not fully applicable to the experience of the non-aligned countries of Asia, Africa, and South America. While in most Asian and African countries, the media (especially the broadcast media) are owned and run by the State, in Latin American countries, commercial ownership of all the mass media is the norm. A common factor in the experience of the majority of the non-aligned countries is the dependence on industrialized countries for both hardware and software. Another common factor is the commitment of these nations to social and economic development on their own terms; they would like to employ the mass media as tools for 'development', for 'nation-building.' The larger national interest and the public good are of paramount importance to them. So certain freedoms need to be curbed in the interest of say national integration, and economic and social development. Hence the stress on 'development communication' and 'development journalism'. According to development theorists, journalists have the responsibility to support national governments in their efforts at eradicating illiteracy, promoting family planning, promoting national integration, and increasing production and employment. The weakness in the theory is that 'development' is often equated with government propaganda.

Democratization Theory—Latin American critics (notably Paulo Freire, Reyes Matta, Luis Beltran, Diaz Bordenave and Valerio Fuenzalida) of commercialized ('commodotized') media have come out strongly against the top-down, one way and non-participative character of contemporary mass media. Like the development theorists, they lay stress on the positive uses of the media, on the need for 'access' and the 'right to communicate.'

They insist on the need for local and community participation in media and news production. The people must speak for themselves, they argue, not through professional journalists and producers.

What is vehemently opposed also is commercial, political or bureaucratic control of the media, which exist to serve audiences, not the interests of government or commercial enterprises. The 'demassification' of the media, according to this theory, is as vital as 'democratization.' The ultimate purpose is to put the media in the hands of communities (as in people's radio) for their own 'liberation' through a process of 'conscientization.' Thus is created, in Reyes Malta's words, a 'critical national audience.'

The Correlationship

Successful media relations involves understanding the media, how they work and what their requirements are. It also involves relating this knowledge to the needs of your own organization and the objectives of its media relations programme. It is important to work out the best strategy and to plan accordingly.

This book is essentially practical. It is concerned with the tools, the organization and the planning of the media relations programme. But it also seeks to show how a thorough knowledge and understanding of the media can make your efforts more effective.

There is, after all, no point in spending a fortune on trying to communicate an important story if you are telling the wrong people, in the wrong way, at the wrong time. Putting yourself in the recipient's place and deciding exactly what will be of interest and what will not will be much more useful from everyone's point of view.

This kind of practical knowledge of the media will put you in a better position to build up a harmonious and helpful relationship with those sections of the media which cover your organization's particular activities. And this relationship will in turn help you to establish a smooth communications channel between media and management.

Unfortunately, the senior managements of some organizations tend to view the press or media relations department as a buffer between the media and themselves. This can only lead to trouble. Very often the Public Relations Officer (PRO) is not qualified to answer detailed and possibly highly technical questions. Nor does he or she have the authority to answer for the company on important issues. Such an attitude inevitably leads to an unnecessarily bad press and a lack of cooperation by the media on future occasions.

Rather, the PRO should be the means by which the two sides can talk to each other more easily and with more understanding. You must stick to your professional guns in telling senior management what the consequences of their actions in the media relations field are likely to be. You must, however, also follow up such a stand with sensible advice on dealing with the media and be on hand to see fair play.

Of course, there are occasions when certain sections of the media behave with some dishonesty and as PRO you must watch out for signs of such a situation arising and warn your management in time. But the vast majority of dealings with the media will not be like this, and management must be encouraged to be as open as possible.

Building up a favourable relationship with the media often involves building up a good personal relationship with key journalists in your field. You cannot hope to achieve this if you are not convinced yourself. If you do not think you can be committed to an organization's activities, do not work for it. Honesty is as important at this level as it is on individual issues.

This applies equally whether you are planning to work directly for the organization or for its PR consultants. Indeed everything in the book applies to both situations, for they differ only in their organization and lines of control. To all intents and purposes a PR consultant must act as though he or she works directly for the client organization. 'Public Relations Officer' has also been taken to be synonymous with Press or Media Relations Officer' for the purposes of this book.

Of course a harmonious relationship with the media does not mean that everything will always go smoothly. Sometimes your objectives and those of your media friends will be in conflict and this is where your powers of diplomacy will be tested to the full. Competent journalists will be probing critically. That is their job. Yours is to present the facts in the most favourable light for your organization and, if the problems are severe, to ensure that ultimately your organization's worst story receives the best hearing.

A good example of successful media relations concerns a multinational oil company, one of whose oil tankers was wrecked, causing extensive spillage along the Californian holiday beaches. Sales at petrol stations immediately started to fall. The company instituted an expensive and wide-ranging mopping up programme including very quick cleaning of the popular beaches and a bird sanctuary, a marine life survey and a restocking operation. Full details of the disaster and the company's prompt action were relayed to the media at once and this, coupled with the previously good relationship between the oil company and the media, ensured that most of the coverage was concentrated on the mopping up operation. This resulted in the company being seen as a responsible, socially conscious organization rectifying an inevitable disaster, rather than as an irresponsible multinational with no concern for the environment. Sales not only recovered but exceeded the previous norm.

There are times when the disaster is less obvious to the public view and this is when there is a strong temptation to deny everything. The short answer is, don't allow your management to do so either. If you or any of the representatives of your organization do lie, your reputation in the media will be shattered and its loss will precede you into whatever industry you go. It is very rare for the truth not to emerge, given time, and once a journalist has been castigated by his or her editor for believing your lies the journalist will, understandably, never trust you again. In future, the journalist will be suspicious of everything you and your organization have to say and will tell associates to be wary too.

negated the whole concept since only the very-well-to-do, the elite can afford to launch the media ventures.

India is a classic example of communication contradictions. Certain media are allowed in the private sector while others are controlled by the Government. Newspapers in India have traditionally uphold the freedom of press. In India, with a low literacy level, the influences of print media are limited to the urban centres. Further, most Indian newspapers being privately owned, are supposed to guarantee free and unbiased reporting. Several defects have been identified. Most of the largely circulated newspapers are owned by big business and industrial houses, and thus political interests take precedence over any other human interests. A study conducted by the IIPA, Delhi, revealed that out of 54 dailies selected, 27 newspapers were owned either partially or totally by business and industrial houses and controlled about 50 per cent of the total circulation. For the purpose of unbiased and objective performance, delinking the ownership of newspapers from large industrial houses was suggested.

However, inspite of all this, the Indian Press enjoys credibility with reading audiences. Public opinion is reflected either in the editorials or letters to the editor published in newspapers. But, with 85% of the population totally unexposed to the press and its accessibility limited to just the elite, it is questionable how accessibility to the media can be a criteria for its high credibility. Further, how can editorials or letters to the editor from the literate few, constitute feedback of the entire nation.

Government controlled electronic media are anathema to the very concept of an open society. Frequent political interference has eroded the credibility of both AIR and Doordarshan. Added to this, bureaucratisation has affected professional aspects of their functioning. These two powerful media can cross the barriers of illiteracy and their reach is the reason why political authorities keep a stranglehold on them.

Community Participation—A community is an assembly of people in an identified geographical area. A community's development hinges on effective communication. The increased use of local media makes communication a vital input of every community development programme. Community participation in media programmes accentuates free flow of information. Consequently, the democratic process acquires more meaning and relevance. Community participation in mass media can be both at the level of decision-making and management.

The mass media are very important component of society. Their use in a developing country like India is considered most crucial in the challenge to mobilize people for development activities. Therefore, there must be a communication policy. The policy should give direction to the programmes which are channeled through various mass media networks.

Practical Difficulties

Technology-oriented Problems—The mass media systems may fail to perform their functions when unplanned use of such technology creates problems. For instance communication resources can be concentrated in a few centres alone. The mass media may be misused by the owners to exercise their power, or the media content may be manipulated to give as a result of the communicators biases. All these problems forced the formulation of a viable communication policy. If the policy itself becomes outdated in the face of technological developments, it will have to be suitably changed.

Problems of Research—Traditionally, communications research in India has shown a remarkable orientation towards social problems. Studies on propaganda techniques, attitude change, effects of mass media, personal influence, diffusion of innovations, flow of information, media uses and gratifications and the economics of communication have been motivated by practical problems faced in society. These studies focus on the need to understand the role of communication in those problems and the desire to apply the knowledge gained from research to solve them.

In spite of a great deal of empirical research, no systematic knowledge about the nature, frequency and origin of communication problems in India is available. However, the situation is changing now. Demands are being made for improving existing regulations, resource allocation principles, institutional arrangements, and defining the rights and responsibilities of professional communicators, commercial communication organisations and the bureaucracies. A communication policy must give importance to these issues. The policy, in effect, is built on the body of knowledge developed by research.

Official View

A Policy is a set of principles, rules and guidelines to help in the tackling of problems which may be faced by a society in any particular field. A communication policy is formulated in response to the challenges of new communication technologies. We can define communication policy as action-oriented principles, outlining objectives and means of achieving objectives, focusing on what needs to be done and what is to be avoided in dealing with current and anticipated communication problems in society. The policies are formulated on authoritative guidelines.

Role of Communication Policy—Given the centrality of communication in modern society, one should rightly expect that communication policy would have a distinct and independent role to play. It would take into account the problems that crop up when using communication in varied activities. Communication policy should be based on an understanding of the totality of communication problems. Such a policy should aim at achieving society's goals and expectations regarding the applications of communication.

Objectives of Communication Policy—The priorities according to which the developed and the developing countries formulate their policies differ, sometimes even contradict each other. The technologically advanced countries like USA and Japan are concerned with mobilizing world markets for their communication goals and services. The developing countries like India, on the other hand, are concerned with building and expanding their communication systems with indigenous and appropriate technology. One major objective of their policy is to eliminate the vestings of colonial dependency. A major thrust area of communication policy of developing countries is the implementation of viable alternatives to the one-way flow of information into their societies. Most of the developing countries are busy waging a constant battle against poverty, malnutrition, illiteracy and indebtness. Thus, communication development receives scarce priority in their national objectives.

Mass Media Policy Formulation—The mass media can be tools of cultural enrichment, national cohesion and advancement. The media policy makers in India first have to bridge the gap between ground realities and ideal situations. Certain paradoxes exist in the field of communication which need to be considered by policy makers. Some of these realities are elucidated here-

(a) Whereas there is an urgent demand to realise the right to equal access to information, there is a widening of the information gap between the richer and the poorer sections of society.

(b) There is misappropriation of the mass media for commercial and political purchases, when the need of the hour is to apply the media to the task of propagating culture, education, information and leisure time entertainment.

(c) There is predominant use of media to impose foreign values.

(d) In India, by and large, the communicators don't desire to find out the reactions of the audience to their programmes.

(e) The increase in the number of channels is not matched by any corresponding increase in the standard of programming.

(f) While communication satellites remove the barriers to information and education across the national boundaries all over the world, the same technology pave the way for cultural imperialism and new communication colonialism.

Policy versus Practice and Performance—The Doordarshan has always suffered from the dichotomy between policy pronouncements and the continuous drift and departure from them in actual practice. In developing and democratic country like India, access to television and the social benefit accruing from it, is a crucial test of the social relevance of such an expensive medium. The importance of utilising TV is not just for the idle entertainment of the elite but for the uplift of the poor. But in effect and in actual practice, the purchase of a TV set is seen as wholesale investment in entertainment which obviates the bother and expense of going to an auditorium or a stadium.

Commercialism vs Social Good—From inception, broadcasting in India has been looked upon as a public service for the promotion of social objectives. The concept of advertisements for the promotion of consumer goods was also considered incompatible with the prevailing philosophy of the "socialistic pattern of society". In a developing country like India, radio and TV should be viewed as a national resource for the uplift of the masses. It is only through a strong media network that the eight kind of information and education can be imparted to the people. But the media in our country, like elsewhere in the world, have buckled under the pressure of commercial interests. Mindless entertainment with little or no educative value defeats the very purpose of building up a strong media network.

Performance of Indian Press—The press in a democratic country plays a vital role in creating, moulding and reflecting public opinion. It is a fundamental institution of our society. Though the press in India is free, it suffers from many ills. There are a few in-built handicaps such as vast geographical area, illiteracy, poverty, multiplicity of languages and absence of adequate communication facilities. Some other bottlenecks exist like –

(a) the linking of ownership of newspapers with other industrial or commercial enterprises.

(b) limited newspaper ownership with closely held share interest.

(c) Urban-oriented expansion of newspapers leaving the vast country side population untouched.

(d) inadequate and expensive newsprint.

(e) the lack of local advertisement support.

Speech and Expression—Man's greatest invention is language. The invention of the script has helped mankind to preserve human thoughts and learning. It has helped society to conquer both space and time. An important product of the script was the book. The books helped older civilisations like the Chinese and the Indian civilizations to preserve heritage. Books spread ideas which set people thinking, as a prelude to individual and group action. For this reason, they met opposition from guardians of political and religious doctrines.

Plato argued that wise men alone could rule and the state would control education. For Machiavelli, the security of the state was supreme. Hegel regarded state as embodiment of morality. John Milton (1608-1674) in Areopagitica gave a solid reason for the freedom of the Press. In his essay on liberty (1859) John Stuart Mill (1806-1873) proclaimed that liberty was the right of the individual.

Today freedom of expression and speech are internationally reorganised rights. The league of nations made the first organised attempt at the international level to proclaim rights of speech and expression by launching a series of conferences. In just a few years of its birth, the United Nations approved the UN Declaration of Freedom of Information (1946) and the Universal Declaration of Human Rights (1948).

With the gaining of independence, freedom of speech and expression were recognised as fundamental rights and were included in the Indian Constitution. They are provided in the Article 19(1) of our constitution. Article 19(2) provides reasonable restrictions on freedom of expression.

In U.S.A., freedom of the press was very clearly recognised for the first time in the Virginia Bill of Rights in 1776. Unlike U.S.A., Britain has no written constitution. But it has been the fountain of all philosophy concerning freedom of speech, expression and the press, as John Milton did most of his work in Britain. The rights of free speech, expression and the press are in a constant process of evolution.

Freedom of the Press—In general press freedom means freedom, unless specifically prohibited by law, together, print and publish information and to set up technologies in pursuit of such objectives, to claim and gain access to information. In practice, freedom of the press means freedom of the owner of a newspaper. Journalists enjoy only that much freedom as is given to them by the owner of their newspaper/magazine.

From the beginning, freedom of the press was sought and obtained on the ground that it was a prerequisite to democracy. The press demand freedom because of the functions they discharge for the benefit of the society. In today's context, freedom of the press is only an extension of the citizen's right to freedom of speech and expression. It is the press alone which can thwart the attempts of any government to deny this right to the citizen. Today, the press, the electronic media, wherever they operate privately, have information-gathering networks spread all over the world. They are the eyes and ears of the people everywhere.

In connection with the limitation, the very first thing is that the right of the freedom of the press is only an extension of the citizen's right to freedom of speech and expression. Therefore, all those laws imposing restrictions on this right of the citizen apply to the press too. It has no special privilege that the citizens do not enjoy in this area. In all western societies and in India, the constitutions as well as the general laws of the countries, set the limits for the exercise of freedom of the press. It goes without saying that with regard to freedom, the press is not on any higher footing than the ordinary citizen. Since the press is also a business and an industry, all those laws which apply to business and industry, also apply to newspaper organizations.

Responsibilities and Social Obligation of the Press—The theory of responsibility is simple that everyone is responsible for the consequences of his actions. 'No Rights without responsibilities'. Therefore, freedom of the press is also linked with responsibilities.' At least, the freedom should not be abused.

Responsibilities and its Rationale—When we say that somebody is responsible, we mean that he has a duty to do something, when we say someone is accountable, we mean that if he fails to do what his duty is, he is accountable to some person or institution. Thus, the right to freedom of speech and expression carries with it, a duty not to disturb public peace. If he so disturbs it he is accountable to the state for such breach of responsibility. Since media circulates information for the consumption of members of the society, it is natural that they should be responsible in the dissemination of the information. With every increase in the power of media, this responsibility towards the society also increases.

Unwritten Understanding—Editors and others often say that they have a right to inform the public. These are self-imposed responsibilities. These arise from an unwritten understanding between the media and society. On the basis of the responsibility of the media to inform the public, media have fought for and gained the right to free speech and expression.

But state has also imposed some obligations on media like not to publish anything that leads to, or has a tendency to lead to, a breakdown of public order. These are responsibilities imposed in addition to, and sometimes in contrast to, self-imposed responsibilities.

Govt's Role

The First Press Commission was appointed in 1952, because after independence the role of the press was changing. It was fast turning from a mission to' business. The commission founded that there was a great deal of scurrilous writing often directed against communities or groups, of indecency and vulgarity and personal attacks on individuals. It felt that the best way of maintaining professional standards of journalism would be to bring into existence a body of people principally connected with the industry whose responsibility it would be to arbitrate on doubtful points and to ensure the punishment of anyone guilty of infraction of good journalistic behaviour. Second Press Commission was appointed in 1978 and it wanted the press to be neither a mindless adversary nor an unquestioning ally. It wanted the press to play a responsible role in the development process. From the role that the two commissions recommended for the press, we can summarise the responsibilities of the Press thus-

— Help the country in its development process both by making constructive suggestions as well as criticism of delays and distortions in the development process.

— Give the widest possible access to people, reflecting the pluralistic composition of Indian society.

— Maintain internal stability and safeguard external security.

— Prevent and deflate social conflict.

Code of Conduct for Journalists—Complaints are heard throughout the world that a section of the press functions without regard to its responsibilities to the society. There is a vast area not covered by any legal regime. Media ethics apply mostly to cases not specifically concerned by law.

Code of Ethics—The Second Press Commission observed that one of the functions entrusted to the Press council was the building up of a code of conduct for newspapers, news agencies and journalists in accordance with high standards of journalism. The second Press Commission lists a number of codes drafted in India, the USA and Britain have through the years. The All-India Newspaper Editors' Conference formulated a Code of Ethics and a Charter for Editors in 1953. The National Union of Journalists (1981), the All India Small and Medium Newspapers Association (1975) had all drafted similar codes. But the Editors Guild of India refused to draft any code arguing that responsible people do not need such a formal code. The second Press Commission said that it would not be desirable to draw up a Code of Ethics for newspapers. The Code of Ethics (1953) of All India Newspaper Editors' Conference asks journalists to serve and guard public interest, to be alive to fundamental human and social rights, to observe restraint in reports dealing with tensions leading to or likely to lead to public disorder, to assume responsibility for all information published, to respect confidence, not to exploit their status for non-journalistic purposes, not to allow personal interest to influence professional conduct, to correct inaccurate information, not to demand or accept bribe. The National Union of Journalists' Declaration of 1981 is also largely on similar lines.

Ombudsman—The idea of an Ombudsman is of Swedish origin. In Sweden the Press Ombudsman at the national level is appointed by all the newspaper organizations together. Ombudsman generally means an intermediary, investigating complaints by private citizens against government officials or agencies. However, at present private or voluntary organizations are also having Ombudsmen to decide public complaints made against themselves or their members. In India, the Lok Ayuktas in some states are Ombudsmen.

Although this concept first originated in Sweden, but it was first adopted by the Press in USA.

Press Council—The world's first Press Council took its birth in Sweden in 1916. In USA, a Press Council (National News Council) worked for 11 years and today there are nearly 50 Press Councils all over the world. The Press Council of India was set up on July 4, 1966 and Justice J.R. Mudholkar, was its chairman. It consisted of 25 members who were editors, working journalists, proprietors etc. In 1970, news agencies were also put under its jurisdiction. The council has powers to levy a graded fee on newspapers and news agencies to meet its expenditure and to reduce its dependence on government's financial support.

The countries of North and South are separated by an enormous gap in their respective communication capacities. The developed countries continue to exercise considerable political, economic and technological control on information flows. Nearly 80 per cent of the information disseminated in the world originates from five largest transnational news agencies as told before. About 15 great media corporations dominate the production of the radio sets, television sets and printing equipment, ten of these corporations belong to the U.S.A. Due to our dependence on the media delivery systems of the West, we also become dependent on the West.

Need for Self-Reliance—Self-reliance in news and information distribution, both in disseminating news to the outside world or in getting news and information from various places in the world, for internal consumption, is essential for the following reasons-

(a) To provide the media a national identity and personality.

(b) To facilitate the analyses of the world events not from the perspective of the West but from the national perspective.

(c) To foster better understanding among the developing countries, which is far more essential now than ever before.

(d) To prevent the unwarranted entry of foreign and alien ideas, cultures and life-styles, that always tend to contribute to shaping public opinion in favour of foreign countries, particularly of the West.

(e) To provide an objective account of the news and developments that were considered newsworthy by the indigenous media.

Non-aligned News Pool—As per the directives of the UNESCO to establish a news pool or consortium of news agencies, the 'pool' of news agencies of the non-aligned countries was formally launched in July, 1976 at the New Delhi Conference of Information Ministers and Representations of the news agencies of the non-aligned countries. The objective of the pool is to expand the mutual exchange of information among the non-aligned countries in a spirit of collective self-reliance.

The Non-Aligned News Pool is not a transnational news agency, but a system of exchange of agency information, based on co-operation and co-ordination among individual news agencies taking part in these activities. The Pool is not based on any formal membership. The Pool has no single directing centre, nor does it have its own budget.

The Restraints

Communication Restraints—Many of the developing countries do not have an extensive and elaborate telecommunication network. For some, high tariffs are major barriers. Optimum information exchange depend on the level of development of communication systems in the individual non-aligned countries.

News Flow—A few year ago, about 85% of the news items received by PT1 from the Pool partners were spiked. The reasons for this were given as delay in news reception, poor quality, low news value, or propaganda material.

Lack of Training—The lack of proper training among the non-aligned journalists and their inability to match the professional standards of the journalists of the transnational news-agencies, are the reasons for the poor quality of material put out by the Non-Aligned News Agencies Pool.

Political Constraints—In many of the non-aligned countries, the news agencies are under the strict control of the governments. The first casualty of such a solution is the objectivity of the news and information put out by their agencies.

The Media's Lukewarm Attitude—The editors of private-owned newspapers in the democratic countries like India, either are not convinced of the need for such an inter-regional co-operation or they do not respect the news coverage of several agencies, which are participants of the pool.

The Systems—While there has been a continuous effort to establish alternative news and information distribution systems in the world, the recent global changes have had a deep impact on the information scene.

The West has been for a long time using the concept of 'Freedom of Information' as an ideological weapon, and successfully deploying it to deflect the 3rd World from its pursuit of a new world information and communication order.

In the matter of broadcasting, the Western powers insist upon the 'open skies' policy, which they claim to be consistent with the principle of freedom of information. On the face of things, this seems a plausible argument. Open skies, seems to connote a situation of an unfettered information exchange of knowledge flowing freely across the national boundaries. On the contrary, the same western countries, show a complete disinclination towards free trade by imposing heavy tariffs to protect their own products.

These developments call for a greater unity among the 3rd World countries to come out of the dependence and dominance in the field of information, and promote self-reliance. The existing world information order provides an opportunity to the richer nations to use the scarce global natural resources, and exclude the poor nations from using the same. An attempt is made through the on going GATT talks to impose stronger forms of monopoly control over the content of information flows.

Global Scenario

The developing nations campaigned for a 'new order' in the field of international information and communication, which would facilitate a 'free and balanced flow' of information capable of breaking through the stereotypes created and nurtured for over 50 years by the western media empires. The new order, they maintained, would create a new international information climate that would foster a closer and better understanding among nations and individuals. The most important step in this direction was the launching of the Non-Aligned News Agencies Pool, in 1975. The 'free flow' concept was amended to 'free-and balanced flow', when a declaration on the role of the media in the promotion of international understanding and peace was approved by the UNESCO in 1978. 'The right to know' was transformed into 'the right to communicate'.

The non-aligned nations coined the phrase, New International Information Order (NIIO). The MacBride Commission broadened the sphere by substituting the term 'world' for 'international' and incorporating 'communication' along with 'information'. Since then the phrase the 'New World Information and Communication Order (NWICO) has been widely used.

Free Flow Ideas—A major factor that helped the growth of US agencies was the wireless transmission technology, which reversed the world communication imbalance to the overall advantage of the American interest. Another factor was a general realization in the US of the advantages that world communication control bestowed on foreign trade and commerce. Following such realizations, ideas on unrestricted How of communication between nations began to crystallize in the US.

Demand for NWICO—The following overlapping and mutually complementing factors are at the base of the demand for a new order in the field of information-

(1) The emergence of new nations following the dissolution of the colonial empires after World War II.

(2) The asymmetrical economic relationship between the new nations and the western industrialized nations which, while strengthening the latters' wealth and power, perpetuated the new nations' dependency, not merely economic but political and cultural as .well.

(3) The coming together of the new nations under the umbrella of non-alignment in the wake of aggressive bloc-building by the US and the USSR.

(4) The new nation's realization that their under-development was related to their dependence on rich nations followed by a firm resolve to assertive actions to correct imbalances in world trade and commerce, and cultural exchanges.

(5) Their gaining in strength in international organization, such as the UN and the UNESCO. Four stages can easily be identified in the history of the NWICO. The first stage (1973-76) marked the evolution of a new order. The second stage (1976-79) saw the accumulation of data and empirical evidence to give credence to the new order demand. The third stage followed the publication of the MacBride report in 1980. The fourth stage is the period following the adoption of the NWICO Resolution in the UNESCO.

Generally, the evolution of the new order concept is credited to the NAM. Much of the credit for the enlarging communication agenda of the UNESCO in the 1970s goes to the Non-Alignced Movement, which saw communication, at least in the early 70s, as a means to an end, the end being economic development of the poor nations.

The Algiers Summit of the non-aligned countries, held in 1973, is a major landmark, in the history of NWICO, for it was here that communication concerns were addressed directly in more than one paper in the context of their economic development programmes.

The 19th UNESCO General Conference adopted a resolution inviting the Director General to undertake a review of the problems of communication in modern society. Director General constituted a 16 member commission for the study of communication problems.

The 20th UNESCO general conference, held in 1978 was marked by a spirit of compromise. The new Mass Media Declaration (MMD) text now retitled as 'Declaration on Fundamental Principles Governing the contribution of the Mass Media in strengthening Peace and International Understanding and in combating was Propaganda, Racialism and Apartheid' was approved.

Character and Content of NWICO—The 21st general conference of the UNESCO, held in 1980, accepted the MacBride report and unanimously adopted Resolution outlining the basic character and content of the NWICO. The establishment of the NWICO depended upon five major factors—(1) the will of the developed and developing countries to bring about changes in all areas of communication within their respective regions; (2) Co-operation between the developed and developing nations for removing all obstacles to a two-way and balanced flow of news and information among nations; (3) sharing of communication resources, including technologies, for countering monopoly of the international news flow by a few; (4) cooperation among the developing countries to correct imbalances with their own regions by increasing horizontal flows and (5) Co-operation between the media-rich and media-poor for mobilization of resources to strengthen communication infrastructure in the latter's region.

The 21st General Conference of the UNESCO approved the establishment of a news agency, the International Programme for the Development of Communication (IPDC) within the framework of the UNESCO to reduce the gap between the developed and developing countries by strengthening infrastructure and services through international cooperation and assistance. The objectives of the IPDC cover all facts of communication development.

Problems and Prospects of NWICO—The withdrawal of the US on December 31, 1984, and Britain and Singapore a year later, from the UNESCO, was not a deterrent to the objectives of the NWICO. Today, the evolving goals of the NWICO rest with not just the UNESCO, but a large number of international organizations such as the Organization for Economic Co-operation and Development (OECD), the International Telecommunications Union (ITU), the IPDC and the Third World and its organizations for moving the aim of the NWICO to a higher plain. The IPDC has done its best to help develop communication capabilities of the media-poor regions. Between the second session in 1982 and the seventh session held in January 1986, it had allocated US$ 9.74 million for some communication projects in the developing countries. Those included 3 regional news agency projects Pan Africa News Agency (PANA), the Agencia Latino American De Servcios Especiales do Information (ALA SEI) and the Asia-Pacific News Network (ANN) and 14 national news agency projects in different 3rd World countries. These agencies and news exchange arrangements operating within the developing countries, no matter how inadequate they are, indicate that the NWICO has set itself on its evolutionary path. But there is more to be achieved.

Imbalances in the flow of news and information at international level have not ceased to exist. The one-way flow is still very much in evidence. Most of the news flowing through the transnational agencies into the developing regions concerns the developing world. The agencies continue to view the developing world's events and issues from their own perspectives. As a result, news everywhere is seen through the prisms of the West, the developed world. The Western media giants continue to set the world's news agenda.

Measures to be Adopted—The developed countries should be more open to redress the ever-increasing asymmetrical economic relations between them and the poor countries. This calls for hastening the pace for the establishment of the NIEO as it is linked with the NWICO. The developed world could make available resources for communication specific projects in the poor regions of the world. New technologies needed to be viewed as resources for the benefit of the mankind, and not as a new tool for exploitation of the disadvantaged.

Steps are needed to establish a balance in the information flow by devoting more space and lime to news and issues concerning the developing countries. The developed countries should join hands with the developing countries in making the telecommunications tariffs more suitable for a better use of existing systems.

The developing world, on the other hand, needs to formulate communication policies, without which the media development would get hampered. The press must make conscious efforts to free itself from the attitudes fostered by the Western news criteria.

Free Flow of Information—The free flow of information is a Western concept, by which almost all western countr es rationalise the operation of their media and information agencies. The term means that any person or persons and any organization or organisations can own and operate any media or information agency, gather any information, and disseminate the same, if they so desire, to any target audience, wherever and whenever they want. The concept is basic to the history, culture and life of the liberal capitalist western society. Any challenge to this concept is rejected on grounds that it is undemocratic, inhuman and even uncivilized.

The philosophy of free flow resulted in the consolidation of the centres of information gathering and dissemination in the western countries. The socialist and the 3rd World countries could see that they were not represented objectively in the western media. Significant happenings in their countries were paid scant attention and whatever done, those were only half truths coloured by the Western perceptions. Slowly, this situation got concretised, and the leaders of the 3rd World countries endured the situation as they were unable to take steps to change the situation. The 3rd World countries had no infrastructure or active network to make a difference.

Concept of Imbalance—There is imbalance in the flow of information between the developed West and the developing 3rd World countries, which can not have any say on the mechanism of gathering information as they do not own and control the technology of the giant information agencies of the West. Moreover, the 3rd World countries, knowing fully well that the information disseminated from these agencies doesn't represent all the truths about them. The imbalance is in terms of volume of information, flowing into the 3rd World countries, when compared to the volume of information flowing out from them.

The root of the problem goes back to the late 1950s and 1960s, when the concept of 'Development Communication' was born. The communication specialists thought that what the West achieved in centuries, the 3rd World could achieve the same in a matter of decades if aided by the mass media. Two eminent western scholars-Daniel Lerner and Wilbur Schramm-were in the forefront to suggest this theory. Their theories were tried in many 3rd World countries. It was assumed that mass media used for creating a stable and sustainable democratic nation and implementing programmes to uplift the living conditions of the common man in society would transform the developing societies into modern, vibrant and stable societies. However, a decade later, it was found that most of the social problems remained unsolved. Instead more problems were created. The western media organizations focused the negative developments of the developing society. In such a situation, an American author, Herbert Schiller articulated something very new. He said that the free flow of communication was essentially meant to safeguard the economical growth of the West. And any attempt to regulate the flow of information beyond borders is seen as a threat to the western economies. Thus, it is termed as interference with the basic human right. Hence, the concept of 'imbalance' is an economic issue, and the international flow of information is just another fact of this issue.

Although the flow is still imbalance, exchanges of TV programmes, specially educational programmes, are quite frequent. More western programmes are seen on the TV screens of the 3rd World countries. Despite the large scale changes brought about by technology, imbalance persists in the media and coverage of the development west vis-a-vis the developing countries of the 3rd World.

11

The Key Players

Every journalist unless he is happy to remain a worker for the rest of his life-carries the dream of being an editor. Who is a newspaper editor?

The Head

He is not, as is commonly believed the man who writes the editorials. He is the man, who conducts a newspaper. Usually at the bottom of the last page of every paper, is what is known as the Imprint Line. The Imprint Line is mandatory and pins responsibility on what goes into print on the men who bring out a daily. Consider this Imprint Line:

Printed and published for the Proprietors, Bennett, Coleman & Co. Ltd., by *T.P. Pithavala* at *the Times of India Press*, Dr. D.N. Road, Bombay 400 001. Editor: Girilal Jain. Resident Editor: K.C. Khanna. General Manager: Dr. Ram S. Tarneja.... Everything is clearly stated.

If a newspaper in any way contravenes the law, the men responsible-the editor and the printer and publisher-can easily be identified and located and will have to obey the court's summons.

The editor's chair in the circumstances, is not necessarily a comfortable one. The man who occupies it does not have an easy job. He bears a heavy responsibility and often has been called upon to pay a heavy price in the discharge of that responsiblity.

Qualification for an Editor : There is no one way applicable to all aspirants. Anyone who has the money to set up shop as an editor can become one. There are no rules and regulations, no memberships to be filled, no examination to pass. A mere declaration suffices.

Editors in the formative stage of the Indian Press were men imbued with a sense of mission. Robert Knight who made *The Times of India* into a great institution early in its career came to his job with experience in civil life and the running of public institutions. *The Pioneer* was started by Sir George Allen, a businessman of Kanpur and his son C.T. Allen. Of the three enterprising brothers Hemanta Kumar Ghosh, Sisir Kumar Ghosh and Motilal Ghosh who started the *Amrita Bazar Patrika,* the first two were working as employees in the Income Tax Department. S. Kasturi Ranga Iyengar who bought *The Hindu* in 1905 was a lawyer.

But there were others, men like Arthur Moore, Kalinath Ray, A.D. Mani, Benjamin Horniman, S. Sadanand and Prank Moraes who came to their jobs the hard way. Devdas Gandhi got his experience assisting his father in the running of *Young India.* Sadanand also had his apprenticeship with the same paper. Prank Moraes first worked as-an assistant editor with *The Times of India* from 1938 to 1946 during which, for a three-year period he also doubled as a war correspondent. He became deputy editor in1949 and a full editor only in 1950. Kotamaraju Rama Rao, who became the crusading editor of *National Herald,* had his apprenticeship as a reporter under T.L. Vaswani of the *New Times* of Hyderabad, Sind. M. Chalapathi Rao worked as an assistant editor first at the *National Herald* and later at *The Hindustan Times* before he became editor of *Herald.* Pothan Joseph worked for a string of papers like the *Voice of India*, the *Indian Daily Mail* and *The Hindustan Times* interspersing his editorial career with a few executive assignments such as that of the Principal Information Officer of the Government of India. These distinguished men give the lie to the belief that editors are born and not made.

An editorship is not a bed of roses and has never been. Easy as his life may seem he works under all manner of pressuresland not all-necessarily coming from the management. Because his is the final responsibility in bringing out the paper he has to bear the brunt of the wrath whether of advertisers or of existing governments', During the Emergency (1975-77) in India, it was the editor who had to shoulder the burden of official wrath. Editors in India have been under pressure for decades, in fact from the very beginning of the British rule in the country. The Vernacular Press Act was passed in 1878 in order to control the *Amrita Bazar Patrika,* then published in Bengali as well as in English-the *Patrika* being bilingual. To get out of the clutches of the Act, its publishers changed over completely to English beginning 21 March 1878.

The *Patrika* has a long history of editorial daring and competence. At one time, the Government of Bengal recommended the deportation of one of the paper's earliest editors, Motilal Ghosh. On another occasion, the paper had to face prosecution in connection with the famous Barisal Conspiracy Case. Ghosh fought the charges and succeeded in getting the case dismissed. In 1932, the *Patrika* was penalized and a security of Rs 6,000 was demanded from it.

Another paper to fall foul of the government was the *Free Press Journal.* So powerful were the writings of its editor-publisher S. Sadanand that he had to forfeit the then phenomenal figure or Rs 70,000 as security. Indian editors were not the only ones to face the British government's wrath. E.G. Horniman of the *Bombay Chronicle* frequently clashed with officialdom and, at one time, the paper's printer and publisher were asked to deposit Rs 3,000 as security which was later forfeited. The history of Indian journalism is full of such instance of editors, fighting valiantly to protect the honour and integrity of the free press.

Many editors have also fallen foul of the owners of newspapers, though, in one instance, when C.Y. Chintamani diffėred from hispaper's Board of Directors and offered to resign, it was the offending member of the Board, Pandit Madan Mohan Malaviya who decided to quit instead.

No two editors are alike. The only common denominator that can be ascribed to them is their humanity, their concern for people, their interest in new. A delicate problem for every editor is the extent to which he can, and should, delegate authority. In a large paper an editor would have from two to six, sometimes as many as eight assistant editors. Each would have specialized in a particular field of activity such as foreign affairs, national affairs, law, finance, defence, agriculture or whatever. No editor can possibly be an expert in all fields and even if he happens to be an immensely knowledgeable man, he just would not have the time to keep up with new developments. It is amazing how much a writer has to put in by way of reading. It could be new books on the subject, documents pertaining to it or upcoming literature dealing with the issue. No editor is expected to be a know-all. It is an editor's task to know who, among his colleagues, is best equipped to write on an event and to assign the task to him. By this the editor is not surrendering his responsibility, he is exercising it wisely. A good editor should know how best to tap the available talent in his office.

It is common in most editorial offices for the editor to have a morning conference with his staff. Often it-is done around the coffee table where assistant editors can sit informally and not only discuss the day's newspaper but engage in a post-mortem of the news. Depending on what the day's most important issues are, there will be a discussion of some of them at the end of which the editor would lay down his own views and give guidelines. If the editorial staff is fairly homogenous there would be no difficulty in arriving at a consensus as to what editorial line should be taken on any given subject. Often, if the assistant editors have worked over a long period with the editor, they would know instinctively as to what angle would be projected. In any event it is the editor who lays down the policy and the subject of the editorials. Who will write what is also discussed and decided on at this conference.

An editor of a party paper will have no difficulty in the matter of policy as it would have been laid down for him. It would be his task to argue the party case as well as he can; he has a brief. An ideal paper, of course, would be one where its owners would let the editor make his own decisions and argue on the merits of a subject. In that event he would have to be as honest and objective as he can possibly be, placing, as he should, the public interest before anything else. He will know that life is not a bed orroses. He must expect to be subjected to all forms of persuasion, not all of them scrupulous, including flattery, bribery, even physical threats, not to mention behind-the-scene wire-pulling.

Though an editor is once removed from the actual production of a paper, it is in his power to decide what should be published and what shouldn't. In a sense he has to play God. This is a tremendous responsibility and cannot be ducked. It is an insensitive man and consequently a poor editor who has on occasion tortured himself over taking a decision that could possibly have harmed many people. The editors of *The New York Times* have admitted publicly their regret that they did not publish information about the US government's plans to abet the invasion of Cuba. If the paper had published the news, they have argued, the country may well have been saved the embarrassment of the Bay of Pigs fiasco.

Most editors may not be called upon to take momentous decisions, yet editing a paper is one long struggle against time, during: which decisions, one way or the other have to be taken. This is both the charm and frustration of being an editor Responsibility ends with him.

Editors have different methods of dealing with the problem of leader writing. Some dictate and then make the final corrections. Some do their own typing. Some others write laboriously in long hand. Some finish their writing by the end of the evening and place a phone call before retiring to bed to see that events have not-overtaken the editorial. Some others refuse to put down a word on paper until midnight.

Real Awareness

The important thing for an editor is always to be keenly aware of the needs of the public and to be able to feel its pulse. It is to him that the reader will look to, interpret yesterday's news. An editor-and certainly a good editor-will offer leadership to the country as only he can. But for that, he will have to offer leadership to his staff, in the first instance. What often makes a news paper great is the right combination of inspiration, emphasis design, control, tone and selectivity. It is the editor who will have to see that through his personal leadership, this combination is,achieved. It is not-and cannot be-an easy task.

An editor will soon learn-if he has not by the time-he has become one-that his time is not always his own. In the office he will have to be in constant, if not continuous, touch with his colleagues. Outside the office he will be in demand as a public speaker,-as a guest at dinners and parties. These are chores that may not always be pleasant for him and more often than not are tiring and time consuming. And yet only by listening to friends and foes in various situations can an editor come to know what the public thinks. Dinners may be hard on the waistline but it is during the after-dinner coffee that an important politician may want to unburden himself to an editor to seek his reaction. An editor must make himself available to those who have something important and worthwhile to say. This may not be very conducive to a settled married life, but it is an occupational hazard that editors have to face. A major problem confronting the "ideal" editor-the editor who 'puts public' interest before everything else is the extent to which he should extend cooperation to the government. It is not the job of the editor to give uncritical support to whatever administration is in power. Neither can it be said that his should be an unrestrained attack. Some journalists pretend that no one but the editor and proof reader read editorials. Such a view is extremely misleading. Whatever the situation be elsewhere in the world, in India there is ample evidence to show that editorials are read with interest. Editors often are more influential than they are prone to tell themselves. It may be that editorial influence is more over policy makers than over the public at large. The fact remains that editorials ("leaders") cannot be dismissed out of hand as mere space fillers.

An interesting comment has been made on the subject by James Reston of the *New York Times.* Speaking about the influence or the American Press on the American foreign policy, Mr. Reston pointed out that in his view this is usually exaggerated. "Its influence" he said, "is exercised primarily through the Congress, which confuses press opinion with public opinon. No doubt the press has great influence on American foreign policy when things are *obviously* going badly. It has very little influence, however, when things are going badly but the impending disaster is not obvious and the government is saying, as it usually does, that all is well or soon will be if everybody only has faith and confidence."

This is largely true. When things are going reasonably well, the tendency for the public is to accept government statements; the public frequently wants to be assured and is willing to believe or, at the very least, to suspend judgement. The crunch comes when things go badly and then it is to the critical editor that the public will turn. This was amply shown when, soon after the Emergency in India was lifted, the sales of newspapers suddenly soared to phenomenal heights. The public was turning to the editors to tell it the whole story unvarnished. The circulation of *The Indian Express,* for instance, showed a remarkable rise in the immediate post-Emergency months.

The important thing for an editor is, to be intellectually honest.

He does not always have to be right; in the nature of things he cannot be so. But as long as he is honest and is seen to be honest, his responsibility to his profession ceases there. Nothing more can be expected of an editor and nothing more should.

The problem of honesty is more complicated than one thinks. What, for instance, should an editor's attitude be towards Mrs. Indira Gandhi at a time when the Janata Government is at sixes and sevens? Should the editor refuse to support her as a possible leader of an alternate government on the grounds that her role during the Emergency disqualifies her to receive any support any time or should he take the stand that as a leader of proven stature and stamina, Mrs. Gandhi deserves support at a time of national instability? It is here that an editor whose credibility is beyond challenge can get respectful attention from his reading public. In other words, for an editor, credibility is all.

Permanent Contact

It is important for an editor to be in constant touch with government officials from ministers downward. Senior editors get easy audience with ministers, since it pays the ministers themselves to nave their policies and views understood in the right perspective by the opinion-makers. The editor who lives in an ivory tower is becoming increasingly rare, if ever such a species existed. He cannot afford to be too far from the madding crowd. The crowd is and should be his business.

Almost all editors to a person, complain of the heavy schedule that they have to put up with. Consider this average day put in by one editor who usually is up around 6.30 in the morning and, goes for a half hour early morning walk. Then as he has his tea, he reads the morning papers, especially his competitors. If, as frequently happens, an item of interest has been missed by his paper, he will make a note of it for later discussion with his staff. He is in his office by 10 a.m.

10.00-10.45 a.m.: Staff meeting. This is the time devoted to dissecting the day's performance with assistant editors and assigning writing work to them.

10.45-11.30 a.m.: The editor meets the News Editor, the Chief Reporter and the Chief of his News Bureau. The discussion will relate to why some stories were missed, or why some were not adequately displayed or why some others should not have been displayed. The *post mortem* over, the discussion will deal with upcoming stories and how to cover them.

11.30-12 noon: Individual assistant editors will stray in to discuss specific ideas and to get editorial approval for them.

12 noon-2.00 p.m.: The editor will do whatever writing he plans to do for the next day's paper, taking a 15-minute break for a quick lunch.

2.00-4.00 p.m.: This is the time to look into copy submitted to him by his assistant editors, to select articles and special features to go for the next day's editorial page.

4.00-5.00 p.m.: This is Visitor's Hour when public citizens, usually those who have previously made appointments call on the Editor with complaints, suggestions or plain gossip.

5.00-6.00 p.m.: Time to look quickly into New Delhi and provincial papers and also at foreign papers and dispose off work with-the Bureau.

At 6.00 p.m. the editor leaves for his home where he will wash, change and relax.

8.30 p.m.: Dinner engagement. This is not an everyday affair but is sufficiently frequent to be taken as part of the day's work. Before going out, however, the editor usually calls the office and tell where he may be found in an emergency. Usually he himself calls the news-editor to check on late news breaks.

11.00 p.m.: Back home and one more late night call to the office to check certain details. Mostly arrangements are made to send him the final proofs of the editorial page so that should last minute changes become necessary they can be quickly incorporated.

This does not permit much time to engage in sports or hobbies. A major complaint of editors is that they do not get the time needed to refurbish their minds. "I am living on my capital" is how Mr. Girilal Jain expressed his frustration. According to him, in 15 months he had taken only four days off and had seen only two films, which is probably a good average for most editors.

There are editors and editors. What makes for a truly great editor? According to Mr. M. Chalapathi Rau, C.Y. Chintamani was one. The following article written by Mr. Rau for *Swarajya* gives us a clear picture of why he thought so.

"Chintamani was a journalist, mostly an editor, with a pontiff's air but without pontiff's pomp. An editor of his period, enjoying considerable reputation, a legislator and political leader, possessing a muscular, vigourous style, he had a right to pontificate, and he pontificated giving a further lease of life to the leading article, before journalism made news techniques dominate the newspaper.

My acquaintance with Chintamani was brief but interesting my irreverence about eminence coinciding with the climax of career. It was my ambition not to be a journalist and neither the Spenders, nor the Chintamanis attracted me much. But style did, style as an extension of personality and not merely as an assembly of words, even if it was proper words in proper places or the best words in the best order.

With my interest in politics, I was reading in Madras with great interest the leading articles in a weekly edition of the *Leader* published from Allahabad. By then, I was forgetting Mill on Liberty and Morley on Compromise and was a convert to the Congress. So I could not but read the *Leader* critically. But an admiration for the argumentativeness, the consistency of outlook and the vigourous syntax of the main leading articles developed.

As an admirer of the orators who could rouse emotions one could not admire Chintamani, a speaker of cold logic, though with warm interjections, when I first heard him in Bombay. Then I heard him in Waltair in 1936 or so when he delivered his lectures which later became his book *Politics Since the Indian Mutiny*, abroad survey with many personalities, sketches and amusing anecdotes. Dr. S.Radhakrishnan presided. I rememher Radhakrishnan making caustic references to the Liberals and Chintamani reacting to them vigorously. I was among the few who listened to his Table-Talk as he sat at his brother's place in an easy chair-and pontificated off the record. He had no doubt about anything. Sastri had intellectual honesty but no intellectual courage. Sapru had intellectual courage but no intellectual honesty. Sivaswamy Iyer, who had both intellectual honesty and intellectual courage was India's most accurate thinker, and came only after Gandhi and Malaviya as a great man. Gandhi, of course, was one of the greatest men the world had known but he had done immense mischief in politics....

I had no prejudice against Chintamani but my irreverence extended to him. There was much talk of what people called his phenomenal memory. I held even then that memory was selective. If one remembered certain things, one did not remember other things. Chintamani was reputed to remember all the Congress Presidential addresses, the list of all the Popes, the birthdays of famous Indians, when and where he had met Gokhale or Malaviya first and so on. He also remembered British constitutional debates on India or the debates in Indian legislatures. And many other things. But I was afraid he did not remember many other things because he did not care for them or did not care to remember them. He did not seem to care much for foreign affairs though India had no foreign policy of its own then as an appendage of an empire. He could elaborate some historical parallels and narrrate vividly some historical anecdotes. But in general he showed no sense of history. My point is not that he was not sufficiently educated but that he concentrated on a few things and did not care for much else.

The Leader was read mainly for its leading articles and Chintamani was admired, even adored, for most of them. He wrote on all important Indian political subjects, leaving South Africa and other matters to his assistants and whenever he wrote, the world knew that he wrote. There was first his vast knowledge of Indian political subjects, there was then no mistaking the conviction with which he wrote, there was finally the force and vigour with which he wrote. To the Liberals, his was the voice of the Mesosiah.... He had read all the best biographies and auto biographies in the English language and remembered them. He did not forget what this Secretary of State or that had said or what this Viceroy had done. The unflagging energy with which he wrote sustained the readers' interest, even when he wrote two columns. My irreverence disappeared whenever I read leading articles written by him.

Above all there was character in whatever he wrote or did. This enhanced his intellectual and moral stature. He would be no turncoat, no Titus Oates. Chintamani had resigned his ministership on a matter of principle, somewhat rare in our history before Independence, and after Independence. The people in D.P. could not forget it. He enjoyed life. He was kind to young people. He was a fine conversationalist.... I found he did not know enough of economics, did not understand what the Gold Standard was. Chintamani had his personal predilections believed in the other world and spirits and while I was hearing, it, he surprised me by saying that Gokhale's spirit had dictated an editorial to him. He wrote even on the transfer of Superintendents of Police and his obituary editorials ended with 'May his soul rest in peace'. When Chief Justice Thorn died, he wrote that 'the summons had come to his Lordship from above' which roused my amusement.

The more I have known of Indian journalism, however, the more reverent I have become about him. As a leader-writer, he was a rare type. Other leader-writers who have given me equal pleasure were Kalinath Ray of the *Tribune* with his logic chopping and N. Raghunathan of *The Hindu,* who at his best reminded me of the leading articles of the old *Times Literary Supplement.*

Chin tam ani was a personality; he had character. He was a great editor".

Consider here the qualities that Chalapathi Rau admired in Chintamani: knowledge, ability, good memory, vast knowledge of Indian politics, adherance to principles at any cost, unflagging energy, courage of convictions; style, character. And an over-riding ego.

Editors, to be sure, have egos that seem to go with the job. An ideal editor, of course, will have opinions (or what is an editor for?) but will not be opinionated. Some of the great editors of our times have been men with strong opinions, men like Sadanand, "Stalin" Srinivasan, S. Natarajan, Frank Moraes or C. Narasimhan. They lent to the papers they edited their strength of conviction. An editor without an opinion is like a river without water. He will go nowhere.

Chintamani confessed a lack of expertise in economics. No editor, it is fair to say, can possibly be knowledgeable in all subjects but it is expected of him to have a lively curiosity and an abiding interest in what makes the world go. Today's editor, besides, must be more than a leader-writer; to be an effective editor he will have to know something of making layouts, or cropping a picture or reviewing a film; in other words, it would not hurt to be a jack-of-all-trades while being master of a few.

In the twenties, thirties and well into the forties and fifties, a paper could still sell on the personality of the editor, though it is pertinent to remember that newspaper circulation was in the mid 50,000s for most papers and a circulation figure of 100,000 was considered something of a distant dream. But editors of that era were well-known to their readers and they carried something of an aura about them. Editors today are less well-known; editorials are read but they are disembodied views rather than the live thoughts of a man passionately committed to truth. Newspapers no more sell on the strength of editorials no matter how well they are written or argued or presented. There was a time when writing in the *Indian Express* Frank Moraes placed his views on the front page. That did not perceptibly increase the circulation of the *Express.* If a paper is to sell it must take into account popular tastes whether in politics, economics, sports or films. That this is increasingly being recognized can be noticed from the fact that the *Express*, again, is devoting a page for features, an innovation in Indian journalism.

People's Mood

We may take a brief *detour* to examine a subject that editors are continuously called upon to face, the public mind.

As all editors know, the public is not as well informed as it should be and it often does not even care. Editors are seldom known.

M.V. Kamath who has edited *The Illustrated Weekly of India* has had letters addressed to him in the name of H.V. Kamath, an older man and distinguished Member of Parliament whose name has long registered in the reader's sub-conscience. A Carnegie Endowment survey once established that many Americans believed and this in a country with a powerful communication media-erroneously that the NATO Treaty was negotiated through the United Nations. And the *New York Times* disclosed that nearly one third of the Americans surveyed by its reporters did not know that Berlin was located in communist East Germany. Social scientists can document such findings also in India at all levels of public intelligence.

If this be the case what is the public that the editor is addressing himself to? If public knowledge is limited should he, as one writer has facetiously suggested, put out papers that look like Mother Goose rhyme-books and write for readers with an intelligence,quotient just slightly above that of a moron? The fact of the matter is that in India, at least, there is a substantial section of the public that is highly sophisticated. This is borne out by the letters that editors get every day, some of which are witty, provocative and often throwing new light on old problems.

Editor's Job

An editor enjoys immense powers such as are not often realized even in editorial sanctum sanctora. He can make or mar reputations. This is difficult to prove statistically. It has been said that even if the average mind could be plumbed for its reaction to any given editorial, no standard could be devised to project its long-term effect. The effect of the written word, by its nature, is incalculable. We know, for example, that newspapers down the years have been suppressed and the only conclusion that we can draw from that fact is that governments have always been conscious of the power of the press. Obviously not every editor is powerful. And the size of a paper's circulation is no guidepost to an editor's influence. The circulation of *Harijan* that Mahatma Gandhi edited was not much to speak about. It never really ever touched even the 50,000 mark. And yet, in terms of moving the governments, it was probably the most powerful paper in its time, certainly as long as Mahatma Gandhi was actively engaged in editing it. But it was the Mahatma who made the *Harijan.* These days, too often, it is the newspapers who make the editors.

Nevertheless, editors have certain responsibilities commensurate with their powers. These are *(a)* to the state, *(b)* to their proprietors, *(c)* to their readers, and *(d)* to their own conscience, and not necessarily in that order. An editor without a conscience needs to be watched. He could be an enemy of the people. Unscrupulous editors may one day get their due, but they can do irritrievable damage to a nation's psyche, while they are in circulation.

The problem of an editor's responsibility to the state has never quite been defined though, when efforts have been made by governments to muzzle the press, it has been loudly articulated. During the Second World War, Arthur Moore of *The Statesman* was sought to be muzzled and the Viceroy even suggested that he be repatriated to England, on security grounds. In times of war, of course, governments will clamp down censorship on the press, but it is the peace-time relationship between the government and the press that call for examination. When senior correspondents asked Mr. V.K. Krishna Menon-after the Goa take-over was completed-why they had not been given prior intimation of the "invasion," Mr. Menon blandly replied. "How was I to know that you would not leak the information to foreign embassies?" Mr. Menon is not alone in the kind of thinking that goes into government press relations. On 2 October 1962, toward the end of the Cuban crisis week, Arthur Sylvester, Assistant Secretary of Defence for Public Affairs (and a former Washington correspondent of the *Newyork News)* called a press conference. It was a tense session. Newspapermen charged the US government with withholding the facts regarding the Cuban crisis and giving out misleading and even untruthful information. Sylvester responded:

I can't think of a comparable situation, but in the kind of world we live in, the generation of news by actions taken by the government becomes one weapon in a strained situation. The results, in my opinion, justify the methods we use. News generated by actions of the government as to content and timing are part of the arsenal of weaponry that a President has in application of military force and related forces to the solution of political problems, or to the applications of international political pressures.

Sylvester and his State Department counterpart, Robert Manning (who was later to become editor of the *Atlantic Monthly)*, signed orders requiring the military and civilian officers talking to the press report to whom they talked and what was discussed. (The State Department order was rescinded a month later but the Defence Department order was in force for full five years). The memorandum for Defence personnel said:

Subject: Procedures for handling media representatives.

The subject of each interview and telephone conversation with a media representative will be reported to the appropriate public information office before the close of business that day. A report need to be made if a representative of the public information office is present at the interview.

In such a situation how should an editor handle his job? Sylvester had suggested, by way of justification of the government's handling of information that there is a need to "speak in one voice to your adversary." Commenting on that-and laying down what an ideal editor should do in the circumstances, the *New York Times* said in an editorial on 31 October 1962: "To attempt to manage the news so that a free press should speak 'in one voice to your adversary' could be for more dangerous to the cause of freedom than the free play of dissent, than the fullest possible publication of the facts."

Another and a yet more fitting answer was given by the chairman of the House subcommittee on Information of the Committee on Government Operations, John E Moss. He said: "Government pronouncements during a conflict of wills obviously have an effect upon the outcome of the conflict, but to imply that the entire government information process is part of the manouvers in international relations is to ignore the working of our democratic system."

That, of course, is not how the US Administration saw it. President Kennedy, for example, thought that by not using the information about the presence of Russian missiles in Cuba which the *New York Times* possessed, the paper had made "far-more effective our later actions and thereby contributed greatly to our national security."

There will always be two opinions as to what the true relationship between the government and the press should be and it will be argued that the circumstances in the end will dictate what such a relation should be. By and large it has been suggested that relationship is best which is adversary in nature. The press which means the editor-is better off to be on guard where the government is concerned than to work in cahoots with any administration.

Inconvenient Links

The relationship between an editor and the proprietor is an even thornier one than that between an editor and the government. Where the proprietor is himself the editor-as it used to be in the *Free Press Journal* when Sadanand was alive-the problem obviously does not arise. But there were times when Sadanand employed separate editors and with his kind of temperament, conflicts between him and them were routine. On one occasion Sadanand without so much as consulting his then editor S. Natarajan, changed editorial policy overnight. Natarajan thereupon did what any self-respecting editor should do, resigned on the spot.

Pothan Joseph who, in his time, had served many masters and was willing to argue any case has been reported to have said that, an editor, like a lawyer, should have no compunction to posit the owner's point of view. Joseph himself at different times edited *The Hindustan Times* (a paper that strongly supported the Congress) and the *Dawn* (mouthpiece of the Muslim League). Pothan Joseph found nothing wrong in this.

Some old-fashioned editors have held the view that an editor is responsible solely to his conscience and to his readers and that any proprietorial interference in the discharge of his duties is an assault on the freedom of the press that should be resisted. Theoretically such a position is unassailable. In practice, however, many editors have learned that he who pays the piper calls the tune. An editor is well advised prior to his accepting his appointment to see that he is on the same wave-length as that of his employer. That is the best way to save later embarrassment and agony. Most editors are hired on contract and an editor who claims special privileges for himself on grounds of editorial independence may soon find that editorial independence and job security do not always go hand in hand.

Role of News Editor

The news editor is a very important functionary in the organisation of a newspaper. He is the real backbone of the newspaper. The news editor is responsible for doing the most important work in the publication of a newspaper. In certain ways, he can be called the number two man in a newspaper organisation. He is solely responsible for the news coverage activities of the newspaper. It is his duty to see that the news service of his paper is always up to the mark and ahead of its rivals.

The news editor deputes the reporting staff for news collecting activities. He also directs the work of the sub-editors. He is the final arbiter to whom all questions affecting the news columns are referred, and ultimately he decides the fate of every report and paragraph. However, much of this responsibility in actual working may be delegated to his subordinates. In the western countries, sometimes, the news-editor performs the functions of a general supervisor, because his work is divided among other employees of the newspaper like copy testers, planners etc. Generally, his time is occupied with administrative work.

Mere Control : He merely controls the activities of his assistants and makes the most important decisions. The rest of the work he leaves to his subordinates. But in India the position is quite different. In our country, the news editor has to deal with many aspects of collecting the news and making use of it. He is responsible for all the news stories that appear in a newspaper. In fact, he performs many functions which were previously performed by a district editor, copy tester and a planner of news coverage. The news editor not only acts as a senior journalist guiding other journalists, but he also has to deal with the administration of the staff under his control. He is responsible for alloting duties, giving assignments and making leave arrangements for them. The news editor is generally a very experienced person. He knows all the ins and outs of his job.

In a newspaper the news is received from various sources like reporters, correspondents, national and international news services etc. The news is continuously received on the teleprinter which is installed in the newspaper office. It is the news editor who plans how to use the news which is continuously arriving in the newspaper's office from various sources. He prepares the dummy for the next day's paper in which the space to be occupied by advertisements appearing in the newspaper is indicated. In fact, on the basis of this dummy, the next day's newspaper is planned by the news editor. For special reports he obtains photographs to be published in the paper. He tries to be in touch with all the events and news which are taking place or the reports which are trickling in.

He also discusses the coverage of news and events with the chief reporter as well as the editor of the newspaper. The timings of the city edition and dak edition are also decided by him. He tries to coordinate with the printer and the production side for bringing out the newspaper in time. He gives instructions to the chief sub-editor regarding the use of important reports and news items. Although the chief sub-editor is the ultimate incharge of the actual shape the edition will take, yet the news editor always tries to know as to what is happening.

It is the duty of news editor to build up the news service of the paper on a sound footing. No doubt, in the fast moving world of today this is not an easy task. He has to keep in touch with his paper's local reporters, correspondents, foreign as well as the numerous national and international news agencies for collecting the latest news regarding the important happenings. He may have to meet many callers as well as attend to immense correspondence reaching his office.

The Responsibility : The news editor has also to make arrangements to cover the unexpected occurrences hurriedly. To meet the rush of work and unexpected situations, things may have to be done in a hurry, yet in a systematic and proper manner. The unexpected is always happening in a newspaper office. It may be report regarding a big air crash or a railway accident, a mining disaster or a huge fire, a gruesome murder or a cyclone involving loss of many lives. Whichever of these occurences it may be, the same has to be dealt with promptly and appropriately, no matter what hour of the night or day the news arrives in the newspaper office. A good news editor evolves cohesion and order, even out of a chaotic situation due to his cool direction.

The successful news editor possesses a highly trained news sense. He has the knack of anticipating events intelligently. A good news editor is a man of tireless and boundless energy. He should have a lot of driving force to direct his staff, sparing neither them nor himself, when a big story is about to break, or when the reputation of his paper is at stake. Above all, he should be able to make quick and accurate decisions in a crisis and remain cool and calm under all circumstances.

Role of Sub-editor

The sub-editor plays a very important role in the publication of a newspaper. He is a very important member of the newspaper's staff. The quality and style of a newspaper greatly depend on the good work done by the sub-editor. It is the sub-editor who prepares the copy for the printer.

Although the editor of the newspaper exercises the supreme direction and legal responsibility, yet it is the sub-editor who performs most of the functions of the editor, as far as the production of a paper is concerned. In a way, we can say that if the editor is the top stone, then the sub-editor is the key stone of the arch. In ordinary matters the sub-editor has undisputed control over every article and paragraph that reaches the newspaper's office. As far as the difficult and important articles of news publicity are concerned, he may be guided by the editor.

The functions of an editor have become very vague now-a-days. His control is now merged into the managenial side of the paper from which side he may exercise both a journalistic and commercial influence. An editor may hardly write much for the newspaper. In fact, it is the sub-editor who does most of the editing work in a newspaper. If the functions of the editor have now become a little less, as far as the production of a paper is concerned, then the functions of the sub-editor have definitely increased greatly.

The sub-editor is mainly responsible for the manner in which a journal or a newspaper is made-up, sent for printing and offered to the public. There is no doubt that the sub-editor must be a man of high ability and judgement. He must know thoroughly the news value of every matter which comes into his notice. He should have the ability to see the importance of even a small paragraph and the competence to reduce a lengthy paragraph to its deserving size. A sub-editor may not generally do much of original writing like an editor, but he should be an expert in revising the news articles as well as supervising the work of those who do the writing work. Thus, a sub-editor must possess the capability either to reduce or to expand a subject matter as per the needs of his paper.

All sorts of news go on trickling into the sub-editorial department all the time. It is just like a raw material out of which a sub-editor produces a finished product (the news to be published in the newspaper).

The sub-editor has the power of life or death over all the newspaper's material that reaches him. Thus, the responsibility of the sub-editor is really enormous. A newspaper receives its copy from a variety of sources like reporters, correspondents, telephones, news agency reports and verbal communications. All this information is filtered by the sub-editor. The sub-editor is actually responsible, more than any other person for what the paper looks like and stands for, to the readers.

There are many ways in which a sub-editor can leave the impression of his personality on the newspaper. The format of a paper is in reality determined by the sub-editor. The sub-editor has the nose for selecting the right type of news. It is the task of the sub-editor to decide as to what is going in for tomorrows's newspaper and in what form. In fact, the sub-editor with a wide experience in his work, is the most suitable person to become the editor in due course of time.

There is always a big pile of news reports and other communications lying on the table of the sub-editor. He is also pressurised by the printing department for the copy. He has to attend to his functions in a very quick manner, using his best judgement as to the relative urgency, importance and the desirability of printing a particular news or article.

Wonderful Job : The sub-editor has to separate the grain from the chaff out of the great number of news material lying on his table. He should have an eye for accuracy. He must check the facts of a story and look out for the errors, if any. If there are certain facts which are missing, he must ask these from the reporters. The sub-editor has to read every story and sometimes contrive to make it interesting and news-worthy.

Mainly, we can say that a newspaper receives the news from two sources, one from the paper's own correspondents and the other from the various news agencies. Generally, out of these two sources preference is always given to the news brought by the paper's own correspondents, because a good report under the headline 'from our special correspondent' indicates the initiative and enterprise and adds to the prestige of a newspaper.

Sometimes, a newspaper may receive a number of versions of a particular story from different sources. The paper's correspondent may give a different story where as the news agencies may give their own accounts. The sub-editor has to put all these conflicting accounts into one coherent and wholesome story. If the reports contradict or conflict with each other, then he has to believe the story put in by the newspaper's own correspondent. It is thus the responsibility of the sub-editor to make the story clear. He should see to it that the news story is based upon facts, it is as complete as possible and is clear from every angle for easy understanding.

A sub-editor checks the news stories one by one. He goes through every single piece of the copy. Then he adds a catch-line, if the reporter has not already provided a suitable one. He also writes a suitable headline for the story. This is a very important and difficult duty of the sub-editor. After this, he edits the story, cutting the unnecessary matter and trimming the length to the right size according to the space where it has to be printed. He checks the spellings of names and places so that these are not printed wrongly. A sub-editor also has to correct errors of grammar, capitalization, punctuation and abbreviations. He cannot afford to allow even the most minor error in the newspaper.

If a sub-editor feels that the intention of the writer of a story is not clear or the message of the story is very vague, then he can refer the copy back to the reporter and ask him to rewrite the story. Sometimes, he may have to refer to books like 'who's who', encyclopaedias, telephone and civic directories, almanacs etc., to confirm the facts of a story. He may even have to telephone the source of the news item to seek any clarification regarding which a doubt creeps up in his mind.

The sub-editor has to take into consideration the policy of his paper before allowing a news item to be published. He has to breathe life into some dead matter lying before him so that the story is made lively. Sometimes, he tones down a story which is too lively. He may also trim down a story, if it is too dangerous, to make it safe. He has also to decide the suitability of the news stories and articles on the merits of their news value to the particular paper. He has to reject a superfluous article and prune another to its justified size. He is always on the look out to print a news story which is a scoop, well ahead of his rivals.

After deciding the main contents of his newspaper, he has to use his utmost skill in their make-up and display. This is just like the window dressing of a shop which is fully stocked. And it is a very important function of the sub-editor. He has to be careful that in the final rush no mistake creeps into the print and no paragraph gets mixed up or overlooked. The maximum attention a sub-editor has to pay is to the layout of captions and the main news page. Balance and proportion are the qualities which should be aimed at before anything else.

The principal test of sub-editorial capacity in the art of make up is, of course, the appearance of the main news page. It is the page which the majority of the readers read first of all. Some very busy readers only read this page and no more—they simply turn the other pages. Although the eye may be arrested by the heading of the principal news, yet the total effect of the whole page should not be crudely sensational. In fact, the make-up of the first page should be in such a way that a reader is helped to find at a glance how the world has behaved during the last twenty-four hours. There is no doubt that the make-up of a newspaper is the reflection of the sub-editor's appreciation of news value. Sometimes, the value and significance of a news feature is largely neutralised by an ineffective handling of make-up.

Extra Knowledge : Side by side with the presentation of the news, a sub-editor should also know something about the gathering of news and arrangement of regular features. He should be fully acquainted with the reporters and correspondents employed by his newspaper as well as with the regular contributors who write special features from time to time, which are published in his newspaper. The sub-editor should also know the principal news-agencies which supply news stories to his paper. In fact, now-a-days more and more news is supplied to the newspapers by one or the other national or international news agencies.

The sub-editor should also be acquainted with the important photographers and photographic agencies which supply photographs of important events and news items to his newspaper. In fact, now-a-days every big newspaper has its own staff photographers, who cover the special functions and events for their newspaper. By knowing these sources of news as photographs, a sub-editor can contact them in case of any contingency without any difficulty.

Of course, many of the troubles of the sub-editor will be lessened, if the correspondents and other contributors take a little more pain to make their copy readable. If the reporters and writers try to follow the style in which their writings are presented finally in the newspaper, then they can greatly save a good deal of unnecessary work and worry on the part of the sub-editorial department. Sometimes, a contributor or a correspondent may even have a complaint against the sub-editor for the way in which his article has been cut down by the sub-editor, who may not be sufficiently acquainted with the importance of the material. Every sub-editor should be careful in the use of scissors and the blue pencils, so as not to give any cause for complaint later on to the conscientious writers.

There is no doubt that ultimately the public is the best judge of the work of a sub-editor. The good work done by him in the selection of the news and views will be much liked by the readers of his newspaper, whereas any fall in its standard may result in a reduction in its circulation. It is, therefore, the duty of every good sub-editor to do his best to put as much exclusive news in his newspaper as possible and as early as possible.

12

Editor's Job

A newspaper office or news agency receives a large assortment of news items. These originate from different sources. The news copy is written by experienced and inexperienced people and hence lack uniformity. In any newspapers, there is always a shortage of space for all news items, which are received in the office. A newspaper's success largely depends on the space and its most efficient, judicious and economic use. Hence, within the space set aside for news, as much news as possible needs to be packed to serve a divergent readership. Considering these factors, editing of the news copy becomes essential.

What is Editing?—All incoming news items, collectively called copy, is sifted, before being possessed, to achieve a balance of news between that originating within the organisation and that pouring in from outside. The unwanted matter gets weeded out and only the newsworthy stories are finally selected.

The Desk Management—The news room is headed by an editor or a chief editor or an editor-in-chief or a chief news editor. He plans and directs the day's news operations. He is supported by a team consisting of the news editors, chief sub-editors, senior sub-editors. In a news agency, news editors and chief subs looks after the smooth functioning of the news desk. They plan and write 'leads'.

What Makes News?—News has a number of characteristic elements—

Proximity: The nearer the origin of news, i.e., the closer it is to home, the more is its impact. For example, on a particular day, there may be 45 deaths in a boat tragedy in Bangladesh. But, on the same day, a local bomb blast that kills five people is sure to have more impact on the readers.

Timeliness: News grows old quickly. It decays and perishes fast. The more recent its occurrence, the more worthy it is. On the contrary, an event that happened six months back, but is discovered and reported now could grab the front page. For e.g. the bank securities scam including Ketan Parekh.

Prominence: Names make news and the newspapers like to use as many local names as possible. For example, if the vice-chancellor of a university gets hurt while playing cricket, few people will take note of the incident. But, if a public figure like a minister is injured in a game, we have a more interesting story.

Consequence: A reader's interest is aroused in a large measure if an event or occurrence affects him, and more so, if he participates in the event. He is eager to know what will this mean to him in the long run. How will it affect him and his family. A steep hike in the prices of petrol, cooking gas, milk or an increase in water and electricity tariffs will have widespread consequences.

Human Interest: Any interesting story about people and their peculiarities, and their infinite variety, make for wider readership. The human interest stories are pure identification. These are the little things that have happened, or could happen to yourself or to your neighbours or friends. These stories are worth little or nothing as news in any strict sense. Yet these are worth telling.

How to Edit a Copy? Ideally read a story, preferably thrice-once for familiarisation, once while you edit and third time to check your work. If the story has no glaring problems and if you fully understand it, you would be ready to edit it.

Format—A news story is divided into two parts-the lead and the body. The lead describes, simply and briefly, what happened and the body documents and elaborates the lead. Adequate attention should be paid to the lead. The intro should be concise and crisp. Details should be dispersed and blended in the subsequent paragraphs.

Opening Para—The most significant information is placed at the top and other details follow in their order of importance. Each succeeding para should add an essential detail without being dependent in content or style on what follows. Next, see if the second para supports the lead. The third para should continue the development implicit in the lead and in the second para.

Rewriting—While editing a story, the subeditor should look for errors in spelling, grammar and correct these. But an instant second look might sometimes compel him to rewrite it. Highlight the news point, taking care to avoid distortion and respect the facts produced by the reporter.

Headlines—When a reader looks for something interesting in a newspaper, it is the heading which catches, his eyes. A story, howsoever well-edited, would not attract him unless it is given a headline. The headline attracts the reader to go through the story. A headline sells the story. Writing a headline is like applying the finishing polish on a well-crafted piece of furniture.

Kicker—Kicker is another conventional headline, usually a one-line heading with a second line (kicker) above it in a different style and half the type size. It extends no more than midway above the main line.

Hammer—Hammer is the reverse of kicker, but, usually, in all capital letters. The big type is the kicker and the smaller type the main headline. One word, or two at the most, will suffice of the hammer. By virtue of their size, hammers impress the readers with their importance. But too many hammers on one page may dilute that significance, and destroy the look of the page.

Leads—This lead is different from the one already talked about. Suppose there is a train accident at a place 60 km from Punjab. Just an hour before the first edition of a newspaper goes to the press. But we cannot wait till the reporter telephones from the spot or comes back to file the story. We can give a short news about it and wait for further details. Many news items are bound to flow in on the same event, details will pour in once the reporter reaches the site, there shall also be eyewitness accounts. All these are tied together, highlighting the major facts and the lead is written for the newspaper's city edition.

A lead is a device, used mostly in the case of developing stories, for changing the story's emphasis in the light of new information of facts as these unfold.

Editorial Desk

A copy editor is a bridge between a reporter and the reader. He has divergent roles to perform and docs one or more of these tasks while editing a copy. He need not execute all these functions simultaneously. A copy editor is a gatekeeper and image builder who protects a newspaper's reputation.

Duties of a Copy Editor—A Copy Editor :

(a) Removes rough edges from the copy and polishes it to make it presentable.

(b) Adjusts the copy to the style of his newspaper.

(c) Should carve out each story in a familiar language so that it runs smoothly through the average reader's mind. Smooth writing ensures smooth reading.

(d) Tailors story length to space requirements.

(e) Detects and corrects errors of fact.

(f) Simplifies, clarifies and verifies meanings.

(g) Adjusts stories to make them objective and fair.

(h) Adjusts stories to make these legally safe.

(i) Rewrites and restructures stories extensively, where necessary.

(j) Follow the policy of the newspaper.

(k) Corrects copy in the interest of good taste.

(l) Avoids sensation.

(m) Removes those points that could be called undue publicity.

(n) Deletes doubtful words and sentences.

Qualities—The production of a newspaper is a delicate and complex process. There is tension since a deadline is to be met. Amidst this tense atmosphere, the sub-editor has to perform his job meticulously. He should possess certain qualities to discharge his functions efficiently.

Calmness—Be calm and composed. You should not get excited when a big story breaks.

Decisive—Take quick and correct decisions. The editorial department has no place for indecisives.

Non-partisan—Never take sides.

Memory—Have a sharp memory for counter-checking facts.

Grasp—Size up the situation as it unfolds, and estimate its relevance.

Know your reader.

Self Confidence—Have confidence enough to correct a bad copy written by anyone.

Mature—Be mature enough to correct only bad copy, and not just make changes for the sake of changing.

Sceptical—Do not accept anything at face value. You should approach everything as a source of potential error.

Knowledge—Be a jack of all trades. A good editor should store most of the information as it comes across, and search for more.

Stability—Have enough stability to work under pressure.

Tools—The copy editor will require a set to tools, the lack of which may lead to loss of valuable time. These aids are indispensable. Often you may come across problems of spellings and facts. You should focus on the errors, and correct the name.

Language—The basic building blocks of journalism are words. You should respect the words, and follow the way these are arranged and strung together. Any misplacement of words could twist the meaning. Hence, you should pay attention to punctuation marks, grammar and syntax. All these are important in the sentence construction.

Punctuation Marks—Punctuation problems start and almost end with a comma. This little mark causes more trouble than the rest put together.

Punctuation marks brings in clarity and better readability. At the same time, too many of these clutter a story. There should be no comma after a verb unless it is immediately followed by a parenthesis.

Technical Knowhow

Slug—A news item or story may run into several paras, and also exceed one page. If running into pages, a news story has to be kept track of from amongst various stories, and chronologically arranged. Hence, these paras, in a page, are divided into two of three parts. Then, these parts are 'slugged' and numbered, i.e., given a label, which identifies that story for that particular day, and helps the editor on duty to bring different parts together.

Related stories are slugged to make the relationship clear. Slug is an identification mark or tag. It is often the key word in a story and written on top left or right of a page.

Editing Symbols—As soon as you start editing a copy, the first symbol you use is for paragraph indentation. Even if your para is indented, you should mark this symbol on every para. This would help the typesetter in knowing that you want paragraph to begin at that spot. Always note that editing marks are large and clear.

Photo Editing—Pictures submitted for publication in the newspapers and magazines have to be edited to fit into the layout of the page, and also the unnecessary portions cut off, which the photographer might have added in the actual composition. The competent photo editor's job is to see to it that he does not waste space, and trims a picture keeping the main essence of the subject intact. This reduction process is called 'chopping'.

Only a Professional—It is the job of the photo editor to select the best photograph which tells the story on its own. The photo editor edits it to suit the space in the page without destroying or distorting the essence of the picture, and gives it a good display. It is the photo editor's duty to give the photographer ideas about the picture possibilities.

Qualities of a Good Photographer—A good photographer must be able to handle every assignment the editor gives him to his own satisfaction. One has to work with a great speed on a location. You should actually shoot a news event from several different angles, and let your photo editor decide which picture to use.

The newspaper photographs are based on factual situation. The photographs illustrates an event, bring depth into it, and probably comment on it. Usually, the photographer is given only an idea to work with, and is expected to create an appropriate photograph to illustrate it. This is where a good memory or a notebook will come in handy. The photographic techniques involved in shooting for magazines are not much different from those in newspapers. The technical skill is again taken for granted, and your primary concern is to illustrate the story clearly and completely.

Creative Cropping of Pictures—The intelligent photo editors adopt different creative cropping techniques to bring out the exact point of emphasis a 'pix'. They try to enlarge the main image, which will have a better visual impact. A photo editor studies the picture carefully, and decides about the cropping. First, he crops the picture mentally and then decides on the final edited photograph. A badly cropped pix can not be repaired. A good photo editor is one who can visualise how the picture will look like when it is cropped and printed in different sizes and shapes.

Choosing a Picture—In a professional organization, the photographers leave contact sheets with the photo editors to enable them to choose the right frame, and mark the composition. Sometimes, the photographers send the exposed rolls, and leave the rest of the job to the photo editors. In most countries, where there is competition amongst the leading newspapers, the photo editor looks for pictures from the freelancers as well. He chooses the best picture, and places it in the newspaper. It leaves no bad feelings amongst the staffers, because they also know that their newspapers should have the best coverage. This system makes every photographer work very hard on the assignments, and be alert with the competitive spirit.

Captions—Even though the news picture is supposed to tell a story on its own, one should say where and when the incident took place. Caption writing is an art by itself, which conies with experience and aptitude. The picture and its caption are complementary to each other, and it is very essential to mention when and where the picture was taken, and who the persons seen in the picture are.

If the photograph is described in the body of the story, then there is no need for a separate caption and the pix could hang in between the paragraphs. Sometimes to box a powerful picture with just a detailed caption brightens the page.

Graphic Illustrations—In most coverages, photographer reaches the spot only after the incident takes place, and is able to take only the result of what had already happened. In such special cases the newspaper or magazine might have to depend upon graphic illustrations to detail the activities that had taken place on a particular spot earlier.

However, with the advancement of technology, photo editing is done by the computer, which eliminates all the unessential elements, and gives out only the section as per the commands. Photos can be stored and recalled on the computer as and when required.

Design and Layout—The newspaper composing and printing methods have gone through major changes during the past few decades. However, the basic function remains the same, to convert the printing matter into printable format. The composing methods used by newspaper industry range from hand composing to computer-guided operations. The major composing processes are-

Hand Setting—Hand setting is the original method of setting movable type. In this the compositor works with a composing stick, a type case and the metal type itself: letters, punctuation marks, figures, and spaces. The compositor adjusts the composing stick to the desired pica measure or line length. After taking out proofs and carrying out the necessary corrections, the next step is to make up the page. Since the composed matter consists of hundreds of individual pieces, it is essential that it is locked up, may be directly on the bed of the press.

Machine Setting—This method involves casting type from molten metal. There are four popular type casting machines-

Linotype and Intertype—These are mechanical methods of composing and casting type in the piece lines called 'slugs'. The name Linotype is derived from casting a line-of-type. In both systems, the operator sits at a keyboard. The machine is adjusted to set type to the desired pica measure and leading. The upper front section of the machine carries a slotted metal container, which holds the matrices and when the operator strikes the keys, the matrices fall into positions to form a line-of-type. After the matter is composed the type is locked up. Any change within a line means that the entire line, or even all the succeeding lines in a paragraph have to be reset.

The basic difference between linotype and intertype is of the intertype of matrices. They can be used for casting headlines as well as body matter.

Monotype—As the name suggests 'monotype' casts the characters one by one rather than as a complete line. It is a combination of two machines, a keyboard and a typecaster. It is a two-machine method of casting individual type characters, mechanically.

To set type the machine is adjusted to the required pica measure and leading. As the copy is typed, it produces a perforated paper roll, which is used to drive the typecaster. A combination of holes dictates the letters, spaces and punctuation marks to be set.

To set type, the perforated roll is fitted on the typecaster, where it directs the casting mechanism by means of compressed air. The air passing through the perforations brings the matrix holder and the specific matrix ready to be filled with molten metal into proper position. Once the type has been cast, it is ejected onto a galley, one character at a time.

Ludlow—This is a combination of handsetting and machine casting operations. The operator sets the type matrices and leading in a composing stick by hand. The composed matrices are then locked up into a casting machine, where they are filled with molten lead to produce the slug.

Phototypesetting—It is also known as cold type-setting, as it does not involve metal casting. Its first phase resembles that of monotype setting. Unless the perforator or keyboard is attached to a video display unit, the operation is limited to conversion of copy matter into a coded perforated tape. This perforated tape is then fed into a programmed computerised unit, which projects the desired images of type characters onto photosensitive film. This film is then made up in mechanicals from which printing plates can be produced. Photo-composing provides a fast, flexible and reasonable economical method of setting type.

Daily Newspapers—Newspapers come in different shapes and sizes. There are newspapers that provide general public interest news to the readers, there are other which cater to the needs of the specialists. Every newspaper has its own way of presenting news, views and features.

The front page of a newspaper should be attractive, which will hold the attention of the readers. The front page is the "face" of a newspaper.

Newspaper Identity—Newspapers have a name and each newspaper tries to acquire a unique identity by observing different ways.

The Mast Head—On the front page, the masthead of a newspaper is much more than just the name of the newspaper. Some of its characteristics are-

— it is in distinctive bold print,

— it is in a big type size,

— it has a fixed place on the front page,

— it remains in the same form for years.

Headlines—Headlines are a means to attract the readers towards the news items. It is the responsibility of the page-designer to make each headline as distinctive as possible. Headlines are given generally by the sub-editors/copy editors.

Placement of Photographs and Cartoons—Picture is worth a thousand words. On the same basis, it can be extrapolated that a good cartoon is worth at least two thousand words. From a page designer's point of view, it is important to realise that photographs, cartoons and graphic have a special significance. Placing a picture or cartoon at wrong place may not only reduce its utility, but also reduce the design appeal of the total page. A page designer has to examine whether the picture, cartoon, graphic, chart, has an independent value or it has to be juxtaposed with a particular news story. The size may have to be adjusted due to placement or space considerations.

Overall Page Design—There is a design in the page, a form and a structure. Each page designer has his own concept of beauty and page structure. To bring it out, he uses different type sizes, white spaces, placement of pictures, graphs, charts, cartoons etc.

Inside Pages—Inside pages of a daily newspaper differ from the front page in their format, structure and presentation of contents. By grouping news items on specific pages we are able to give the newspaper a structure. The inside pages under one group often tend to cover as many news items as possible. Hence, often these pages may seem cluttered.

The Editorial Page—The format of this page looks similar in many newspapers in India and abroad. There is a section, on this page, where the editor(s) write their analysis of the major national and international news items. Along with that, there may be one or two articles written by prominent people on current topics.

The design of the inside pages of a newspaper is relatively much more structured than the front page, which is dependent on the major happenings during the past few hours.

Advertisements—Advertisements have special significance for commercial publications. The very existence of newspapers and magazines depends on the revenue from advertisements. Hence, special care must be taken with regard to placement of advertisements along with the news stories on the pages. Advertisements are placed on these pages according to the product or service to be advertised. Large colour advertisements have special significance in page design.

Readability—Newspapers are meant to be read. As far as possible the news item should be contained in a neatly defined area. Each letter, each word and each story has special significance. Readability for a page-designer has a different meaning than that for a reporter, sub-editor or proof-reader. Readability from a page designer's point of view depends on placement of the news stories, typography and the overall page layout.

Typography—Today with the help of computers one can develop new type faces by incorporating variations in size, form and shape of each letter. It is the size, form and shape that determine and distinguish the type face of a letter. As page designers, we must select type by analysing its visual appearance as well as readability of its type face. While the choices may be many, editors of daily newspapers for the sake of economy, workability and convenience to its readers, make deliberate attempt to limit the variations of type faces used in their page make-up. Many newspapers adopt just one type face in different sizes throughout the newspaper.

Typography Enhancing Design—Each letter or alphabet has immense potential to be used as a piece of art.

Matching and Contrast—Because of economic and managerial reasons, newspapers use very limited type faces. Some newspapers may use only one. The only variation being the size. However, with the popularity of phototypesetting and offset printing, newspapers have a wider choice in matching and contrasting of type faces.

Emphasis and Highlights—In page layout, when we want to emphasize or highlight a word, an expression, a sentence, a paragraph or even a portion of the news item, we have many options before us. Some of them are-

— Use of different type form of the letters such as italics.

— Use of bolder type face for the word or portion of the news item to be emphasized.

— Underlining the word or sentence.

The portion to be emphasized may be displayed with the wider margin, different colour or a combination of above alternatives.

New Trends

Speedy transmission of news is as important as the actual news gathering. It has been made possible by the advanced electronic equipment. News is a perishable commodity. The newspaper staff have to be on their toes to ensure that important news items are processed quickly, to meet the deadlines of publication.

But rapid transmission of news becomes meaningless if information being imparted is inaccurate. In this context, the accuracy of the data and apparently minor details of spellings and language, assume importance. Such correction work is done with the help of the computers and 'fax' machines.

Computers—The computer are an ideal system for storing data in their memory and this data could be retained at a later stage. The computers act as the data banks, and are very useful sources of reference for the newspapers.

A computer is an automatic electronic apparatus for making calculations, besides storing and processing information. For this data along with instructions on how to process the same have to be fed into the computer. That is called the 'input'. The result obtained from the computer after processing of the data is called the 'output'.

The hardware components of the computers refer to all the physical parts viz. electronic and mechanical parts.

The software components of a computer refer to the set of instructions given to it to perform a specified task. These are fed to the computer in a language understood by it called a 'program'.

Page Designing—The arrangement of captions, photographs and graphic on a page would have to facilitate easy reading, besides being visually appealing. Certain parameters of format are fixed for any newspaper, such as those of the page size, print area, number of columns, positions of masthead, allotment of articles according to their categories and page titles.

Computer in Use

The Desktop Publishing, the DTP for short, refers to both hardware and software that are involved in preparing high quality prints of pages, once these are composed satisfactorily. The prints are used as artwork, and the actual duplication is done by offset printing, owing to the high costs involved in the DTP operations. The hardware of a DTP includes a large-sized colour monitor of the VDU (Visual Display Unit) and a laser printer apart from the CPU, which is programmed to suit the DTP software. The laser printer involves a high-speed, high-quality printer technology.

The DTP software consist of programmes to compose pages and their layout. These perform the function of the word-processing and automatic margin alignment, providing a variety of type-faces, page-numbering, etc.

Limitations—Although DTP is considered incomparable when it comes to composing a page according to specifications. It handles the entire process with ease, completing the tasks at a rapid pace. But a few limitations persist in the new DTP packages too, like-

(a) It is not possible to obtain on the VDU an exact copy of the colours, as they would appear in the final print.

(b) The monitor is capable of showing the character in white against a background, whereas the actual product is black & white.

(c) The monitor shows only a restricted areas of each page. Such fragmented views make it difficult for an entire page to be visualised.

(d) A change once made in the typography might not eventually be printed as the package would not be programmed for it.

The appearance of a newspaper contributes to its having greater or lesser readership. There are number of readers who get addicted to their daily papers just because they take a liking to its layout and design. Each publication has a tradition which is flexible enough to accommodate innovative changes in the design layout with the passage of time. However, the readers might welcome such change only to a certain point. Both content and style of presentation matter in attracting readership.

13

Social Aspects

Humane Media

The present concept of human rights took shape in the end of the 18th century. Human Rights may be defined as those privileges which can justifiably be claimed by any person. Everyone is entitled to these rights. Any one can make fair claim to these rights.

U.N. Declaration of Human Rights—The United Nations, Universal Declaration of Human Rights was adopted on 10th December, 1948. It is the only official document of its kind, world wide, till date. It proclaims economic, social, and cultural rights in addition to political and civil rights and freedoms for the people of the world. These rights are considered the foundation of freedom, justice and peace in the world.

The United Nations reaffirmed their faith in the worth of human beings and in the equal rights for men and women, through this declaration. They expressed a determination to promote social progress and better standards of living, for the large majority of the people.

The declaration states that all are equal before the law and are entitled to equal protection from it. There is special emphasis on the basic provision of the right to a standard of living adequate for the health and well being of individuals and their families.

It is important to note that these rights are universally accepted. The UN has also adopted two International Covenants effective from 1976. These are the International Covenant on Economic, Social and Cultural Rights and the International Covenant on Civil and Political Rights.

Effective Role—In order to perform their role effectively, the media personnel need to be fully conversant with the various aspects of human rights issues. They should arm themselves with the necessary information and then present the facts and analyses before the public. It is never possible to bring about favourable changes with just one stroke of the pen, or an infrequent programme or two. What could be hoped for, is to make every citizen aware and conscious of their rights and to enable them to recognize a violation of human rights, when they come across such events in daily, life. The news media can then bring about and maintain a healthy Human Rights Movement.

The Electronic Media transcend the barriers of literacy and enjoy a widespread reach. However, government ownership and lopsided programming are its major drawback. Firstly, informative programmes need to be based on healthy debates and discussions and not on propaganda and image-building exercises of leaders, as is usually the case. Secondly, only sensitive personnel can put across a point clearly and in a wholesome perspective. Such sensitivity can not be found in people who equate a career in communication to a mere 'job'. The electronic media have the potential to act as information disseminators. To fulfil this role, they have to provide complete information to the audience. The piecemeal treatment of issues causes both confusion and harm. In general, there is inadequate coverage of human rights issues and problems.

The print media, quite naturally have literate audience. Big industrial houses have a monopoly over ownership of the press.

This fact determines the nature of relations between the press and the government. Newspaper openly takes side for or against the policies of the government.

The nexus between the print media and the government is strengthened by a sort of 'give and take' policy. The press receives government patronage in terms of supply of newsprint and advertisements of human rights for favourable write-ups about the government. In such a situation, violations of human rights by the state are unlikely to surface.

However, themes like caste system, subjugation of women, rural poverty and the feudal system, all of which are concerned with the area of human rights, have been dealt with time and again through the film medium.

Films like 'Chandidas' and 'Achhoot Kanya' carried a crusade against untouchability. 'Sawakari Pash' was a shocking exposure of the exploitation of the poor peasants by unscruplous money lenders. 'Duniya Na Mane' voiced a strong protest against the marriage of young girls to old men. But it was only in late sixties that a new wave or parallel cinema movement gathered momentum. Realistic films were made on short-string budgets. A more realistic traditional path was followed by Shyam Senegal whose films have been relatively realistic in form and deeply committed to socio-political themes.

By the 80s, a new generation of film makers was setting a new trend. They began to use the medium to focus attention on grave socio-economic issues and raised questions against social injustice and atrocities, with passion and compassion.

The film medium has a potential to portray the ills of society, frequently in the narrative format. This is how the films serve the cause of human rights and ensure their just implementation in society.

Social Pressure

A consumer is the user of an article. The act of purchase confers on the buyer, the right to expect a certain standard of quality from the product. If consumers are dissatisfied with the performance of an item after its purchase, they have every right to seek redressal of their grievances. The government and voluntary agencies have to involve the general public in the consumer movement. This they do by informing the people about the quality that they can expect, when they buy any item.

Consumerism is an organised movement of concerned citizens and the government, to enhance the right and powers of buyers in relation to sellers.

The reasons for the origin of consumerism in India are—

(1) The shortage of essential commodities and inflation during early 1973-74, which gave a fillip to the consumer movement.

(2) The lack of high standards in technology and advertising which prevents a range of alternative products and claims from flooding the market.

(3) Possession of lesser disposable finances and time when compared to consumers in the west.

The thrust of consumer movement in India has been on availability, purity and pricing of essential articles. Since the majority of consumers in India precariously balance income with expenditure, it is important to safeguard their interests.

Role of Law

(a) Protection of consumers under the Code of Civil Procedures 1908.

(b) The sale of Goods Act 1930

(c) The Agriculture Procedure Act 1937

(d) The Prevention of Food Adulteration Act 1954

(e) The Protection of Civil Rights Act 1955

(f) The Export Act 1963

(g) Protection of Consumers under the Code of Criminal Procedure 1973

(h) The Water Act 1974

(i) The Standards of Weights and Measures Act 1976

(j) The Air Act 1981

(k) The Bureau of Indian Standards Act 1986

(l) Consumer Protection Act 1986

Advertising and Consumers—Advertisements are a powerful means by which to influence the choice of customers, especially in the competition between product brands. But some advertisers may put out false claims, to increase sales. Consumer activities keep a close watch on advertisements to caution unwary customers when necessary. A code has been evolved to serve as a guideline both in creating advertisements and solving disputes over their content. It is applicable only to Indian advertisements. A Code of Self-Regulation in Advertising, formulated by the Advertising Standards Council of India in December 1983, lay down that advertisements should be honest, truthful, fair, responsible and not offensive.

Consumer Organisations—Some Voluntary and Government agencies supervise the implementation of consumer rights. These consumer organisations as they are called, work in the areas of—(a) consumer education, (b) product rating, (c) liaison with the government and producers.

(a) Consumers are provided with information about various goods and services. This may be regarding prices, quality, standard trade practices etc.

(b) To help consumers choose from a range of products, some of these agencies even carry out tests on the products and report their findings. The consumer guidance society of India brings out a journal on similar lines.

(c) The task of consumer organisations is cut out for them.

They need to present the consumer's case to the government and to producers. The government looks after the prices of smooth distribution of essential commodities. Therefore, consumer right activities approach the government to sort out problems of consumers in these matters.

Phenomenal Increase—The phenomenal increase in consumption of goods and services in urban centres, has created a demand for information about them, a demand which media can and must meet. They must identify and fulfil the information needs of the public. Media can nurture an informed view only when they equip their audience with the right kind of information. Media exposure inculcates in consumers a sense of awareness about their rights. Also, the role of the media is emphatically brought out when aggrieved customers turn to media programmes and columns to seek advice, justice and compensation. The media need to provide tips on access, quality, pricing etc. and be a reference point for accurate information. In their coverage of consumer issues, the media can explore general trends in acquisition and also in its exhibition in society. The media could conduct consumer research surveys to investigate purchaser needs and opinions. This could be in coordination with consumer organisations.

The media should play a complementary role to consumer education, comparative testing, ranking and evaluation of consumer products and in maintaining a liaison with both the government and producers. The media could also be used for investigative reporting of perceived and unperceived consumer problems. This could lead to consumer complaints in the media, ultimately resulting in investigation, both by the government and consumer groups. Consumer organizations and the media should evolve and follow a code of conduct, in order to justify the confidence that consumers repose in them.

New Atmosphere

There are many facets of environmental pollution, like, oil spills over the oceans, holes in the ozone layer, denudation of forests, extinction of wildlife species, topsoil erosion etc. Every phenomenon listed above has long term implications and effects. None is a natural disaster. Each is wrought by human interference with the precarious balance in nature. Several governments and groups of citizens have expressed the need to reduce the ill-effects of our lifestyles on our environment. However, it is not possible for a few, isolated groups to achieve their aim of cleaning the environment. The entire population has to be made aware of this danger to their very survival. The media comes into the picture here. They can help by shouldering the responsibility of informing and educating the people, making them environmentally conscious.

Media Promoting Environment Issues—Due to our actions the world's oceans are already polluted beyond repair. The ozone layer that protects us from harmful radiations of ultra violet rays of the sun is also being destroyed. Global temperature is rising leading to changes in the climate. The earth has neither the resources to provide for our unlimited greed nor the capacity to absorb the ever increasing pollution.

One of the finest examples of how the mass media have shaped society's responses to the environment is Rachel Carson's Book 'Silent Spring' published in 1962. Carson wrote about the dangers of pesticides and how their use can destroy the nature. 'Silent Spring' is a mass medium, a book that reached millions not only in U.S. but all over the globe. In this way the media focus our attention on issues which may otherwise escape our attention.

In our own country, the media have done well in reporting on issues and persons. It is through the media that we come to know about the contributions of environmentalists. Through investigative journalism the mass media help reveal matters of vital public interest, that are at many times concealed by relevant departments or institutions. In our country the focus on large dams is one such example. All of India's 1574 large dams are dying prematurely and so will similar new projects. Further, almost all our rivers are degraded and so are our soils. These large dams have been found to have an adverse affect on the local climate, flora and fauna. Due to investigative journalism we are made aware of the hidden costs attached to many projects that seem affordable at the planning stage.

'Nai Duniya' a Hindi daily from Indore, took up for discussion the problems of the state industry workers of Mandasaur, Madhya Pradesh. The newspaper succeeded in obtaining medical and monetary relief for the workers who were affected by the fine slate dust. Now the question is how the environmentalists themselves make use of the mass media. Most environmentalists recognize that the mass media are a powerful means of reaching large numbers of people. This is especially true in the case of television. TV affects its audience most profoundly because it has the capacity to show people events and things, which otherwise they may not be in a position to see. Thus, any action of the environmentalists which is caught by the camera is viewed by millions over the TV screen. The more dramatic the activity and the more controversial it is, more are the chances of it being covered by the mass media and thus one can get more publicity out of the exposure. Keeping this basic law in mind the environmentalists have learnt to use the media as a strong weapon in their hands in their fight for environment protection. Such activists indulge in dramatic activity in order to attract attention.

Drawbacks of Media—Various environmentalists undertake dramatic activities to attract the attention of the mass media. Such activities frequently involve indulging in antics which may not always be desirable. But to attract the attention of the mass media, the environmentalists often have to undertake such activity. It is a drawback of the mass media that they select only those events which are likely to evoke inters and captivate audiences. On the other hand, they ignore events which may be very beneficial to the society though they are not perceived attractive enough. Another drawback of the mass media is what is called the corruptive influence of the mass media. For e.g., in some of the advertisements of cigarettes, the producers of the ad want to link in their viewers minds, qualities such as gallantry, courage and kindness to animals, with the manly puffing of a cigarette. Since both smoking and wild life are popular, chances are that more people may be attracted by them.

Publistic Media—It is a false notion that the environment problem exists because of lack of technological advancement and economic progress. On the other hand there is ample evidence that the blind race of technological development and economic drive are largely to blame for the environmental ills. The question is, as to why society undertakes such development. The answer is, because the select few who control most of the resources stand to gain the maximum out of such an exercise. Thus, unless the silent majority is able to see through this game and exert itself against such development, the environmental problem can not be solved.

The powerful elites are using the mass media, in order to maintain the status quo in which they remain in control of the situation. It is in the interest of our environment that the mass media be used to further the aims of those who believe in universal justice.

Rich and developed nations have been using the mass media to perpetuate various myths regarding environment degradation. According to them, the poor and developing countries should follow a path of development which is approved by the nations. Such development largely involves transfer of outdated technologies of which developed nations have no use. This technology is sold to the poor countries in return for agreements which force them again to ask for loans from the developed nations. These agreements are of such kind that benefit the rich nations at the cost of the national development of the poor countries.

To change perceptions and to persuade people to adopt processes that are environment oriented, we need to have a deeper understanding of how the mass media affect us.

Feminine Aspects

In India of the 19th cent., women suffered from the denial of freedom in their own homes. It was in such an oppressive scenario that movements for social reform developed within different religions. Eminent persons like Ishwar Chandra Vidyasagar and Jotiba Phule wanted to rid Indian society of the twin plagues of religious superstition and social inequality. A progressive movement to make educational opportunities available to women, took shape in the latter part of the 19th century. On the work front, women are faced with gender-specific work areas and roles. In India, a series of laws have been enacted to encourage women's participation in different activities of society. Legislations have been enacted to ensure that women get the same rights and privileges as are enjoyed by men. However, discrimination against women continues to exist. The status of women can not be elevated by the sheer number of legal enactments and constitutional sanctions in their favour. These legislative policies need to be translated into reality to improve the status of women. The general public ought to be made aware of these rights. It is generally accepted that the economic status of women is an indicator of a society's stage of development. The extent of women's empowerment determines-their political status.

Women in Media—There have been several studies of media with reference to the manner in which they present women. Usually women are shown as playing a secondary and passive role in various programmes, episodes and films. The reality reconstructed by the media, does not match the one encountered by women in their daily life. Disparity in the actual living conditions of women and those presented over the medium of television in perplexing and disquieting at the very least. One can see for oneself the truth in the argument that television programming doesn't include the image of the working class woman or pleasant woman.

In India, print media does not enjoy as widespread a reach as the electronic media because a majority of the population is non-literate. Yet, they leave their impression on both general readers and policy-makers. It is unfortunate that events rather than processes make news. Most issues of special concern to women, do not fit into the traditional concepts of what constitutes news.

Media as a Tool in the Crusade for Women's Education—Non-formal education especially on matters of nutrition, health, family welfare etc., is an effective method of teaching. It is here that the media comes into the picture. They can educate the large number of women in their audiences through regular programmes.

Illiteracy is often considered a cause of poverty, the prime reason for the inhuman conditions in which the poor live. This need to be strongly challenged.

Health programmes telecast on Indian television, focus on social problems, with a specialist doctor to answer queries in an interview format. These programmes provide information on common diseases and their treatment.

All India Radio, broadcasts special women's programmes from all its stations, at least twice a week, meant for rural women. 'Nutrition' is a topic of special interest to them. The Family Planning Units of AIR, produce programmes on the small family norms for rural audiences, industrial workers, women and youth. Information on family welfare, maternity, child health and nutrition is provided through these programmes.

Employment of Women in Media—Research has indicated that the world-wide employment of women in the media is low, particularly in decision-making levels. Employment figures of individual media institutions in the U.S.A. show that the common employment pattern is one in which proportionately more men are hired, especially at the top levels. The dominance of males in some sections of media is defended by arguing that the major carrier ladders to top positions usually involve professional and educational skills which are more common with men than women. However, the number of women hired in the media can not be considered in absolute terms, since the number of women looking for such jobs is still small as compared to men. Media are not the fundamental cause of the subordinate status of women. But they can and should work together with the rest of the society to help reduce the suffering of women kind.

Contradictory Media Policy and Practice—The working group on software for Doordarshan popularly called the P.C. Joshi Committee, has commented in its report (1985) on the status of women. The report has a chapter on women which notes the failure of efforts to raise the women's status through development measures and constitutional guarantees and emphasizes that despite such interventions the position of women has deteriorated as brought out by the 1974 report of the committee on the status of women. The report made the following observation:

A number of television programmes revolve round middle class ideologies that limit women's roles to wives and mothers. Only domestic duties are deemed their 'work'. The plurality of Indian culture and the diverse roles that women play are neither acknowledged nor communicated.

Urging that Doordarshan should formulate clear-cut guidelines and policies at the earliest, regarding the positive portrayal of women, the Joshi Committee Report recommended that this portrayal take note of all facets of women's lives. It pointed out that the need of the hour was to integrate women in terms of equality in all sectors of national life and the development process.

Growth Factor

It is necessary to note that development does not mean mere increase in the per capita income or more industrialization but a process involving a number of qualitative changes, nothing less than the upward movement of the entire social system. The development must be seen and felt. Proper development always helps people to be self-sufficient and self-reliant.

Characteristics of Developing Countries vis-avis Development. The common characteristics of developing countries are—

- low levels of living
- low levels of productivity
- high rates of population growth
- high and rising level of unemployment
- underemployment
- high dependence on agriculture and other primary production.

Development, in contrast, is associated with some of the characteristics of the developed capitalist countries. These are—

- high levels of living
- high levels of productivity
- lower population growth
- predominance of industrial or non-agricultural activities.

Theories and Paradigms of Development—The central task of development theory is to explain why some countries are underdeveloped and how these countries can develop. Since the end of World War II, leading to the independence of many countries, different theories have come up and it is possible to group these theories on the basis of the vision and direction of development and then sub-divide them further on the basis of certain shared analytical approaches i.e., paradigms common to these theories.

Unilinear World View of Development—It simply means that underdevelopment is.a condition preceding development. All developed countries are late comers to the process of development, which had already taken place in the developed west. For becoming like the west, there are certain institutional or economic hurdles, whose removal will initiate the development process in the underdeveloped countries.

Theories falling under Unilinear world-view may be divided into two broad categories-

(1) Theories which consider development as harmonies and non-contentious processes. The development process benefits all rich as well as poor people and rich as well as poor countries. There is harmony between different groups of people and different countries.

(2) Theories which consider development essentially as a conflicting process. These theories refer to the rich exploiting the poor as much as the rich countries exploiting the poor.

Mainstream Paradigm—Theories under category which suggest development to be a harmonious process, lead to two paradigms, one which advocates state intervention as an essential requirement for development. It includes theories like "Big push" "Vicious circle", "Unbalanced growth", "Stage theory", "Dualism theory".

Counter-Revolution Paradigms—It emphasizes non-intervention by the state and advocates the efficiency of the market in promoting development, which favours "free market" for development.

The Structural Paradigm—It suggests that underdevelopment is a consequence of the internal as well as the international structure (system of production). Internally, the less developed countries are totally dependent on the production of export of primary products e.g., raw materials. On the international front, the developed countries produce and export "manufactured" goods. These theories suggest that if the less developed countries want development, they are required to change the structure of production in favour of manufactured goods through capital based technology and industrialization.

The Orthodox Marxist Paradigm—It considers that conflict and contradictions in the development of capitalism are inevitable, and that these can only be resolved through a revolution, which will then usher in the next phase of development.

Non-Unilinear World-View of Development—The Populist and Neo-Marxist are the two paradigms of non-unilinear world view.

Populist Paradigm—The term populist is used here in the absence of any other term that is adequate to describe this approach. The theories under the populist approach question either the need or possibility of the less-developed countries developing on the lines of the already developed capitalist countries.

Contributions of E.F. Schumacher, who wrote, Small is

Beautiful, inspired by the Gandhian thinking, may be considered as part of the 'populist' paradigm. Populist paradigm is discussed as an alternative strategy but not housed by the mainstream paradigm in the initial stages of independence, and the creation of an impression among the people that development means becoming like the West.

Neo-Marxist Paradigm—A serious challenge to the Unilinear world-view of development did not arise until the emergence of the Neo-Marxist paradigm. There are quite a few economists who can be called Neo-Marxist, but here, we are concerned with the writings of Paul Baran, A.G. Frank, and the related "dependency theory". The essence of the paradigm lies in the fact that, at present, the less developed countries can not develop like the west. It stresses the inter connectedness of development and underdevelopment, of traditional and modern and indeed many other social, political and economic factors. Paul Baren declared that under-development of most of the world was a direct result of the dynamics of monopoly capitalism, which had blocked the primary accumulation of capital in the underdeveloped regions, and smothered their novice industries. A.G. Frank contents that underdevelopment as we know today, and economic development as well, are the simultaneous and related products of development on a world wide stall, and over a luxury of more than 4 centuries, at least, of a single integrated economic system, capitalism.

Gradual Evolution

Communication is an important input in development. Proper use of communication can foster the pace and process of development. In general terms, communication means interaction between two individuals or within a group or a community or a nation. Development communication is a relatively younger field of study within the discipline of communication. It is mainly concerned with the role of information and communication in social and economic development of an individual, society and nation. It identifies what mass media can do directly or indirectly to improve the quality of life to both urban and rural masses.

Nora Quebral said that development communication was the 'art and science'. Development communication is an 'art' because one has to create his-strategy and programme to communicate to his target audience and it is a 'science' because it follows a process, a system.

Rogers says that "development communication refers to the uses to which communication is put in order to further development".

Development Communication has two primary roles—

(a) A transforming role-as it seeks social change in the direction of the higher quality of life.

(b) A socializing role-by seeking to maintain some of the established values of the society.

Philosophy of Development Communication

Development Communication is Purposive—In Development Communication one looks for specific behavioural objectives, such as getting farmers to go in for a specific variety of seed, pesticide etc.

A non-purposive message is one, which is transmitted to a receiver directly or by means of a channel without any intention to influence the receiver.

Development Communication is Positive—In Development Communication, positive value is attached to what one communicates about. For e.g.. high yielding variety of seeds, once adopted, the farmers can increase their harvest manifold.

Development Communication is Pragmatic—In Development Communication, the purpose of communication is important. The evaluation of communication does not rest on the mere invention of communication activities performed. Findings have showed that mere increase in the flow of information doesn't necessarily result in those behavioural changes, which are desired to be achieved.

The role of media changes in Development Communication. It plays following responsible roles-

(a) Circulate knowledge that will inform people of significant events, opportunities, dangers and changes in their community, country and the world.

(b) Provide a forum where issues affecting the national or community life may be aired.

(c) Teach those ideas, skills and attitudes that people need to achieve for a better life.

(d) Create and maintain a base of consensus that is needed for the stability of the state.

To perform these roles, the media keeps the development orientation in its perspective. Three approaches have been identified in relating communication to development.

Empathy—Daniel Lerner (1958) in his book 'Passing of Traditional Society', saw the problems of 'modernizing' traditional societies. He saw the spread of literacy resulting from urbanization as a necessary precondition to more complete modernization that would include participatory political institutions. Development was largely a matter of increasing productivity. And to increase this productivity one must aspire, and it must begin in the psyche of the people. Hence it is basically 'Psychological'. Every change in society must originate and begin in the hearts of the people. If the people would like to change, only then the development would begin. Lerner saw the media as filling the need of promoting interest among the people for a better life. He said 'empathy' endows a person with the capacity to imagine.

Diffusion—Everett M. Rogers (1983) approached this with a perspective that had much in common with Lerner, but differed with him somewhat in emphasis. He saw the diffusion of the new ideas and their practice as a crucial component of the modernization process. It has been found that when a message is propagated a segment of the population adopts it and develops a positive attitude towards it.

Magic Multiphlier—Wilbur Schramm's (1964) Mass Media and National Development which was produced from the UNESCO, became almost a blueprint for development communication for Schramm it was the content of media output that was the key to their use in development. Information must flow, not only from people but also from them, so that their needs can be known. Here is where the mass communication enters the calculus-the required amount of information is so vast that only by making effective use of the great information multipliers, the mass media, can the developing countries hope to provide information.

Development Support Communication—The origin of the development support communication is traced to the agricultural extension, which was initiated in the fifties in many of the developing countries. The DSC was a concept popularised by the UNDP and other UN institution like FAO, UNICEF etc. The World Bank also supported the DSC. It stands for linking all agencies involved in the planned development work. Thus, the routes of communication envisaged are not only vertical from top to bottom and bottom-upwards, but also horizontal between the institutions and personnel connected with the process of development.

System Approach in Agricultural Communication—The communication support for agricultural development is intended to provide knowledge and skills about improved agricultural technologies so as to induce change in the existing farm practices for increasing agricultural output. In our country, agricultural communication forms a part of the overall agricultural extension strategy.

The Intensive Agricultural Distinct Programme (IADP)—It was launched in early sixties. Initially, it was assisted by a number of subject matter specialists (SMS). Later it was renamed as IAAP and these SMSs were redesignated as Assistant Directors and the number of VLWS was reduced for extension work in the villages. The main contributions of IAAP programme were the better supply of inputs like seeds and fertilizers and reducing the gap between the extension staff and the farmers.

Agricultural Extension under the Panchayati Raj System—In this the District Agricultural Officer at the Zila Parishad level was responsible for planning and implementation of agricultural schemes. Information flow from radio, agro-service centres, and local newspapers was high and was rated to be very useful. The credibility of the VLW was found to be low.

Agricultural Extension under the Training and Visit System—The operation of the T&V system, studies in the Kota district of Rajasthan, reflected that the contact of the farmers with the VLWS was limited. It was observed that the extension workers were not working through the contact farmers, as envisaged by the T&V system. The contacts with VLW were almost the same for all types of farmers-both contact and non-contact farmers. The level of knowledge of the farmers about the improved practices relating to the major crops of the area was low. The T & V system did not help the farmers to increase their knowledge. It is necessary to use other effective extension methods like demonstrations.

Diffusion of Innovation—Development underpins change and acceptance of innovation-ideas, practices and technologies. Hence facilitating diffusion of innovations is an essential aspect of the development support communication. An innovation refers to an idea perceived as new by an individual. Diffusion is a process by which an innovation spreads.

While some factors stimulate and facilitate quick diffusion of innovations and transfer of technologies, some others inhibit adoption. Certain social systems do not encourage adoption of innovations. Individuals in such a system are very slow and rigid in accepting new ideas, practices and technologies. Cultural incompatibility is another hurdle to change.

Adaptation of innovation is a time-conserving process, and it requires the best efforts to provide knowledge and change human behaviour. So, one has to take care that the new ideas, practices and technologies fit in and match with the existing social system and cultural practices.

DSC Activities in Population Control—DSC activities in the population control and family welfare are gradually losing their informational components and becoming propaganda, in the eagerness to reach a wider audience. Its efforts in the family welfare programme seldom use the knowledge and the talent available at the local levels. Expensive mass media technology is receiving higher emphasis at the cost of the traditional media. Usage of the traditional media is not only acceptable, and creative but affordable also. The urgency of containing the population did not allow the planners to pay due attention to the needs of different socio-economic and tribal groups, spread in different regions of the country. Thus, proper attention might not have been given to proper communication planning. In addition, the media habits of the target audience, their access to the media, the appropriateness of the channel have not been researched properly and adequately.

Thus, the most important issue is to provide linkage between the DSC strategies and different welfare programmes as part and parcel of the larger whole. In philosophy and principle, this approach has been accepted, but it has always lagged behind in implementation for various reasons. The family welfare programme has come to a stage where rural people appear to be aware of the benefits of the family welfare, but the socio-economic pressures operate against it.

DSC and Health Behaviour—Realizing the complexity of health behaviour, which, in the case of Indian society, is largely guided by informal but deep-rooted socio-cultural values, the country has adopted such measures which help the people to keep themselves healthy. Thus, the process of motivation of the people is attempted through the mass media and interpersonal communication, based on development-support strategy.

Looking into the limited role of mass communication in the changing health behaviour, one can think of interpersonal communication, which, in the context of the complexity of health behaviour assumes greater significance. In this communication, word of mouth and personal communication from a trusted source is significantly more effective than mass communication from a remote source. Health and development support communication are closely interlinked and mutually interdependent. In a country like India, a DSC strategy needs to be developed in a manner that can cater to the needs of the diverse groups based on social and cultural backgrounds. The goal of achieving health behaviour change should be a central point of the DSC strategy, and it needs to be operated in that spirit.

DSC and Education—Education is the process of bringing desirable change in the behaviour of human beings. In education, the greatest emphasis should be placed on the development and growth of a person, both physically and psychologically. With the development of society, education has focused on various aspects, such as child education, adult education, technical education in arts and crafts, health education, physical education and several others.

Communication for development purposes should be distinguished from communication for the sake of entertainment, such as chitrahar, commercial advertising of soap and tooth paste or news dissemination news bulletins, surabhi and entertainment-oriented communication also has a powerful social influence and possible effect on the attempt to meet the national objectives.

It was agreed that the DSC should be taken to embrace the infrastructure, the information processing and transfer systems; the media, the personnel, the communicators; the recipients; the supporting communication services; organized interpersonal communication and extension services; the contents; the purposes or objectives. It was recognized that the central focus was on mass communication, and that a multi-media approach with inter-media comparisons was necessary. To sum up, the DSC for education can play a powerful role in nation-building and development, and can contribute significantly to bring about social change in the desired direction.

DSC and Environment—The environmental problems that countries face vary with their respective stages of development, the structure of their economics, and their environmental policies.

The challenge is to accelerate equitable income growth and promote access to the necessary resources and technologies. Another challenge is to build the recognition of environmental scarcity into decision-making with or without development, rapid population growth may make it more difficult to address many environmental problems. Rapid population growth can worsen the mutually reinforcing effects of poverty and environmental damage.

Ignorance is an important cause of environmental damage and a serious impediment to finding solutions. It is necessary to know the facts, to determine values and analyze the benefits and costs of alternative measures and finally to ensure that information is available on the public and private choices. The DSC regarding environmental issues increases access to information.

Thus, any DSC strategy, set it family welfare health or education, should be such that the communicator treat the rural people as intelligent, conscious and capable of learning new things. This naturally implies that unless the media originate in and relate themselves to the world of values and environment of the community they are bound to be irrelevant and ineffective. Thus, DSC has to be a dependent rather than an independent variable.

14

Legal Aspects

Historical Background

The foundation of the Press Law in India had been laid even before the first newspaper began publication in the country. In 1795, censorship was introduced for the first time. In 1799, the first Press Regulations were promulgated by Marquess of Wellesly, which required the newspapers to print the names of printers, publishers and editors. In 1823, Governor General John Adams introduced licensing of the Press. Similar regulations were introduced in Bombay in 1825 and 1827. However licensing was abolished in 1835 and was reintroduced by Lord Canning in 1857.

In 1860, a comprehensive law, the Indian Penal Code (IPC) was enacted. It contained offences like defamation and obscenity which must be avoided by writers, publishers and printers. The oldest surviving Press Regulation, 'Press and Registration of Books Act' was passed in 1867. The Vernacular Press Act was passed in 1878 which meant to curb the Indian language newspapers. But was repealed in 1881.

The present Criminal Procedure (Cr. P.C.) was first enacted in 1882 and then consolidated in 1898. The Newspapers Act was passed in 1908, empowering magistrates to seize a press. In 1910, the Indian Press Act was passed. It empowered the government to ask for a deposit of security from the press and where it deemed fit to forfeit it. After Independence, the Press Act, 1951 was to be a temporary law for two years but was extended upto February 1956. Following the recommendations of the First Press Commission, a law was passed in 1955 seeking to ameliorate the conditions of working journalists and other newspaper employees. The Working Journalists Act, 1958 was passed to overcome certain difficulties in respect of fixation of the rate of wages.

In 1956, Parliamentary Proceedings Act, known as Firoze Gandhi Act, was passed, which protected a newspaper from legal action for the publication of substantially true reports of the proceedings of Parliament. The Act was later repealed in 1976 during the period of internal emergency. In 1961, the Criminal Law Amendment Act was passed imposing certain restrictions on the freedom of Press on grounds of security of the state and public order. Press Council Act was passed in 1965 with the objective of protecting the freedom of the press and raising standards of journalism.

Press and Registration of Books—The oldest surviving Act in this regard is the Press and Registration of Books Act, 1867 and remained the fundamental law governing the rules for the regulation of the publication of newspapers and of having printing presses.

The Act requires that the name of the printer, the place of printing and name of the publisher and place of publication must be legibly printed on every book or newspaper printed and published in India.

Two conditions are necessary to be fulfilled for publishing a newspaper. One, the name of the editor must be clearly printed on every copy of the newspaper. Two, a declaration must be made before the District Precedence or Sub-divisional Magistrate within whose jurisdiction the newspaper is to be published, stating (a) name of the publisher (b) premises where printing and publishing is conducted (c) title, language and periodicity of the newspaper.

Every time the title, language or periodicity is changed, a

fresh declaration must be made. Similarly, a new declaration is necessary as often as the ownership or the place of printing or publication of the newspaper is changed.-

The magistrate can cancel the declaration and order closure of a newspaper for irregular publication. In any period of three months, a daily, a tri-weekly, a biweekly or a fortnightly newspaper publishes less than half the number of issues, then it shall cease to publish. A fresh declaration must be filed before it can be started again.

The magistrate's decision can be challenged in an appeal before the Press and Registration Appellate Board, which comprises a chairman and another member nominated by.the Press Council of India.

Registrar of Newspapers—There is a provision for appointment of a Press Registrar by the Government of India for the whole of the country. It maintains-title, language, periodicity, name of the editor, printer and publisher, place of printing and publication, average number of pages per week, number of days of publication in the year, average number of copies printed, sold and distributed free, retail selling price, names and address of owners etc. of each newspaper. It also issues a certificate of registration to the publisher of the newspaper. He does this on receipt of a copy of the declaration from the magistrate who has authenticated it.

The newspaper is also obliged to furnish returns, statistics, and other information as the Press Registrar may from time to time require.

Official Secrets Act, 1923—It is a comprehensive document relating to official secrets and defines a number of offences. The Act is aimed at maintaining the security of the state against leakage at secret information, sabotage and the like. However, many of the acts prohibited by this law may be committed by newspapers and journalists, as private individuals, while performing their duties.

The OSA, 1923, broadly has two parts-one relating to spying for the enemy (Sec. 3 & 4) and the other relates to unauthorised communication of any other secret official code or pass words, or any sketch, plan, model, article, note, information (Sec. 5) The second one is more important from the stand-point of the freedom of the Press. The government whose administrative culture is secrecy, has an interval of dividing its document into 'classified' and 'non-classified' categories. The classified documents are considered secret and are restricted for publication. The OSA also prohibits publication or communication of any information, which may be directly or indirectly useful to the enemy.

In India, it has been widely demanded that Sec. 5 of the OSA should be done away with as it may be in the public interest to publish certain information which, in the opinion of the authorities, should not be revealed. The second Press Commission and the Press Council of India have recommended that Sec. 5, be scrapped. After the internal emergency period, during the Janata Party regime the government set up a working group to examine the question of official secrecy. The group reported that in view of the present situation the provision of the Official Secrets Act should be made more stringent and rigorous.

Contempt of Courts—Judiciary is the most important of the three arms of the government as it interprets laws. In order to enable the judiciary settle disputes properly and efficiently, its independence must be ensured. According to Sec. 2 of the CoC Act, 1971, contempt is of two kinds, (a) Civil contempt, (b) Criminal contempt.

Civil contempt means wilful disobedience to any judgement, decree, direction, order, writ or other process of a court, or wilful breach of an undertaking given to a court.

Criminal contempt means publication of any matter or doing of any other act whatsoever which (i) scandalises or tends to scandalise or lowers or tends to lower the authority of any court or (ii) prejudices or interferes or tends to interfere with the due course of any judicial proceeding or (iii) interferes or tends to interfere or obstructs or tends to obstruct the administration of justice in any other matter.

Publication of anything which tends to create in the minds of the people an apprehension about the integrity, ability or fairness of a judge or which tends to deter litigants from complete reliance upon the court's administration of justice, amounts to contempt.

However, the power to punish for scandalising the court, is to be used sparingly arid in reference to the administration of justice only. It can not be used for indicating personal insult to the judge.

A judgement can be criticised as erroneous, but dishonesty on the part of the judge in delivering the judgement can not be alleged.

Punishment can be awarded for interference with the due course of justice only if the interference is substantial. Similarly, a person will not be guilty of contempt of court for innocent publication of distribution, during the pendency of civil or criminal proceedings of a matter which would otherwise deem to constitute contempt.

Punishments—A contemptor can be punished with simple imprisonment, term extending upto six months or with a fine upto two thousand rupees or with both.

In case of civil contempt, the contemptor can't be sentenced even to simple imprisonment. He can be detained in a civil prison for not more than six months.

Legal Remedies

Defamation, of taking away the fame from someone, is an offence punishable with imprisonment from the earliest times of civil government. Kautilya has called it 'Vakarushyam' in his book Arthashastra and prescribed punishment for it.

The modern law pundits have regarded defamation as an injury to the reputation of a person. Reputation is considered as a property and any damage to it can give rise to both criminal and civil action. There is no separate law of defamation in India, although the Indian Penal Code (IPC) has four sections defining defamation and what the defences and the punishments are Section 499 defines the offence of defamation.

There are two kinds of defamation—Verbal and Written. Verbal defamation is known as slander while written defamation is termed as libel. There is no civil action if defamation is of the spoken word. The press, being a written and printed medium, is likely to commit an offence of libel only. The main difference between civil suit and criminal proceeding for defamation is pertaining to the compensation while the object of civil action is to adequately compensate the person defamed for the loss of reputation by damages, the object of criminal prosecution is to punish the offender, by way of imprisonment or fine or both.

Defence Laws

In section 499 of IPC there are four explanations and ten exceptions. The offence of defamation can be committed not only by spoken words or written statement but also by signs and visible representations.

That means an offending cartoon or photograph may also give rise to action for defamation. The ingredients of the offence of defamation are-

(1) An imputation concerning the person must have been made.

(2) Such imputation must have harmed, or there is reason to believe that it has the tendency to harm, the reputation of the person concerning whom it is made. Imputation means an accusation against a person and implies an allegation of fact and not merely a term of abuse or insult. In order to constitute the offence of defamation, it is enough if the offending statement is made with the intention of harming the reputation of the complainant or with knowledge or reason to believe that it will harm his reputation.

But there are also certain exceptions to Sec. 499 of IPC.

(1) It is not defamation to impute anything which is true concerning any person, if it be for the public good that the imputation should be made or published.

(2) It is not defamation to express in good faith any opinion regarding the conduct of a public servant in the discharge of his public functions or regarding his character, so far as his character appears in that conduct and no further.

(3) It is not defamation to express in good faith any opinion regarding the conduct of any person touching a public question, and regarding his character so far as his character appears in that conduct and no further.

(4) It is not defamation to publish a substantially true report of the proceedings of a court of justice or the result of any such proceedings. This exception comes under absolute privilege. Only thing is that it should be a mere report of the proceedings without any comment. And it should be substantially true.

(5) It is not defamation to express in good faith any opinion regarding the merits of civil or criminal case, decided by a court of justice; or regarding the conduct of any person as party, witness or agent, in any such case, or regarding the character of such person, as far as the character appears in such performance and no further.

(6) It is not defamation to express in good faith any opinion regarding the merits of any performance which its author has submitted to the judgement of the public or regarding the character of the author, so far as the character appears in such performance, and no further.

(7) It is not defamation if a person having authority over another either conferred by law or arising out of a lawful contract, passes in good faith, any censure on the conduct of that person. This exception is not related to the work of a journalist and is related to an officer writing confidential reports about his subordinates.

(8) It is not defamation to prefer in good faith an accusation against any person to those having lawful authority over that person, regarding the subject matter of accusation.

(9) It is not defamation to make an imputation on the character of another, provided that the imputation be made in good

faith for the protection of the interest of the person making it, or of any other person, or for the public good.

(10) It is not defamation to convey a caution in good faith to one person against another, provided that such caution be intended for the good of the person to whom it is conveyed, or of some person in whom that it is conveyed, or of some person in whom that person is interested or for the public good. Here again imputation published for the public good in good faith is expected.

Scope of the Law—The four explanations given in section 499 of IPC are—

(1) It may amount to defamation to impute anything to a deceased person, if the imputation would harm the reputation of that person, if living; and is intended to be harmful to the feelings of his family or other near relatives.

(2) It may amount to defamation to make an imputation concerning a company or an association or collection of persons as such.

(3) An imputation in the form of an alternative or expressed ironically, may amount to defamation.

(4) No imputation is said to harm a person's reputation, unless that imputation directly or indirectly, in the estimation of others, lowers the moral or intellectual character of that person, or lowers the character of that person in respect of his caste, his calling, or lowers the credit of that person, or causes it to be believed that the body of that person is in a loathsome state, or in a stale generally considered disrespectful.

In addition to the defences discussed above there are four special defences available to journalists in an action for defamation. They are- (1) Justification; (2) Fair Comment; (3) Privilege; (4) Apology.

Justification—The defence that the statement is true is called the plea of justification. In a civil suit, truth of the defamatory statement is a complete defence. The burden of proof is on the defendant. If the impugned statement is provided to be substantially true, it is enough. But if the plea of justification is taken in a criminal complaint, the evidence rendered should be such as would result in the conviction of the complainant for the alleged offence. If the defendant doesn't succeed in proving every material part of his statement, the very fact that he has taken the plea of justification, may be treated as aggravation of the offence and may result in the award of increased damages.

Fair Comment—Fair comment on a matter of public interest doesn't amount to libel. In a plea of fair comment three points arise-

(a) The comment relates to a matter of public interest.

(b) It is only a comment and not a statement of fact.

(c) The comment is fair.

Any matter that effects the public at large is a matter of public interest. Conduct of persons in public office or sanitary conditions, public performances of dance, drama or publication of books or release of films for public exhibition etc., are all matters of opinion. Everyone is entitled to comment on such matters. Comment, being a matter of opinion, is enough if it is fair and honest. Others may agree with the comment but the commentator is not called upon by the law to justify it. Criticism should not be actuated by malice. It should be a reasonable inference from the facts, which must be truly stated.

Privilege—There are some occasions when a person will not incur the liability even if the report or statement published is defamatory. Such immunity is conferred by law for protection of public interest. A defence founded on such immunity is called the 'privilege'. It is of two kinds-Absolute and Qualified.

Absolute Privilege—On grounds of public policy no action is taken for publication of reports or statements, however false they may be in cases covered by absolute privilege. Reports of parliamentary proceedings and coverage of proceedings of state legislatures are protected by Art. 361-A of the constitution. But the report must be substantially true. But this protection is not available for the statements made by MPs and MLAs outside parliament or legislature.

Qualified Privilege—Judges, counsels and parties in judicial proceedings are absolutely privileged and immune from liability for statements made even if they are defamatory. But newspaper reports of court proceedings come under qualified privilege in our country. Publication of statements relating to affairs of state and reports of public meetings are also given protection of qualified privilege, but care should be taken that-

(a) the meeting is lawful,

(b) the proceedings relate to matters of public importance,

(c) the report is fair and accurate.

Who may be Sued? The Proprietor, Editor, Author, Publisher and Printer of a newspaper or journal would be jointly and separately, liable for any defamatory matter published in the newspaper or journal and may be sued as such. But the aggrieved person may sue anyone of them singly. The only thing is, he can not recover damages from the others for the same offence subsequently, though all are separately liable. But a complaint for defamation should be lodged within three years of the date of commission of the offence. Otherwise it would be time-barred. This is the only limitation under Sect. 499 of IPC. In the case of dignitaries, public servants etc., the limitation for filing the complaint by Public Prosecutor is six months.

Damages in a Civil Suit—Damages in a civil suit depends on the assessment of the reputation of that person by the judge. There are certain principles laid down by case law. The amount of damages depend on the nature of imputation, mode of publication, social standing of a person defamed and mitigating circumstances. A person of high social position and the aggravating circumstances may call for exemplary damages. In cases such as loss of business etc., compensatory damages may be awarded. In other cases general damages are awarded for the annoyance or mental pain caused to the defamed person.

15

Role of New Technology

New Communication Technologies are those which are of recent origin. Interactivity is their distinguishing feature. The use of computers in one form or the other, as an integral part of their system, is what enables them to be interactive.

Role of Computer

The idea of interlinking and communicating with the aid of computers was as old as the mainframe computers of the 1970s. But the mainframes could be owned only by mega-establishments, individuals could not afford them for personal use. The networking of computers, it was found, allowed simultaneous access to a single mainframe by any number of users. This development suited owners and users alike. In the decades that followed, computer technology advanced by leaps and bounds. This resulted in the invention of much smaller computer.

In our own country, computer networking are widely used by public sector organizations. On a global scale, Internet is the largest computer network which permeated almost all parts of the world. Internet can offer any immense range of information services such as electronic mail, file transfer, data bases and multi-media. It also provides connectivity to mobile receivers. Computer network thus has several advantages over interpersonal communication.

Teleconferencing—It is a means by which individuals or groups located at different places can exchange data, speech, visual materials like graphs or diagrams and other relevant informations. Teleconferencing is made possible by the integration of computers and communications in such a manner as to form a hostile system which can work in real-time.

It is gaining popularity due to the minimal physical travel demanded of its participants. The time-saving involved in this process is also a significant factor. Teleconferencing can be classified under the following types:

(a) Computer Conferencing

(b) Audio Conferencing

(c) Audio-Graphic conferencing

(d) Video Conferencing

Teletext—It is a form of broadcast technology by means of which several 'pages' of textual information can be transmitted on an already existing television channel. The teletext information is encoded in the so called 'Vertical blanking internal' of the TV screen which is invisible in the normal course of television viewing. Facilities exist in teletext to enable viewers to choose a particular page of teletext containing relevant information.

Teletext is a simple technology which can be used to advantage for public communication.

Radiotext—Better known by the term 'Radiodata systems' (RDS), Radiotext is a technology similar to teletext but with a difference that it works in conjunction with FM Radio while teletext works on television. Radiotext is to be seen as a value-added service on FM Radio. This technology essentially consists of transmitting data and other textual material on the FM carrier so that the listeners/ viewers who are equipped with a Radiotext 'decode' can extract this signal from an ongoing FM transmission and watch the same on a computer screen which forms a part of the Radiotext receiving system.

Videotex—It is another form of interactive communication technology which is in wide usage in several advanced countries. This works with the help of the public telephone network. The integral components of this system are-home computer, telephone connection and domestic TV set. It is essentially interactive and has much more to offer than teletext or Radiotext, which provide only selective information exchange and retrieval.

Interactive Cable Distribution Systems—Dissemination of television programmes via cable to a community of households started in the 1950s. The cable distribution was seen as improving the reception conditions of television in isolated mountainous regions. Later, TV signals received via satellite were put out on cable distribution systems. The spread, of cable distribution system grew dramatically. Advancement in digital technology and fibre optics have resulted in further improved versions of cable distribution.

Communication Satellites—Transmission of television programmes from one country to another, became a reality with the development of communication satellites. These satellites are stationed in an orbit above the earth's equator at a height of about 36,000 km called the geostationary orbit.

Communication Satellites are owned by various individual nations as well as collectively by groups of nations to cater to several applications like broadcasting, television and telecommunications. INTELSAT (International Telecommunications Satellite Consortium) is an international body consisting of more than 90 member countries of which India is one. Our country has also developed its own satellite system called, INSAT (Indian National Satellite System). It is a multi-purpose satellite service catering to telecommunications, radio and TV transmission and weather forecasting.

Mushrooming of satellite-based transnational television in recent years is a cause for concern as well as hope. Many national newspapers which are published simultaneously from multiple locations take advantage of satellite communications for instant transmission of their pages from one publishing centre to another.

Latest Devices

Every technology has its distinct attributes, advantages and disadvantages, because of which an optimal technology selection is possible for any given application.

A relative assessment of the various technologies has been discussed below on the basis of interactivity, asynchronicity and demassification.

Interactivity—It is a property in which the new communication technologies excel over the traditional ones. Teleconferencing and video-teleconferencing can be cited as the most interactive while, teletext or radiotext can be placed at the other end of the interactivity scale.

Asynchronicity—This term refers to that property of the medium whereby the simultaneous presence of all the participants in a communication exercise is not compulsory. The degrees of asynchronicity, however, varies from one technology to the other. It is highest in teleconferencing where all computers are required to interact without live human intervention, but least in a two-way video teleconferencing.

Demassification—Traditional media like press, radio or television are instances of 'one-to-many' kind of communications. Therefore, they are unsuitable where the communication needs are more individualised. Demassification refers to the extent to which a given technology can lead itself to such individualised communication. The normal telephone system is an ideal example of a technology endowed with a high degree of demassification. Teleconferencing or computer communication are high in their demassification while teletext is at the lower end of the demassification ladder.

Societal Aspects

The new communication technologies have not yet penetrated sufficiently in Third World countries like ours. Therefore it is not able to determine their likely impact on our society with any degree of certainty. Communication scholar, Everett Rogers says that the new communication technologies have a marked social impact in the following respects, especially during their adaptability stages:

(a) As the new technologies are relatively costlier and knowledge-intensive, they will be adopted only by the higher strata of the society at first, who can afford them.

(b) Advanced countries which are already information-rich tend to become richer, thus, widening the information gap between countries. This may lead to unfavourable situation for the 3rd World countries.

(c) Information overload is likely to happen, which in turn poses problems of coping with selective retrieval of required information, from heaps of randomly accumulated information. Here again new technologies help us.

(d) Unemployment may abound in certain sectors as the new technologies would eliminate or render surplus certain traditional jobs and occupations. Some new jobs and occupations may be created in their place, but not in numbers sufficient enough to compensate the loss of traditional jobs.

(e) The universal presence of computers and easy access to them is likely to raise problems concerning privacy and security of communications. Use of special passwords and the like are of course an obvious protection, but they too have their limitations. Clever use of special software may also enable computer miscreants to break the secret passwords and get the information.

(f) Greater use of the new technologies may enable the organizations concerned to become more decentralized in their decision making and other functions. But again, an exact opposite may be possible as the new technologies permit much tighter monitoring on the movements and performances of subordinate staff.

16

Application in Life

After it assumed power in 1989, the National Front government came out first with a Cabinet Paper and then introduced the Prasar Bharati Bill in December 1989. According to P. Upendra, the Minister for Information and Broadcasting, the Bill borrowed from the Prasar Bharati Bill of 1979 and took into account the changed circumstances and the present ethos. Many, however, felt that the bill was put before the nation in a hurry. A national debate was initiated, in many cases with the active encouragement of the government to arrive at a consensus on the framework and the modalities of media autonomy. The Bill, after incorporating some amendments, was unanimously passed in both Houses of Parliament. But following a change of government in October 1990, the lack of political good will to translate the concept into a working proposition was apparent. While there was no official pronouncement, the interim government headed by Chandrashekhar continued to maintain the status quo. The dissolution of the Lok Sabha in April 1991 signed the death warrant of the Prasar Bharati Bill, which then had needed only the Presidential assent for becoming Law. The death of Rajiv Gandhi and the advent of Congress rule in June 1991, under P.V. Narasimha Rao, put an end to any hopes about the issue.

Meanwhile, the question of broadcasting autonomy has become irrelevant as other sources of information and entertainment viz., STAR TV, CNN and BBC have burst into view in the wake of the Gulf War. The invasion from the skies has begun.

Today, the rapid expansion of television in India in terms of availability (7 channels) and sheer expansion (545 TV stations) speaks of unqualified success by any standards. TV has often reached a high degree of professional excellence in its news coverage. The 32-hour continuous election telecast in May-June 1991 involving on-the-spot reporting from the counting booths even in the remote corners of the country and the swift shuttling between the national network and the local centres was a refreshingly dramatic experience for the viewers. But barring occasional and isolated instances, it has steadily developed an urban bias and an elitist approach, popularising, in the process, an alien life style and culture far removed from the realities of Indian life.

The Doordarshan has always suffered from the dichotomy between policy pronounce-ments (which emphasize the use of the mass media for social progress) and the continuous drift and departure from them in actual practice. In a developing and democratic country like India, access to television and the social benefit accruing from it, is a crucial test of the social relevance of such an expensive medium. The reason to the establishment of the Doordarshan in India, according to official statements, is to create a sense of participation in our efforts to usher in a new social order. As early as February 1973, a seminar on software objectives sponsored by the government recommended that, "Television must be used in the development process as an instrument of social change and national cohesion by unhesitatingly upholding progressive values and involving the community in a free dialogue. Indian TV has to shun an elitist approach and consumer value system and evolve a truly national model."

Officially the task assigned to the electronic media is three-fold. First, "the AIR and Doordarshan should inform people about happenings in India and the world, objectively, fairly and without any bias, as adequately and quickly as possible." Second, "the electronic media should get across to the people the policies and programmes that the government has framed for accelerating the process of socio-economic transformation." And finally, the broadcast media should pursue "an open policy and a policy that does not shirk issues and the responsibilities connected to these issues in order to develop an informed and participative citizenry; so that people know and think for themselves what is good for them and for the country." There can be no serious difference of opinion on these objectives. The reach of the electronic media together with the high percentage of the illiterate population make the broadcast media the most appropriate vehicles of national communication.

Mrs. Indira Gandhi, who played a leading role in the growth of TV in India, saw its role primarily as a promoter of development and education in a backward country. She repeatedly affirmed the national importance of utilising TV not just for the idle entertainment of the elite but for the uplift of the poor, especially in the inaccessible rural areas. But in effect and in actual practice, the purchase of a TV set is seen as wholesale investment in entertainment which obviates the bother and expense of going to an auditorium or a stadium. Even a cursory examination of its programmes during any week makes it clear that the order in which Doordarshan fulfils the three functions of the medium are entertainment first, information second and education third. This is true even after the introduction of the five Metro channels.

Even a casual viewer cannot but notice that the Doordarshan does not practice what it preaches and evidently such guidelines are honoured more in the breach then in the observance. The official media, despite occasional airs of openness, are generally identified as the propaganda wing of the party in power. These media do not present a balanced and non-partisan view of the events and happenings, which an average citizen so badly requires in order to arrive at an informed judgement. India may demand free and balanced flow of information at the international level.

But at home, the distinction between the ruling party and the government, between the party interest and the national interest often gets blurred. In addition to the lack of objectivity and frankness, the news on Doordarshan also suffers from an overdose of elite and urban values.

From inception, broadcasting in India has been looked upon as a public service for the promotion of social objectives. The concept of advertisements for the promotion of consumer's goods was also considered incompatible with the prevailing philosophy of the "socialistic pattern of society." What causes alarm today is the proliferation in the mass media of these very advertisements for consumer goods.

In a developing country like India, radio and TV should be viewed as a national resource for the uplift of the masses. It is only through a strong media network that the right kind of information and education can be imparted to the people. But the media in our country, like elsewhere in the world, have buckled under the pressure of commercial interests. As a result, besides discrimination of information or the 'haves' from the 'have-nots', there is erosion of regional and cultural identities and ethics. Mindless entertainment with little or no educative value defeats the very purpose of building up a strong media network. For one, it is definitely not in the interest of the people to provide them with unproductive media fare. For another, it is nothing but unjustifiable use of invaluable resources.

The question that inevitably arises is whether we should use TV for promoting a humane social order or to create synthetic needs.

Under the existing system Doordarshan has become a tool for the promotion of crass consumerism. It is a strange paradox that this public investment, which facilitated the rapid expansion of the TV network in a poor country, is now being exploited by the big businesses for building their own corporate images. While it is conceded that ad revenue makes a network viable and independent, the same advertising also dictates the nature, form and content of the media software. Every noble intention to arouse social consciousness through the media gets traded for unhealthy programming. Here is an example.

Advertisers would always prefer to sponsor those programmes which create the proper mood in the viewers to buy their products. Their choice, invariably, falls on entertainment programmes. On rare occasions when serious programmes on topics like environment preservation, public hygiene or any significant social issues like land reforms or minimum wages are telecast, no sponsor is usually available. This is in stark contrast to the situation when advertisers lined up to spend a total of Rs. 35 crore on the serial 'Mahabharat' alone. To play the role of communicator-cum-educator in developing countries, broadcasting media have to provide software that would enrich the lives of the people. A communication policy would have to specify some guidelines to our communicators regarding balanced programming. Here, 'balanced' would mean the right mix of entertainment, information and education.

Press in Action

The press in a democratic country plays a vital role in creating, moulding, and reflecting public opinion. It is a fundamental institution of our society.

Though the press in India is free, it suffers from many ills. It has yet to identify its true post-independence role so as to ensure against haphazard growth and directionless expansion.

There are a few in-built handicaps such as vast geographical area, illiteracy, poverty, multiplicity of languages, and absence of adequate communication facilities. Some other bottlenecks exist, like the linking of ownership of newspapers with other industrial or commercial enterprises; limited newspaper ownership with closely held 'share interest'; urban-oriented expansion of newspapers leaving the vast country side population untouched, inadequate and expensive newsprint, and the lack of local advertisement support.

Eminent journalists have pointed out several drawbacks which stand in the way of making the press in India an independent and impartial instrument of communication of news and views. Some of these drawbacks are: the present system of accreditation of journalists; the government's allocation of newsprint; fixation of advertisement rates; favours to journalists in the form of perquisites such as subsidized housing, medical facilities, etc., heavy dependence of the press on official releases.

For a comprehensive and an in-depth examination of the state of the Indian press and the steps that need to be taken for its development on sound and healthy lines, the Government of India appointed the second Press Commission on 18 May, 1978, headed by Justice K. M. Mathew.

The appointment of the Second Press Commission had become necessary as the Indian Press had undergone several changes, had taken new strides, and acquired an added significance with an ever-expanding readership.

One of the recommendations of the Second Press Commission was to include both positive and negative aspects of an event in development reports. This implied that these reports should investigate the reasons for success as well as failure at different places and under different conditions of various development programmes affecting the lives of the common people. But most of our newspapers merely carry official handouts giving statistics of man-days of employment provided, persons made literate or area brought under irrigation.

The reporting of non-official initiatives in rural development, education reform, struggle against superstitious beliefs. Evil practices like dowry and Sati or other areas of social campaign, is even less extensive than in-depth reporting of the implementation of official development programmes. The Commission says: "our newspapers usually become aware of such non-official activities only after they have been honoured by a Jamnalal Bajaj Foundation award or Magsaysay award."

Another long standing criticism of the press is that it carries too much bad news at the expense of the good. To gain maximum readership, the press emphasizes the exceptional rather than the representative; the sensational rather than the significant. Many activities of the utmost social consequence are not considered reportable incidents. But, as Indira Gandhi never tired of pointing out, "the meek may one day inherit the earth, but never the headlines." This brings us inevitably to the question of social responsibility. Certainly, the press has travelled a long way from the arrogant attitude of the newspaper owners who said, "A newspaper is a private enterprise owing nothing whatsoever to the public, which grants it no franchise. After all, responsible journalism is journalism with a conscience." Nikhil Chakravarthy, an eminent journalist, had said that, "Even if you don't like someone or disagree with him ideologically, you must be fair." A journalist is confronted with ethical decisions almost daily. Should a news source go unnamed? Should a "leak" possibly affecting national security be used? Does the public interest override individual privacy? Should a rape victim's identity be disclosed? Should communities be identified in a communal clash or gory details of violence reported? General professional codes call for truth, accuracy, impartiality and fair play. Unlike most countries where a free press exists, there is no universally accepted code of conduct in enforcement in India. Even the professional bodies have not been unanimous in developing any. Nor has any serious effort been made by the press to find out what the society thinks of it let alone identify the possible areas of disagreement.

The Indian press had always been known for its sanity over sensitive issues like communal disturbances. But on the threshold of the nineties, it appeared that a large section of the press lost its sense of balance and fairness while reporting such highly explosive issues and events. Barring a few glorious exceptions, most of the newspapers betrayed a distinct and dangerous slant in reporting the Ram Janmabhoomi-Babri Masjid controversy.

For all this, the absence of a code of professional conduct in our country is more or less made up for by the adherence of the press to the social responsibility theory. And the performance of the press can be evaluated on the basis of this single criterion. Such accountability to the public serves as a self-regulatory mechanism in place of an explicit policy.

Modern Practice

What is the role of the government in making the mass media truly effective vehicles of culture, creativity and expression? Whatever the nature of media ownership-whether government, public corporation, or private enterprise-it is the government which is ultimately responsible for ensuring the use of broadcasting frequencies in the public interest.

Programme content is based on the objectives of the medium, these objectives form the basis for media policies. In our country, the Ministry of Information and Broadcasting monitors the content of the print and electronic media to ensure that all the mass media serve their noble purpose; to be tolls in the process of development and change. The improvement and expansion of the media network is directly linked to this goal.

From time to time various Committees and Commissions have been set up for the purpose of evaluating the working of the communication network. Attempts have been made to formulate a mass media policy based on their recommendations, whether or not these suggestions will be incorporated to the working of the media system depends on the authorities. In response to some of the policy considerations the government may decide to make resources available through direct budgets, or grants or provided fiscal advantages to quality productions, or offer preferential customs duties when importing hardware or software, etc. Alternatively, the media policy itself may be the outcome of such decisions and regulations.

Public participation in the formulation of national mass media policies may be achieved by setting up Mass Media Policy Council, with representatives from among media professionals and others concerned with the role of communication in society.

To implement policy initiatives, institutions may be started or existing ones improved for training and research in the media of film, radio and television broadcasting, printing and book production, etc.

It is of utmost importance to chalk out a detailed communication policy to guide the growth of the communication networks. Piecemeal initiatives only harm the functioning of the media system. A comprehensive policy would help bring about more effective and purposeful communication.

For effective mass communication it is essential that mass communications have as much information as possible about the audiences or receivers. Although mass audience for each medium is seen as a large group of unknown people, there are also specific audience for particular contents.

Information technology has advanced so much in the years that it is now possible for people, while sitting in their drawing rooms, to witness the events taking place in any part of the world or even in space. We can watch the live coverage of sports events or music concerts taking place thousands of miles away. Indira Gandhi was able to talk to Rakesh Sharma in the space shuttle and the whole of the world could watch them in conversation. The war in Iraq was shown live by CNN. Teleconferencing makes it possible not only to watch events far away but also to participate in the action.

Technology has expanded the audiences manifold. Today we think in terms of audiences spread over the whole world, a phenomenon which Marshall McLuhan called global village. National boundaries hold no barriers for mass communication.

Still communication cannot be without targets. Mass communication is effective if it is produced for specific groups people. Thus, on the one hand, audiences of mass communication are spread across the national boundaries; on the other hand media content has to be target oriented.

We have seen that each of these media has certain advantages over the others. We have also seen that different people exhibit different preferences for media use.

The term mass in used to denote different things. In physics, the word mass refers to the quality of matter or material contained in an object. It may also mean a quantity of matter of indefinite shape and size—a lump.

Sometimes the word mass is used to refer to common people, specially the lower classes. Mass also has both negative and positive meanings. In the negative sense, it refers to the ignorant and unruly mass. Mass implies a lack of culture, intelligence and even of rationality. In socialist tradition, mass has a positive meaning. It connotes the strength and solidarity of ordinary working people when organised together for political ends.

In general usage, the word mass refers to people in a large number. If we say masses are ignorant, we mean that a very large proportion of the population ignorant. Similarly, when we say mass destruction means destruction on a very large scale. Mass awareness programme refers to a programme that aims to create awareness amongst a very large number of people. In fact, the important feature of mass is its very large size in terms of the number of individuals. It will be appropriate if we say that mass refers to an infinite number of individuals. The size of mass is very large and unknown.

Secondly, masses are geographically distributed. Very large number of large of people may be attending a public meeting. They are physically present anywhere and everywhere. When we say masses in developing countries are poor we refer to the people living in Africa, Asian, Latin America and perhaps some other and perhaps some other parts of the world as well.

Since the masses are very large in size and in physical terms the people are distributed all over, they are anonymous to each other. They are not even conscious of the presence of one another. There may be a vague feeling of others like us but it is not well defined. Since the people are anonymous to one another, the masses are unorganised. Unlike the people in a public meeting, there is not organisation and therefore no leadership or hierarchy in mass. Further, the masses are not capable of behaving as one unit.

We can conclude that for our purpose that mass to an infinitely large number of people who are physically located at different places and are not organised at all as a group. In fact scholars like Roymard Williams have summarised that masses actually do not exist, it is only a way of conceiving large groups of people as masses.

Society is a large and complex system. With modernisation the complexity of the society further increase. The traditional society has a well defined social system in which individuals are closely tied to each other, mainly through kinship ties. But industrialisation and urbanisation lead to the formation of society where interdependence of numbers in economic terms increase manifold but kinship ties gradually fade away. The individuals become more self-centred. The socially, economically and politically isolated. The modernising societies experience an increase in individuality. The individuals develop a strong alienation with the community as a whole. There is an increased growth of segmental and contractual relationships. Such a society which is very large in size but where members are isolated and relationships are contractual is called a mass society.

However, the concept of mass society is not to be equated with of massive society. It is more than the massive society. There are many traditional society that are very large in a numbers but are not necessarily mass societies. The individuals in a traditional and Selznick have explained the concept of mass society as follows.

"Modern society is made up of masses in the sense that there has emerged a vast mass of segregated, isolated individuals interdependent in all sorts of specialised ways. Yet lacking in any central unifying value or purpose. The weakening of traditional bonds, the growth of rationality and the division of labour, have created societies made up of individuals who are only loosely bound together. In this sense, the mass society is something closer to an aggregate than to a tightly knit group.

In fact, as stated earlier, mass society has no continuous existence, except in the minds of those who want to reach as many people as possible. It will be useful to further understand the concept of mass society using a set of contrasts with other kinds of units in social life, like group, crowd and public.

In a small all members know each other. They are aware of their common membership, share the same value, have a certain structure of relationship which are relatively stable. The members of a group interact other for a purpose.

The crowd is a spontaneous collection of individuals. It is temporary and never reappears with the same composition. Members of a crowd may strongly identify with each other. More important, they share the same mood. But there exists no order or structure in the crowd. In many cases the actions of the crowd are emotional, sometimes irrational also. Crowd is physically present within observable boundaries, that is, at a particular place.

Unlike crowd, public is widely dispersed. Its size may be small or large. Generally public is identified with some cause, purpose or activity. Public may be quite heterogeneous and members may not be aware of each other. Usually public is identified by the people who want to perceive a large of people as targets.

Let us illustrate each of the above discussed concept with example from our day to day life. Each one of us belongs to many groups simultaneously. Family is the primary unit and basis for all social life. We are all members of our families. Along with this we are also members of class, team, peer group, club etc. On a railway platform we are a part of the crowd. A crowd is also formed when we together to protest against the non-availability of goods.

Political parties treat us as public when they tell us about their policies and plans. We are public for public for police when it informs us about the imposition of curfew. We move in small group of friends or families in a mela. In the mela, we become a part of the crowd but for those displaying their items we are a public.

The Clientele

The commonly used meaning of the term media audience is the aggregate of persons forming readers, listeners, viewers of different media, that is, the content of different media. In other words, audience is a group if individuals with a common pattern of media consumption. Such individuals share common access or exposure to the same mass communication products.

There are four different ways of looking at media audiences. These are media reach, media access, media exposure and media exposure and media effects. We shall discuss these approaches one by one.

Journalistic Access

The owners and producers of the mass media conceive the total population whom their communications can reach. The signals of All India Radio are available to about 95 percent of the population living in about 85 percent of country's area. So the total population of India may be treated as audience for All India Radio. Similarly, Doordarshan can claim more than 80 percent of the population as its audience because its signals can reach that many people. For a newspaper, audience would be defined in terms of all individuals who are within the distribution range of the papers. For a cable TV system the audience reach will include all residents within the wired area.

Mass media may be available but the capacity or willingness to us the media may not be there. A large section of the population does not have the radio receivers or television sets. Thus, only those who own the radio sets may be treated as audiences of All India Radio. But access may not overlap ownership. In fact, there are many people who watch television programmes at the houses of neighbours or friends or in community centre. Groups watching a popular television at television shop is a common sight.

Many families do not buy newspapers but their members may read newspapers at various places like teashop, barbershop, library or even at neighbours' or friends' house. This, those who have direct access by virtue of ownership along with those who are non-owners but get exposed in other ways accessible audience. Who are non-owners but get exposed in other ways constitute the accessible audience.

Everyone who has access to radio or television does not necessarily use them. In a family that subscribes to a actually expose themselves to the media audiences. Again, no one is exposed to the total content of any medium. No one listens to all the programmes broadcast by All India Radio. Similarly, it is impossible to watch all the programmes of Doordarshan. Many people do not even glace at the commerce page of the newspapers. There are many young people, specially students, who read only the sports page. So audiences can also be seen as programme specific or content specific, that is, populations actually exposed to specific media contents.

Another important aspect of media behaviour is that all users of media content are not uniformly exposed. There are people who listen to news everyday without fail. Others may listen to news, says on an average of five days a week. Still others may be people whose exposure to news or radio is nil.

Real Effect

Another way to think about audiences is in terms of individuals who have been exposed to mass communication products and have undergone a change in their knowledge, opinions, attitude or behaviour. A person may not recall anything of the person, after watching an advertisement, may immediately rush to buy the advertised products. Voters generally do not change their voting preference after listening to election broadcasts by the representatives of political parties.

Readers' Response

The most interesting feature of a mass communication audience is its dual nature. At one level media audience is a collectivity formed in response to media content and defined by attention to that content. When a new newspaper is launched, people gradually start reading it. MTV, STAR TV, and ZEE TV have created their own audiences.

Alternatively, audience may be conceived as collectivity that exists already in the systems and mass media may begin to cater to its information and entertainment needs. Krishi Darshan may aim to cater to the needs of the farmers. Yuvvani attempts to cater to needs of the youth. Femina is meant for the women whereas seminar is meant for the intellectuals.

In the first case, media or its content is the cause of the creation of the audience, but in the second case, the audience become the cause of the creation of the media content.

In many case, it is very difficult to determine whether audience is responsible for creation of the media content or the media content has created the audience. The fact is that the audiences are both, the cause as well as the response to the mass communication process. A new newspaper creates its own readership but at the same time it tries to the needs of the targeted readers.

The original audiences were the sets of spectators for games, stage plays or dispension of justice by the king. Such pre-media audiences existed in all cultures in one form or another. Audience for religious discourses have played a very significant role in the spread of social and political ethos.

Invention of printing revolutionised the whole character of audience. This was the beginning of mass audience. The most important change that the took place was that the audience participation as a private act became possible. People could now take the printed materials to secluded places and undergo a totally private experience. This led to another important change.

The audiences become delocalised. It was no more necessary for all members of the audience to be present at one place. A book had readers spread all over the world.

The advent of newspapers created mass audiences in the real sense. Newspapers also converted mass audiences into potential receivers of commercial message or advertising. The advent of electronic media further delocalised the audiences. The information carried by electro-magnetic waves could cross the national boundaries. The audiences were now spread over the whole world. The members were separated from each other and their distance, physical and social, from the communicators also increased.

The audiences now not only took the form and character of masses but they also acquired the features of a mass society. The satellite communication, coupled with cable network on the ground, has brought a situation where the whole world population can be treated as one audience.

The types of audiences can be distinguished based on their demographics characteristics and mental make up.

Elite audience are composed of the people who are decision-makers and trend-setters in the society. They are economically well to do and are highly educated. They have high status in the society. Their numbers is very small but their influence is very strong. They may also be the owners or controllers of the mass media institutions. The members of the elite audience are the early adopters of communication technologies. Their actual media consumption is generally low.

General Audience—They are very large and highly divers groups that represent the broad cross-section of the society. Majority of the people to this category. The media content is generally targeted at them. Their participation determines the success or failure of content or medium.

Specialised Audiences—These audience are composed of individuals who possess similar characteristic. They are relatively small in number. Mass media generate special contents for these audience groups. Programmes for tribals, for housewives, for college students, etc. are example of programmes for specialised audiences. Similarly, journals like Mainstream, Femina and Economic and Political Weekly have limited but known readership.

The Consumerism

Rise of consumerism has led to a situation where audiences are treated as markets. The media products is a commodity or service offered for sale to a given body of potential consumers, in competition with other media products. Their potential or actual consumers can be referred to as markets.

With the commercialisation of broadcasting and telecasting in our country, the audience are being treated more as markets. There is competition between Doordarshan, STAR TV, ZEE TV, MTV to capture as big an audience as possible. Drastic changes in the programme content of Doordarshan main and Metro channels is an indication of the fact that even the state controlled medium is forced to view audiences as markets. Audience, according to the market concept, can be defined as an aggregate of potential consumers with a known socio-economic profile at which medium or message is directed.

Audience has a dual significance for the media. Firstly, as set of potential or actual consumers of media content and secondly, as the audience for advertising message. Thus a market for media content is simultaneously a market for other products; media serve as advertising vehicles for delivering messages to the potential customers of other products. Advertising is the largest source of revenue for all media. In fact, no medium can survive if not supported by advertising or some other sources. Till the time AIR and Doordarshan were not commercial, the government used to subsidies their services. The most popular programmes of radio and television attract the maximum advertising. Not only that, advertising rates are the highest for prime time programmes. The treatment of audiences as markets has social and moral implication as well. First, when the relationship between the media and audience is that of producer and consumer, the character if relationship become manipulative. The aim is torn sell as much as possible.

Secondly, the members of the audiences are markets and are treated as passive receivers. The audience are lured by cleverly designed message, Thirdly, the success of the media is measured not in terms of needs fulfilled but in terms of sales of the products. Lastly, the market view is that of the media owners and media producers. Audiences never see themselves as markets.

Audience is the single most important element in any conception of mass communication. The development of the relationship between the mass media and the audience can be seen in two contrasting ways. We may consider the availability of a large number of media units as media explosion. In this conception, the media occupy the central position and information from the various media is seen as acting upon the audience.

But if we observe the media audience relationship carefully, we find that the audiences actually exercise their choice as to which medium is to be used and also which content they would like to be exposed to. Marshall McLuhan saw the audiences at the centre of the numerous attacks by different media. He referred to this as media implosion as against the media explosion.

The efforts required for attending to mass communication may be considered in terms of the availability of the media and the ease with which we may use the media.

Expense involved and the time required are also important factors in "the effort required." Watching a film on television is less expensive, less time consuming and little efforts is required for it as compared to watching a film in a cinema hall.

The uses and gratification theory of the media effects proposes that basic human needs motivate individuals to attend to particular forms of mass media and to select and use messages in ways they find personally gratifying. Thus, audience members make a conscious and motivated selection amongst the various mass media and also amongst the various item of content.

The producers of mass communication keep a hand on the pulse of their audiences in order to make their products more and more acceptable. Audience feedback systems are the mechanisms through which information regarding audience reaction is taken back to the owners, controllers and producers of the media. There are two distinct feedback system; market-based feedback system and research based feed-back system. Mass Communicators receive the following information through the market-based feedback system: (a) audience access to the media; (b) audience exposure to the media

The above mentioned information is received by the communicators by three methods:

Audiences decision to subscribe to newspapers or magazines is a direct feedback about the popularity of the publication. Rise and fall of circulation is a very important feedback that the market provides. More and more houses paying for cable TV connections indicate the increased popularity of the. satellite channels. At the same time, it may also indicate that the audiences are not very happy with the Doordarshan programmes. Increased circulation of a news paper implies endorsement of the style and editorial policies of the new paper. Sales at box-office is a good feedback about the popularity of a film.

Sometimes, audience reactions to, mass communication are very actively solicited. Coupons, rebate offers, bring-this-and-get-a-discount and similar practices are used to measure the impact of particular promotional efforts.

For books, magazines, papers, video and audio cassettes, film and cable TV connections, the audience behavior has a direct bearing. More consumers mean more revenues. In case of radio and television and even news papers and magazines, the largest share of revenue comes from advertising. But again the advertising rates are determined by audience size, and thereby audiences exert their influence, through indirectly.

Direct Feedback—Mechanisms of direct feedback are provided in each media system. Newspapers and magazines have columns reserved for letters to the editor sent by the readers. Similarly, radio and television networks have programmes reserved for comments, reaction suggestion from the audiences. Unsolicited letters and telephones also provide important feedback. In some cases, casual conversation between employees of mass media and members of audience may provide important feedback.

A careful observation of the media in our country over the last two decades would reveal the felt needs for direct feedback from the audiences increasing. Space devoted to the letters to the editor column in newspapers and magazines has increased. Similarly, more and more air time is being given on radio and television for programmes where representative of the audience are allowed to give their reaction and suggestion.

Media Reviews—Media give the greatest importance to the feedback through the reviews. Every news paper and magazine has media review column written by a media critic. In these columns, the media critics examine the mass communication of radio and television. Similarly, there are regular review of films, audio and video cassettes published in newspapers and magazines.

The role these media reviews is two fold. One, the owners, controllers and specially the producers of radio and television programmes take the comments very seriously. Secondly, these reviews provide information to the audiences. They, in fact, provide expert opinion and influence audience to notice and use particular mass media content. A radio or television programmes or a film or book or a song sequence commented favourably becomes acceptable to the audiences. Many people buy or read a book after reading its review.

In our country, there were no reviews of the print media except in academic journals till recently. Now, some newspapers have introduced these. For example, The Pioneer has a weekly column Blue Pencil by G S Bhargava. It appears on very Sunday and critically comments on the coverage in different newspapers.

Firstly, the critic acts as a link between the producers and the audience. At this point, the critic performs the role of calling attention to the availability of information and recommending responses. Secondly, the critic may provide his expert comments to the producers. At this point, the act is an interpretation of how and why the audiences reacted positively or negatively to the content. Various functions performed by the reviewers can be listed as follows:

(a) Informing audience what is new and interesting.

(b) Raising the cultural level of the community.

(c) Advising the audiences on how to use their time and money.

(d) Helping artists and performers to understand how their efforts are being received by the audiences.

(e) Recording the history of mass communication.

(f) Entertaining audiences with their articles and reports.

The market-based feed back and the reviews are more or less passive systems. Feedback information gets generated without the producers making efforts for it. They leave many questions unanswered. A newspaper will get information that its circulation is decreasing but it is not known as to who are the people who have stopped subscribing and why have they done so. Similarly, media critics may not comments at all on a programme or their comments may be considered subjective. Research based feedback systems are created to provide systematic information about audience response to a particular mass communication products of services.

Many media organisations have their own audience systems. For example, there are Audience Research in All Radio and Doordarshan. These units keep on collecting audiences responses to various programmes. Based on the research finding, the producers may improve their programme; some programmes may be discontinued or their timings may be changed.

Reliable and systematic information collected about the listenership or viewership leads to ratings of different programmes. The use of the media by advertisers and made to reach the desired audiences in a more cost effective manner. In our country, programmes regularly. It is hoped that soon it will evolve into an authentic and reliable system.

Mass communication does not mean communication for everyone. The media and their audiences come together through a process or natural selection. Media tend to select their audiences by means of content. The audiences also tend to select among and within the media primarily on the basis of content.

Different media may different audiences but there is a considerable overlap between the audiences of one medium with those of the other. Researchers have shown that persons who are above average in exposure to one medium to other media as well. A person who reads a news paper is likely also to read magazines, listen to radio and watch television. Lazarsfeld and Merton called this phenomenon as all-or-non principle. A person interested in escapist entertainment will find it in books, magazines, films and televisions. Anyone who has little opportunity to use one medium because of poverty, illiteracy, ignorance or lack of time or interest-will probably have little opportunity to use any medium.

Newspapers attract very heterogeneous audiences. Children and young people generally do not read newspapers. Most of the readers read only the headlines or at the most read the introductory paragraphs. The finance page has a special readership composed of businessmen and those involved in economic and commercial activities. Sports page has an audience of predominantly young people. Editorial and edit page contents have a very small readership.

Magazines are generally read by people with more education and those belonging to higher economic strata, in general, young people are likely to use newspapers and magazines for entertainment, older people for information and views on matters of public life. Adults do more news reading than young people; the latter pay more attention to photographs and visuals like cartoons and comic strips.

More males read newspaper and also at greater length than females. Higher economic status is generally accompanied by increase in the reading of public news, sports news and society news. People belongs to low and very low socio-economic strata generally read local newspapers or they more attention to local news in regional or national news papers. Middle-class readers to read national news papers. Highly educated and rich people tend to read international newspapers and magazines or the newspapers and publications of other countries.

Before the advent of television, radio was the medium for all classes. However, many people neither owned radio sets nor did they have access to radio in any other way. Transistor revolution spread the ownership of radio receiving sets very widely. But in our country at no time more than 60 percent of the families owned radio sets.

Not-so-poor people and belonging to lower middle classes generally owned single band or two band radio sets. As a consequence, their exposure was mostly confined to local radio station or medium wave stations. People with efficient receiving systems listened not only to AIR but also to foreign systems like BBC, Voice of America, Radio, Moscow.

After the advent of television, radio listening in television owning households has fallen drastically. Many television owning households do not use the radio sets at all. The predominant use of radio today is for music in the background while people are engaged in other works. Many people use radio as an announcer or time. Unlike in U.S and other western countries, radio is not much used in motor vehicles in our country. Audio-tape players have become more popular in cars, buses and trucks.

Young persons use radio to listen to film and non-film music. Adults also listen to music but they tend to use radio as a source of news and information. Housewives may use radio as a companion during the day when they are alone. Young men and women appearing in competitive tests use radio as an important source of information, specially news and current affairs programme. Spotlight and Samayaki are very popular among those sitting in civil services examinations.

The tremendous popularity of television is at the expense of radio. With the advent of television, total time devoted to the media has increased. All sections of the population wish to watch television. Many have their own sets. Others watch television at neighbours or friends houses or at community centres.

News and current affairs programmes of Doordarshan are seen by more educated section of the society. Common people tend to watch entertaining serials. Ramayana on Doordarshan had the largest ever largest ever audience. DD Metro is more popular than the main channel of Doordarshan. Generally, people now subscribe to cable network systems. ZEE TV has a wide audience in Hindi-speaking middle and lower classes. The audience of STAR TV is restricted to middle and upper middle classes. MTV has an audience of young and rich who are relatively more exposed to western culture and values. Research has shown that programmes like Krishi Darshan have very small audiences even among the farmers. It is important to note that the viewers of television also become the audience of the films. A number of films are shown on various channels of television. Besides there are many programmes that the based on films. The television and films industries have become closely related and there are films now produced only for television.

Till television spread its networks, films were the most widely used mass media. All sections of the population, very poor to very rich, went to cinema theatres to watch films.

With the advent of television, VCR, VCP, satellite transmission and cable networks, the films watching in cinema halls has decreased considerably. But the total exposure to films has perhaps increased.

Different types of films have different audiences. Common people generally like to watch masala-films that have an adequate mixture of emotions, comedy, violence, dance, music, sex etc. The new-wave films, the art films and low cost films have an audience that is composed of more educated, socially conscious and intellectual section. Religious films based on epics have an audience composed mainly of rural people, women, illiterate poor etc. Similarly, informative films or films with social messages have different audiences.

Books attract people who are above average in education and also in their use of the serious contents of other media. Books are more likely to attract young adults than older ones, people living in urban rather than in rural areas, people or high income rather than low income. Readers of English books attract audiences more from highly educated, well-off people. Books in Hindi languages are read mostly by the people belonging to these language groups. Generally, book-readers have a high exposure to other media.

Communication is one of those human activities that everyone recognise but few can define satisfactorily. Communication is talking to one another, it is television, it is spreading information, it is our hair style, it is literary criticism: the list is endless. This is one of problems facing academics: can we properly apply the term 'a subject of study' to something as diverse and multi-faceted as human communication actually is? Is there any hope of linking the study of, say, facial expression with literary criticism? Is it even an exercise worth attempting?

The doubts that lie behind questions like these may give rise to the view that communication is not a subject, in the normal academic sense of the world, but is a multi-disciplinary area of study. This view would propose that what the psychologists have to tell us about human communicative behaviour has very little to do with what the literary critic has.

This lack of agreement about the nature of communication studies is necessarily reflected in this book. What we have tried to do is to give some coherence to the confusion by basing the book upon the following assumptions.

— assume that communication is amenable to study, but that we need a number of disciplinary approaches to be able to study it comprehensively.

— assume that all communication involves signs and codes. Signs are artefacts or acts that refer to something other than themselves, that is they are signifying constructs. Codes are the systems into which signs are organised and which determines how signs may be related to each other.

— assume, too, that these signs and codes are transmitted or made available to others: and that transmitting or receiving signs/codes/communication is the practice of social relationships.

— assume that communication is central to the life of our culture: without it culture of any kind must die. Consequently the study of communication involves the study of the culture with which it is integrated.

Underlying these assumptions is a general definition of communication as 'social interaction through messages.'

The structure of this book reflects the fact that there are two main schools in the study of communication. The first sees communication as the transmission of messages. It is concerned with how senders and receivers encode and decode, with how transmitters use the channels and media of communication. It is concerned with matters like efficiency and accuracy. It sees communication as a process by which one person affects the behaviour or state of mind of another. If the effect is different from or smaller than that which was intended, this school tends to talk in terms of communication failure, and to look to the stages in the process to find out where the failure occurred. For the sake of convenience we shall refer to this as the 'process' school.

The second school sees communication as the production and exchange of meanings. It is concerned with how messages, or texts, interact with people in order to produce meanings; that is, it is concerned with the role of texts in our culture. It uses terms like signification, and does not consider misunderstandings to be necessarily evidence of communication failure—they may result from cultural differences between sender and receiver. For this school, the study of communication is the study of text and culture. The main method of study is semiotics (the science of signs and meanings), and that is the label we shall use to identify this approach.

The process school tends to draw upon the social sciences, psychology and sociology in particular, and tends to address itself to acts of communication. The semiotic school tends to draw upon linguistics and the arts subjects, and tends to address itself to work of communication.

Each school interprets our definition of communication as social interaction through messages in its own way. The first defines social interaction as the process by which one person relates himself to others, or affects the behaviour, state of mind or emotional response of another, and, of course, vice versa. This is close to the common-sense, everyday use of the phrase. Sometimes, however, defines social interaction as that which constitutes the individual as a member of his culture or society.

The two schools also differ in their understanding of what constitutes a message. The process school sees a message as that which is transmitted by the communication process. Many of its followers believe that intention is a crucial factor in deciding what constitutes a message. The sender's intention may be stated or unstated, conscious or unconscious, but must be retrievable by analysis. The message is what the sender puts into it by whatever means.

For sometimes, on the other hand, the message is a construction of signs which, defined as transmitter of the message, declines in importance. The emphasis shifts to the text and how it is 'read.' And reading is the process of discovering meanings that occurs when the reader interacts or negotiates with the text. This negotiation takes place as the reader, brings aspects of his cultural experience to bear upon the codes and signs which make up the text. It also involves some shared understanding of what the next the text is about. We have only to see how different papers report the same event differently to realise how important is this understanding, this view of the world, which each paper shares with its readers. So readers with different social experiences or from different cultures may find different meanings in the same text. This is not, as we have said, necessarily of communication failure.

The message, then, is not something sent from A to B, but an element in a structured relationships whose other elements include external reality and the producer/reader. Processes is that they occupy the same place in this structured relationship. We might model this structure as a triangle in which the arrows represent constant interaction, the structure is not but a dynamic practice.

At one time or another almost everyone has responded to the question "How did this [disaster] happen?" with a statement like "Don't ask me. I just work here." In some cases the excuses is a legitimate one. Someone other than the person making the statement made a decision or took a step which created a problem, but far too often it is a decision, action, or lack of action by the person offering the excuse that led to the inefficiency or failure. Although the performance of every member of an organisation is in many ways influenced by the activities of other members, in the final analysis it is the individuals' choices which decide their destiny in the organisation. It concentrates on communication in organisations because it is through communication that individual employees gain the information on which they base choices and exercise the influence which translates their choices into action. The goal of this book is to give readers a sense of how organisational communication is used strategically, that is, how individual employees analyse the situations thy face at work and choose the appropriate communication strategies to use in those situations. The book assumes that all employees are goal-oriented in some important ways and that if they understand how communication functions in their organisation they will be better able to use their communication skills to achieve their objectives and those of their organisations. The book explains when it is appropriate to use a variety of communication strategies, including the denial or responsibility and the claim of ignorance ("I don't know. I just work here"), and more important, when not to use them.

One of the most important recent developments in the way people look at organisations has been the increasing amount of attention paid to different aspects of communication. Managers and researchers alike have recognised that businesses must maintain at least an adequate level of communication in order to survive, that increasing the effectiveness of communication within a firm contributes to the efficiency of its operation, and that in some cases highly effective communication can increase productivity and eventually profitability. Perhaps more important has been the realisation that people who understand how communication functions in a business, who have developed a wide repertory of written and oral communicative skills, and who have learned when and how to use those skills seem to advance more rapidly and contribute more fully to their organisations than people who have not done so. As a result the number of college courses and professional training programs concerned with organisational communication has mushroomed. Of course employees cannot function effectively unless they possess the technical skills that their positions require.

But more and more it appears that being also able to recognise, diagnose, and solve communication-related problems is vital to the success of people in even the most technical occupations. Accountants must be able to gain complete, accurate, and sometimes sensitive information from their clients, supervisors of production lines must be able to obtain adequate and timely information on which to base their decisions, managers of different divisions must be able to give their subordinates clear instructions, make sure those instructions are understood, create conditions in which their commands will be carried out, and obtain reliable feedback about the completion of the tasks that they have assigned. In a recent survey of 700 middle managers, almost 85 percent of the respondents reported that it was their subordinates' communication skills (or lack or them) which determined their success or failure in critical situations. Although these managers also noted that factors like their subordinates' job-related expertise and loyalty to their supervisor and organisation also had an important impact on their effectiveness, it was their ability to communicate effectively that was crucial in most cases.

However, being able to communicate effectively at work requires two kinds of knowledge. First, it requires an understanding of the relationships that exit between communication and the operation of organisations. Since communication processes influence the way an organisation operates and are simultaneously influenced by key characteristics of the organisation, neither organisations nor organisational communication can be understood adequately if they are examined in isolation of each other. Second, effective communication depends on employees' understanding how to choose appropriate communication strategies in different situations. This book intends to provide readers with an understanding of strategic communication skills, the ability to analyse a situation, select an appropriate communication strategy from a number of available options, and employ that strategy in an optimal way. However understanding strategic communication demands that an individual understand how communication functions in organisations, how it creates and solves problems, how it makes some situations occur and how it prevents others, how it makes some outcomes more probable and others improbable. This chapter will introduce these two most important concepts: the role of communication in organisations and the characteristics of strategic organisational communication. Subsequent chapters will expand each of these concepts and explain how they contribute to the success of complex organisations and their members.

Historically, formal organisations have been examined from two very different perspectives. One view has depicted them as the combination of a number of different components, each of which is linked to each other on the basis of some carefully planned and clearly articulated design. People who accept this perspective believe that organisations are designed in three distinct steps. Designing an organisation begins with an analysis of a potential market and a decision about what products-goods or services the organisation should produce. Designers then decide which tasks must be performed in order to produce the desired output and determine how each of these tasks can be completed most efficiently. Finally, designers organise the various tasks into structures and sequences which are intended to maximise the efficiency of the total operation. Since many of the components of the organisation are people, someone must be assigned the job of seeing that all who are involved in each part of the production process understand the tasks they are to perform, how they are to accomplish those tasks, the fact that they must accomplish them in a timely and efficient manner if the organisation is to function properly. In this perspective, communication is important for instrumental reasons. It functions in ways which allow members to share the information necessary for the successful completion of a complex array of interdependent tasks. Although the end products, task requirements, employee skills, or relationships among these components may change when market conditions or technologies change, this perspective assumes that the rational design of an organisation will stay relatively constant. At least, the organisation will stay stable enough so that the designers can draw a picture, usually in the form of an "organisational chart," which accurately reflects its operation.

Another viewpoint describes organisations as complex, interdependent matrices of ongoing process, not as a rational, carefully planned combination of interrelated static components. This distinction is important for two reasons. First, it leads to a view of the members of an organisation as actors, not as relatively inert components of the organisation. Employees constantly are making choices about how they will act in the variety of situations they face. Second, organisations are networks of interdependent human actors whose actions both create situations they face allow them to respond to those situations. Although organisations can be designed by objective, outside planners, their designs constantly are in a state of change. Businesses are composed of large numbers of people who constantly are monitoring their own actions and the actions of others, processing that information, and choosing those courses of action that they think are appropriate. This description of organisations does not imply that their members are either manipulative or Machiavellian although it would admit that some of them are. Instead, it suggests that people are active agents who have their own reasons for acting as they do. They are not mechanical components of the production process, doing only what they are designed to do in precisely that way in which they are designed to do it. They are choice-making members whose actions are part of a complicated array of ongoing processes.

Within this perspective, communication is important to an organisation for two reasons. First, communication is the means through which people acquire the information and develop the criteria by which they decide how to act. Second, communication is the process through which they put their choices into practice. That is, through communication members of organisations learn that there are precedents in their organisation which constrain their choices, and they learn what those precedents are. Through communication with others, they develop and express the purposes which guide their actions. They are able to consider the potential effects of different actions only because they are capable of communicating. In addition, it is through communication that members of an organisation are able to coordinate their actions with other members of the organisation. Because the complex array of tasks that must be performed in an organisation are independent, each member of the organisation can perform only if other members do also. In almost situations, only a small proportion of the activities of any one employees will be necessary preconditions for the successful action of other employees. However, for each member of the organisation, there are some actions that must be taken if the organisation is to operate. And, because all members must depend on the actions of some other member(s) in order to do their jobs, they must be able to predict accurately what those other people will do in different situations. Being able to do so requires employees to understand why they act as they do and to recognise that they regularly respond to certain situations in predictable ways. Communications is the process through which people make sense out of the actions of other people, it is the means by which they are able to understand how they can coordinate their actions with the actions of others.

Human action is contextual, it is the result of the choices people make within the situations they perceive themselves to be.

Unfortunately, these two views of organisations and communication often are seen as being mutually exclusive. Scholars who focus their attention on the design or structure of organisations and the functions of communication in organisation that have been described in this chapter often overlook the complex processes through which people decide how to act at work. Conversely, when scholars concentrates on understanding the relationships between processes of communication and processes of organising, they often deemphasise the tasks people perform at work and the function communication plays in the completion of those tasks. Understanding strategic organisational communication requires an analysis of both the functions of communication in organisations and the processes through which communication guides the actions of members.

System at Work

In some important ways communication functions as a tool for members of organisations: It allows them to issue, receive, interpret, and act on commands; it allows them to create and maintain productive business and personal relationships with other members of the organisations; and it allows them to manage ambiguity and uncertainty.

Two types of communication make up the "command" function: direction and feedback. People perform necessary task effectively only when they choose both to initiate action and to limit their actions in clearly prescribed ways. Some members of organisations, usually those given the formal titles of supervisor or manager, issue messages which tell other members to take action and to limit that action to a particular series to be taken at a specified time and at a specified place. If the person to whom the message is directed does not act, or if the person acts inappropriately, the command function will not be wholly successful. It is inevitable that people will resist commands to some degree. In order to function, organisations must influence people to act in ways in which they otherwise would not act. For instance, few humans would choose on their own to perform seemingly minor, repetitive tasks hour after hour, day after day. But a large proportion of production-oriented organisations could not exist if it was not possible for some people to persuade other people to perform these tasks at a predetermined rate for a predetermined period of time with a minimal amount of creativity. Assembly lines operate successfully only because a complex array of very specific commands are communicated to a large number of people in a way that somehow persuade them to follow those commands exactly. If any worker a does a job in a new, varied, unanticipated or creative way, the productivity of the assembly line is reduced. When automobile workers respond to the boredom of their jobs by choosing to install parts backward, upside down, or not at all, the quality of the final product usually us reduced. When they respond by celebrating the end of monotonous week with a Thursday afternoon or Thursday through Sunday visit to a local bar, their ability to follow commands exactly on subsequent days usually is reduced. Although these deviations from expected behaviour often do little damage, they create enough problems that most Americans learn at an early age "not to buy a car which was built on Friday." Other types of organisations involve even larger numbers of people whose actions must be initiated and controlled if the organisation is to function. Consequently, the command function of communication relies on process of persuasion and influence. Its effectiveness depends on the availability of some form of influence and some communication strategies through which some members organisations can persuade other members to act in specific and unnatural ways.

The command function also involves the production of adequate feedback about the actions that actually are taken by people who have been issued commands. Supervisors often assume that their subordinates will carry out their commands. This assumption is especially strong when the supervisor has issued a set of routine instructions. Comfortable in the knowledge that their commands will be carried out, supervisors instruct other people to take actions which, when completed, will allow the task that the unit has taken on to be accomplished. If any of the people who are involved in the command process fail to carry out the commands they were given properly or promptly, the supervisors will need to modify the commands that were given to the other people and accurate feedback about the extênt to which each of their commands has been carried out.

Almost all people who have worked in organisations which produce tangible products can remember instances in which they found themselves surrounded by piles and piles of partially finished products because some person or group of people failed to receive, understand, or carry out commands. These situations usually strike the workers who are gazing at the piles as being terribly funny, both because they know that the error is someone else's headache and because they have been allowed to take a lengthy break while waiting for the bottleneck to be eliminated and the unfinished products to reach their stations. Rarely does the supervisor who issued the commands find the situation quite as humorous. The piles of unfinished products do, however, give this supervisor feedback about the effects of the commands. Organisations do seem to function more efficiently when supervisors have access to more timely and less tangible command-related feedback.

Command-related communication typically comes in one of two forms: publications and instructions. The differences between the two forms are important because employees' reactions to a command are related in part to the form in which it is issued. Organisations produce a variety of formal written policies and procedures. The published communications have three important characteristics. First, they create the impression that the commands is directed to a general audience. No one has been picked out as the recipient; the message seems to be addressed to anyone. Second, they create the impression that the command is official; that is, it is written by the organisation or by someone who represents the organisation rather than by any one individual. Finally, They suggest, both that the command is a relatively permanent injunction and, indirectly, that the problem it addresses is important and recurring.

In contrast, instructions are oral commands, generally given in a face-to-face encounter and addressed to a single person or clearly defined group of persons. Instructions are highly flexible commands which seem to be transient rather than permanent. They are viewed as being linked to a specific problem which is relatively new, rare, or unprecedented and are from an individual rather than from the "organisation." Because publications and instructions are different forms of commands, they are appropriate to different kinds of situations. The success of any command depends on part being issued in the proper form.

One function of communication in formal organisations is the command function. Because organisations are composed of large numbers of people who play interdependent roles, their actions must be coordinated effectively. Successful coordination is achieved when members initiate the actions they have been directed to undertake. It occurs when some members of the organisation communicate in ways that create the kind of situations in which other members of the organisation will choose to take the precise actions that are envisioned in the commands. Both the process of creating a appropriate situation and the creation of clear and influential command messages depend on the strategic competence and communication skills of the participants. The command function of organisational communication relies totally on complex processes of constructing, interpreting, and choosing actions in response to a particular type of communication.

Organisational communication also fulfils a relational function, businesses are composed of human beings who are involved in interpersonal relationships with other human beings. Unlike non-work relationships, in which people have a relatively wide degree of freedom in deciding who to form relationships with, the structure of formal organisations dictates that each employee must form relationships with a clearly defined group of people. Sometimes, perhaps most of the time, members of organisations are required to form effective "working relationships" with people with whom they never would choose to form personal relationships. For a number of reasons, imposed relationships are less stable and more prone to friction than are "natural" ones.

Like natural relationships, working relationships can succeed only if the parties involved can achieve at least a minimal degree of understanding and cooperation. To do so they must be able to comprehend the meaning of the messages they exchanges with each other, assess each others' motivations with some degree of accuracy, and negotiate some agreements about how they will act toward one another. Unless these minimal requirements are met, the development of effective working relationships is impossible. Like all relationships, working relationships inevitably will involve some friction, misunderstanding, and conflict about the proper nature of the relationship. However, in non-working relationships the parties usually develop a degree of commitment to each other and to the continuation of the relationship. Typically they will have voluntary started relationship and will made a number of decisions to continue it in spite of conflicts and frictions because they continue to receive benefits from it. To some degree at least, their commitment is mutual and intrinsic to the relationship. In working relationships, the parties may have very little commitment to the relationship itself. Someone or something else, a supervisor of the organisation-initiated the relationship, the parties stay in it because their roles in the organisation seem to demand that they continue to work together, and the benefits they receive from it are derived from their place in the organisation rather than from the relationship itself.

When people lack an intrinsic commitment to a relationship, it is more difficult to resolve their differences and the degree of communication skills necessary to maintain it is greater. Minor irritations are not overlooked, minor conflicts are not easily resolved, and major disagreements erupt into open confrontation because neither party is as concerned that an open conflict might threaten the continuation of the relationship. Fortunately, and almost inevitably, people do form close personal relationships with some of those with whom they have effective working relationships. Although this means that their work situations will be more pleasant than otherwise would be the case, it also adds a number of complicating factors to the relationship. They must negotiate boundaries the two dimensions of their relationship, arriving at some mutual agreement that they will communicate differently with each other while at work than they will while in other contexts. In addition, they must cope with the fact that their personal relationship is being observed by a large number of people with whom they have working relationships and that the existence of the personal relationship may further complicate some of their working relationships. "Don't have an affair with your boss, or at least don't let anyone know you are" really is very good advice.

Through processes of communication, working 'relationships are formed, maintained, and in some cases, transformed into personal relationships. As these relationships begin and develop, the participants in them begin to perceive their jobs, their organisation, and their roles in that organisation differently. These perceptions combine to define the situations that each individual believes one faces at work. Perceptions provide the parameters and guidelines within which each individual makes decisions about how to act. These choices influence the character of the relationships with other members of the organisation, and these changed relationships influence other members' perceptions of their organisation and thus influence their actions. Other members' actions in turn alter the character of their relationship and consequently influence the parameters and guidelines within which other members make their choices. In a complex matrix of processes, communication, relationships, perceptions, and choices, the "situations" in which people find themselves at work are created.

In addition, the relationships that people form at work influence their performance in complicated and important ways. Employees' perceptions of and satisfaction with the tasks they are asked to perform are affected by the quality of the relationships they form with the people around them. Similarly, their satisfaction with their jobs will influence their ability to form valued and stable relationships with their co-workers. The quality of employees' relationships with their co-workers influences their ability to gain the information and support they need in order to perform their job and influences their willingness to provide the information and support their co-workers need. The nature of supervisors' relationships with subordinates influences their ability to understand the messages they exchange and the probability that any particular command will be carried out. For all these reasons, the relational and command functions of organisational communication are interdependent and interactive. The success of one depends largely on the success of the other.

The third major function of communication in organisations is the management of ambiguity. Humans are essentially choice-making beings, and their activities at work are essentially choice-making activities. Each day they face a series of decision-making situations. In some of these situations they make choices for the organisation; in others their decisions are more personal. Their choice making is complicated by two factors. The first involves the multitude of motivations an individual generally incorporates into decision making. In each organisational choice-making situation, a person simultaneously must consider the effects selecting one of a number of available options will have on one, one's co-workers, and one's organisation. In some situations the personal concern will be more important than the relational or organisational ones; in others, the decision maker will be concerned primarily with the interests of the organisation and only indirectly concerned with one's own interests. Some different situations will involve different combinations of self, relationship, and organisational interest, organisational choice-making is a complex and potentially confusing process. If the individual faces a situation which provides clear and explicit guidelines for determining how these interests should be balanced, it is relatively easy to make effective choices. However, choice making typically takes place in situations in which the guidelines for action are either unclear or contradictory. Communication then becomes the process through which an actor manages an ambiguous situation.

Second, organisational choice making is complicated by the ambiguity of the organisations themselves. The objectives of an organisation at a particular time often are not clear to its members. In addition, the objectives of a particular unit in the organisation or of particular members also may be ambiguous. In organisations which are undergoing rapid change or which exist in rapidly changing environments, these objectives may be particularly confused.

Also, the complex histories of modern organisations complicate the choice making of their individual members. Most situations are not completely unprecedented. The people involved have faced similar situations in the past and can draw on those experiences to help them make effective choices in the new situation. But precedents sometimes hurt choice making more than they help it. Individuals will recall that in similar situations in the past they made a certain choice. They also remember that their choice was followed by a certain good or bad result. They will tend to believe that it was their decision that led to the result. If the outcome was favourable, they will tend to repeat the decision. If the outcome was negative, they will tend to avoid taking any similar course of action. But in most cases, choices made by a single individual are only one part of a complicated series of events and decisions which lead to an observed outcome. Not realising this, individual tend to make subsequent choices based on the mistaken belief that it was their choice that cause a particular outcome to occur in the past. In this way the availability of precedents can reduce the quality of the choices that are made.

Precedents complicate choice making in another way. When faced with a decision people tend to search their memories for similar situations. When they discover a precedent they feel a great sense of relief because the new situation suddenly becomes clearer and easier to manage. However, people often discover precedents which really are not precedents at all. They recall past situations that they were able to manage and then define the new situation in a way which makes it seems similar to the past, comfortable situation. Through this process they often overlook important differences between the two.

Organisational choice-making situations are inherently complex and almost always ambiguous. They are simplified and sometimes distorted by characteristically human thought processes. They also are simplified and sometimes distorted by typical communication process. Members of organisations use communication in two primary ways in their attempts to manage ambiguity. First, they communicate to each other in order to structure, to make sense out of, new situations. They seek out information which will help them gain a perspective on the problem, and they seek out support from others which will confirm their interpretation, of the problem and strengthen their commitment to a particular course. In addition, they use communication in favour of a particular way of looking at the problem and in support of a preferred option. Through communication with other members of the organisation they are able to create a shared mutual understanding of what a problem is and how it should be addressed. If the information they gain through communication has been sufficient, relevant, and accurate, and if the shared perspective that they have created has been appropriate to the problem, communication will have improved their decision making.

But if the information gained has been inadequate in any significant way, or if the perspective that has been adopted by the people who were involved in the communication is flawed in any important respect, the availability of communication will have reduced the quality of the decision and further complicated choice making in the future. In the latter case, organisational communication has been used to reduce ambiguity artificially; it has not been used to manage ambiguity successfully. Sometimes processes of communication allow members of organisations to make foolish decisions and become comfortable with and strongly committed to them. In other instances communication allows members to make choices which satisfy their needs and the needs of their organisations. In some cases organisational communication even may provide the basis for making the best possible decisions. A variety of processes inevitably influences the potential effectiveness of the ambiguity-management function of organisational communication.

Communication fulfils three major functions in formal organisations—a command function, a relational function, and an ambiguity—management function. For any organisation to succeed, each of these functions must operate at or above some minimal level of effectiveness. For any individual members of an organisation to perform their roles successfully, they must be capable of using a variety of communication skills to issue effective commands and respond adequately to commands issued by others, to develop and sustain efficient working relationships, and to manage ambiguity strategically. However, some kinds of organisations are designed in ways which lead their members to rely most heavily on one of these three communication functions. Some organisations rely most heavily on the command function, others on the role of communication in the management of relationships, and others on the effective management of ambiguity.

Every organisation must have adequate command, relational and ambiguity managing communication. However, the relative importance of these three functions varies in the three different types of organisations. "Traditional" organisations, rely most heavily on the command function of communication and less heavily on the other two. Human relations and resources organisations depend on effective relational communication. Some versions of this type also rely heavily on the command function. In most versions the ambiguity-managing function has a limited role.

The final type, "systems-contingency" organisations, relies heavily on ambiguity-managing communication. In this type, relational and command functions, are important in some situations and less important to others. In fact, it is the assumption that command and relational communication must be combined in different proportions in different situations that distinguishes the systems-contingency type from the traditional and human relations and resources type.

The ideas of the German sociologist Max Weber have been an important part of the study of organisations for decades. In America

Weber is best known for his analysis of bureaucracy and bureaucratic organisations and for his discussion of the relationships between the characteristics of a culture and the uses of three different types of leadership-traditional, rational-legal, and charismatic authority. An equally important but less well-known component of Weber's work is the overall perspective that he took in studying organisations, the theory of "ideal types." This perspective rests on a particular set of assumptions about the nature of organisations and the appropriate means of studying them. His ideas provide a method through which employees can understand their organisations and make effective decisions about how to act on them. Weber's primary assumption was that organisations are composed of human actors who are enmeshed in independent activities and who continually are making decisions about how to act. Their choices are based on the meanings they attribute to the actions of others and on their interpretations of the organisational situations in which they are involved. When people enter formal organisations they bring with them a long history of monitoring their actions and the actions of others, of processing the information they obtain, and of choosing from among a number of options. People from a particular culture develop ways of monitoring perceiving, and acting which are very much like another. These perceptual "filters" are not identical, of course, because every individual has had unique experiences and has been part of a particular group of relationships with others. To some extent all members of a culture will have developed their own beliefs about what actions are "normal" and proper and about what meanings can be attached to different messages. However, within all this diversity and individuality lies a common core, a culture-bound framework for making sense out of people's actions and of deciding how to act in response. It is this common interpretive schema that defines a culture and distinguishes it from other cultures.

When employees from a particular culture come together within a formal organisation they bring with them a common way of interpreting and responding to one another. But once they come together, their interpretive frameworks begin to change in subtle but important ways. Human develop their interpretive frameworks through their experiences with other people. Relationships formed with people at work provide us with additional experience communicating with and making sense out of the communication of others. As a result, people drawn together in a formal organisation begin to form new "mini-cultures" at work. These new ways of interpreting and acting both retain the basic frame-work of the employees' general culture and reflect the more specific frameworks that develop through working relationships. The complicated interrelationship that exists between the broad patterns of action that characterise a society and the patterns that develop within an organisational "culture" was the basis of Weber's theory of ideal types.

Weber argued that researchers can understand organisations if they can understand how actors (employees) in them interpret their surroundings and choose among the wide variety of different courses of action that are available to them. The study of organisations should begin with careful observations of the choices that employees make. Eventually these observations will reveal that different groups of employees use different sense-making schemes. Researchers will begin to recognise that members of some organisations typically interpret and act in ways which are different from those in which people act in other organisations. At some point these observers will begin to construct mental images of organisations whose employees share the same basic interpretive frameworks.

For example, employees may perceive that their organisation is like an army—a formal structure with a clearly defined administrative staff which, for some as yet unexplained reasons, is obedient to commands issues by superiors. This type of organisation would function properly if it exhibited a number of necessary characteristics: each member of the staff occupies a specific position in the organisation which has been clearly defined, written duties and a clear place in the hierarchy of the organisation: each person knows who the supervisor is? who the subordinates are? and how each of them fits into the hierarchy of the organisation: each employee is selected on the basis of qualifications for the job, determined by some "objective" measure like educational background or a score on an examination; works under a contract which can be terminated if performance is inadequate; and can be promoted to a more responsible or higher paying position only on the basis of performance or seniority.

Of course, there may be no "real" organisation anywhere which has all these characteristics. Because this type of organisation is an abstraction, which represents the perceptions of a number of different groups of employees, it exists only in the mind of the observer; it is an "idealised" example of a particular "type" of organisation. It is an image of how a certain type of organisation should be designed and how it ought to operate, note a summary of the characteristics and operations of a group of real organisations. But these mental conceptions of ideal types can be useful for researchers. If researchers or managers or any other members of a real organisation understand how different types of organisations should be designed and operated, they can use that knowledge to detect and solve problems in their own organisation. To do so, they would examine their organisation, looking for features of its design or operation which do not correspond to the necessary features of the most relevant ideal type. Armed with perceptions of the essential features of a number of different types, the researcher or manager can discover cases in which the members of the organisation do not choose to act in the ways that are necessary for the organisation to function efficiently. Once these discrepancies are discovered the observer can make careful decisions about how to alter the organisation or change the conditions under which the members make decisions about how to act. When these changes are implemented, the real organisation will begin to operate more like the ideal type to which it is most closely related.

Unfortunately, these are very abstract ideas. A summary of them might increase their clarity. Weber's approach to the study of organisations rests on his theory of ideal types. It suggest that an observer can begin to understand how an organisation operates by attempting to understand how its members interpret and respond to the situations they face in the organisation. The observer then can design the organisation to increase the probability that its members will choose to act in precisely those ways that are in its best interests. Employees always will make their own decisions about how to act. They are human, and consequently they will continually be involved in observing, processing, and responding to their surroundings. But they make their choices based on their interpretations of the situations they face. Both their perceptions and many of the key characteristics of the situations they face can be created strategically through communication. However, appropriate situations can be created only if the people who design organisations know the elements that must be included. The search for these necessary features begins with the construction of a group of ideal types of organisations. Observers ask "What kinds of organisations do employees' interpretive frameworks suggest are possible?" and construct a list of features necessary for each of these "mythical" organisations to operate most efficiently. The most important features will involve the conditions under which employees will choose to initiate and limit their actions in desired ways. Among these necessary features will be certain characteristics of organisational communication. After observers have delineated the features of each ideal type of organisation, they can begin to examine existing organisations, searching for points at which the real organisations differ from the ideal type. If they can detect important differences and determine the reasons for them, they can begin to isolate problems in the real organisation and develop strategies for reducing them.

Of course, Weber assumed that most of the "observers" would be scholars involved in academic research. But his perspective can just as readily be used by employees. The social psychologist Fritz Heider once argued that human beings think like researchers think, that the same analytical tools that theorists use to understand the world around them can be used by other people to understand their environment and to decide how to act in the situations they face. Heider's notion that people are "naive theorists" suggest that all theoretical perspectives, of which

Weber's of ideal types is one, are based on our interpretations of reality and can be used by us to understand the realities that surround us. This assumption underlies the ideas that will be presented throughout the book. If readers can understand how communication functions in different types of organisations, they can examine their own organisations, determine how communication functions there, and choose the best communicative strategies for responding to the situations they face. Equipped with an understanding of how communication functions in different types of organisations and explanations of why communication functions differently in real organisations, readers can intelligently observe their own organisations and ask themselves these questions: how does communication operate in any organisation? How must people, including myself, act in order for this organisation to operate successfully? Why do they sometimes act in those ways and sometimes act differently? How can I act in order to make the organisation work more effectively and to make the greatest contribution to its success and to my advancement?

These are the kinds of questions. Weber suggested that researchers must ask; the questions provide the kind of information from organisational theory has made. More important, they are the kinds of questions that members of organisations must ask themselves before they can choose the best communication strategies to use in different organisational situations. Through understanding how different types of organisations operate and why a particular organisation functions differently, the "naive theorists" who make up an organisation can adopt the best available communication strategies.

Real Endeavour

For more than two thousand years communication scholars have argued that people communicate most effectively if they adopt the communication strategies that are most appropriate to the situations they face. Plato's intellectual rival, Gorgias, argued that knowing how to adapt to different situations was the only kind of knowledge that was available to human beings and, consequently, should be the focus of education. Some equivalent to Gorgias' concept of adaptation, an idea he labelled Kairos, has been important to the study of human communication since his time. Historically, training students in the art of adapting their communication to different situations has involved two steps: (1) teaching them to analyse the situations they face and choose the best strategies for those situations, and (2) equipping them with the repertoire of communication skills needed to implement those strategies. This book will concentrate on providing readers with the first kind of knowledge. It will examine the myriad of features which make up organisational situations, plan the kinds of communication in which employees must be competent, they and their organisations are to function effectively, describe the strategic through which they can gain the information necessary for them to adapt intelligently to the situation they face at work, and provide guidelines for choosing the optional communication strategies to use in those situation. Although it will discuss a variety of communication skills and suggest when and how those skills might be used by members of organisations, it will make no attempt to provide detailed training in the skills themselves.

17

International Scene

There is now an enormous amount of communication about communication-a literature which relates *inter alia* to cybernetics, neurology, linguistics, psychology, social anthropology, physics, group dynamics, semantics and the sociology of culture. We must also add library studies and documentation. The librarian is indirectly concerned with communication because his collections of material need to be organised for use, and until they are so organised an important agency in the communication process breaks down. The information role of the librarian involves him in the world of communications, and that is why students should study methods and types of communication. What follows is an outline of some communication problems, but I have been particularly concerned to make clear that the sphere of information is a limited one, whereas communication is basic to our culture in a different and more fundamental sense.

Journalism in the World

The ability to communicate is a key element in culture, and most living things have developed rudimentary methods of communication which include sound as well as visual display.

The communications of animals include cries, gestures and thumps which express simple responses to stimuli such as the mating call, or the alarm signal, or the warning display. The purpose has apparently gone beyond this stage of development and uses a language which linguists are trying to decipher. Claims are even made for the domestic fowl, which according to one authority, possesses an international 'language' made up of thirty basic sentences. The social insects such as the ants have communications systems, and the bees do their 'dance' to indicate the locations of a new source of nectar.

But non-human creatures have not evolved a formal language in the true sense, and it is this which in this context distinguishes them from humanity- In the beginning was the word. Apes possess several characteristics which are necessary for culture, such as the ability to walk and to use thumbs and vocal cords. In addition, their children mature slowly and they share with man the dubious blessing of a continuous sex urge. Indeed, sexual activity may well be the most basic of all forms of communication. The vast literature of sex probably owes its origins to the fact that sex relations represent an attempt at total communication, and an escape from isolation. Further more, sexual union exhibits one important characteristic of true communication insofar as it is, or should be, a two way process: to use the current jargon, feed-back occurs.

Hence the only valid objection to solitary masturbation as a practice is presumably that it excludes communication with others. McLuhan's otherwise dubious dictum that the medium is the massage is perhaps most applicable in this sphere. But to return to the animals, they cannot be said to possess true culture because they cannot symbolise, and the essence of human culture is accumulation-the retention and passing on of cultural manifestations from one generation to another. The extraordinary cries of birds, for example, can be recorded and even preserved in libraries, but this, of course, is for our benefit, not theirs.

Significance of Medium

It is established, then, that when homosapiens uttered his first words human culture really began, just as the child enters the cultural heritage when it begins to speak. But the original ,cause of spoken language is not known. Conflicting theories have been advanced and they are commonly and seriously known by fanciful names. The 'bow-wow' theory claims that men learnt speech by imitating animal cries. The 'pooh-Pooh' adherents believe that language developed as a result of involuntary noises provoked by violent stimuli, in contrast to the 'ding dong' people who propose that men must have imitated all kinds of noises in an onomatopoeic fashion. The 'yo-ho-ho' explanation is that men acquired speech to assist in co-operative labour, just as songs are used in the same manner today. Finally, other linguists have suggested that the first words were used to accompany gestures which must have long preceded speech.

Whatever the origins, we know that the languages of the world can be classified into families which were produced by the wandering of tribes and peoples. The resultant babble of tongues is one of the most obvious barriers to communication, when our earliest fore-fathers built the city and the tower of Babel, the people had one language and were therefore building a true community wherein 'nothing will be restrained from them which they have imagined to do'. But in developing their isolated city culture they were neglecting their global responsibilities as laid down, which required that they should be scattered abroad upon the face of all the earth. Accordingly, the Lord said "Go to, let us go down and there confound their language that they may not understand one another's speech." So the Lord scattered them abroad.

That was long ago, yet we are still confounded and are likely to remain so. The proposals for an international language (such as Esperanto) ignore cultural realities, particularly the fact that languages are not artificial creations but reflections of a way of life in time and place. The foreign language barrier is, of course, a great obstacle to all forms of international communication, and is felt so particularly in the field of scientific research where speed of communication is important.

There is in consequence a bibilographical problem with which we are not concerned here. What is more-relevant to our theme is the fact that obvious foreign language barriers may be less dangerous than the other divisive elements in culture mentioned elsewhere. In most countries people officially speak to write the same language as each other, but the use of language may vary so much that communication fails. Groups in one country often have more in common with groups in another country than with their own compatriots, in spite of the language complications.

After the invention of language the next step was the development of the ability to produce pictures to correspond with a thing described in words. Those symbols which literally represented things pictorially are called pictograms, whereas what is called ideogrammatic writing used symbols which indicate by association. The ancient Egyptian hieroglyphic contained both forms, and the Chinese language to this day is based on the dual principle. Such methods of writing have the advantage that they are 'international', in the sense that algebra or chemical formulae or musical scores are, but the corresponding disadvantage is that there is no link with words. It is an entirely visual medium-and those who used it had to learn two 'languages' which were not at all related. Modern scholars can decipher early pictorial languages, but they do not knew what they sounded like when 'read' aloud. If visual communication had remained pictorial, written languages would have remained separate from spoken languages and the latter would have succumbed to a proliferation of dialect and jargon. That is what happened in China.

The Egyptians hieroglyphics included some signs which represented sounds, but they did not develop a phonetic linear alphabet. This was the achievement of the Phoenicians, who produced a practical alphabet, the main limitation of which was that it contained no vowels. Modern sematic languages such as Hebrew also have this characteristic. The final development-that of providing vowels-was carried out by the 'Greeks, and the alphabet had by that time become substantially what it is now. Usage in the Western world was fixed by the Romans, who wrote horizontally from left to right in descending lines and used the letters which we still use,

The Technology

The fourth stage in the evolution of media was the invention in the fifteenth century of printing from movable type. It has remained the main medium of visual communication for the last 500 years. Its significance is too well known to warrant description. It is because of printing that the repository role of the library became so important, since libraries were able thus to accumulate culture. The role of the librarian is to make communication possible. In our time the mass media of communication are to some extent modifying the role of print.

So far we have been discussing what is mainly rational communication involving the conscious levels of the mind. There remain those regions where people communicate by means which involve other faculties and other types of perception. Some of these are still a matter for conjecture and dispute, so that I shall omit telepathic communication or psychic phenomena such as messages from beyond the grave or from supernatural beings. In any event, these are not normally considered to be part of a librarian's responsibility. It is however impossible to ignore the fact that, even though language or print may be used, messages are sometimes conveyed by indirect means, often in order to try to express the inexpressible. Thus the literary artist will use words to reflect a multiplicity of human experiences which has many levels and many meanings. This incorporates both the aesthetic sphere and the technique of suggestion used by the advertiser and the propagandist.

Social State of Affairs

Pre-literate communications were oral, and when human memory is the cultural connecting link we invariably find it impossible to distinguish between history and legend. Indeed history without written records it myth (unless it can be substantiated by precise archaeological research); who knows whether King Arthur ever did ride to Camelot? Having noted this it should be added that many myths have been explained in other ways without reference to history; they have been variously described as parables, allegories and early scientific theories. Fraud, basing his theory on the remarkable similarity of content in the myths and folk tales of the world, and on his analysis of individuals, claimed that myths are thinly disguised representations of unconscious fantasies common to all mankind, Lung carried this theory further with his concept of the collective or racial unconscious, which lies below the personal unconscious, and beyond this yet again the deepest levels common to all humanity. For him the collective unconscious is the deposit of ancestral experience for millions of years, and he calls certain themes which recur in dreams and in mythology 'archetypes'. The postulation of a collective unconscious seems to suggest that certain 'ideas' may be inherited, and it is not one which scientists will normally accept, but Lung's work has been influential and much of his terminology has passed into our culture.

The Preacher, then, apparently overstated his case when he asserted that 'There is no remembrance of the former generations, neither shall there be any remembrance of the latter generations that are to come, among those that shall come after'. But his words serve to remind us that those, who invented the alphabet also invented Time, which eventually became fully mechanised with the arrival of printing and with the invention of the clock. When this happened the old organic cycle of generation, birth, development and death lost its full meaning. Non -literate cultures do not have this impatient sense of time as duration.

As soon as we consider language as a medium of communication it becomes apparent that language and reality are not the samething. Language is not a mirror of experience, not even a destroying mirror, because it exists in its own right, and interacts with other social realities. A word is in fact a thing-in addition to being a symbol of some other thing. As Jesse Shera says (in

Documentation, p. 66) 'We do not know the effect of the symbolic structure that is language upon the behaviour patterns of society'.

We do know, however, that language can be used consciously or unconsciously to conceal objective truth. This is obvious enough in the case of detectable untruths, and psycho-analysis has made us all familiar with the processes of rationalisation by which individuals deceive others and, make particularly, themselves. If people are unable to communicate with one another, it emerges at once that language (or the thinking based upon it) serves many other purposes than external communication, and many of these purposes are either evil or supersitions. The word itself, as Ogden and Richards emphasised in 'The meaning of meaning, may gather round itself occult powers and the aura of taboos.' There have been many deities whose names are held to be unmentionable, and so on. As a thing the word is inevitably a conservative force, and produces a kind of cultural lags, because it reflects (insofar as it reflects at all) a reality which no longer exists. In a time-of rapid change, such as the present, this is one reason why the middle aged (*i.e.*, anyone over thirty) cannot understand the young-and why the young try to invent a new language.

It follows, therefore, that words are not labels but social tools, whose use and meaning depend on conventions which differ according to the class and group affiliations of individuals. If this relates to education at all it only does so insofar as the education structure may reflect (or modify) diverse social backgrounds. In fragmented societies there are various partially separate groups or subcultures who use language in a way which may not be comprehensible to other groups. For complete understanding, a community of experience and thought is required, and when this is absent we state literally that people 'are not speaking the same language', even though their vocabularies may be identical. It is the understanding which is lacking, and this is nothing to do with language as such. This is commonly appreciated with regard to conversation: many people, particularly those past middle age, either do not talk at all, or else rarely finish their sentences, because they have lost faith in language as a means of communication. The other groups have gone beyond the pale-and one group, or one individual (the 'outsider') or one class becomes culturally alienated. This overworked term (alienated) expresses a variety of meanings, but the common factor in all of them is a psychological condition produced by social isolation. Where no real community exists there can be (by definition) no communication, and alienation is therefore very relevant to communication problems.

The concept of cultural alienation as originally used by Marx, and before him by Hegel, Schiller and other German philosophical idealists, is worth a further note, since it is a part of Marxism which has become relevant at the present time and one which has brought about an attempt by some European Christian thinkers to continue a 'dialogue' with Marxism. According to Marx, man has become self-estranged, or dehumanised, or alienated, because what he produces becomes objectified-turned into a 'thing' or 'reified' as something separate from him which he can no longer control. Marx, at least in his early work, blamed Christianity for this process, because of its 'other worldly' nature and because of the emphasis on the individual which meant that collective social life was ignored. But ultimately and more particularly in his later work he regarded alienation as fundamentally economic in nature, "So that it could only be healed by political revolution. These ideas have been developed and modified in Sartre's influential Critique of dialectical reason, 1960, and, like many American writers also, Sartre automatically supports the 'anti-social' alienated individual (such as Genet), which the English tradition, as exemplified in Leavis, does not Raymond Williams, for example, has always stressed social values and his belief that alienation need not occur even now, and will be overcome in a return to a true socialist community.

It will be seen that the term 'alienation' as commonly used at present means something much less precise than this, and may simply refer to cultural or social fragmentation which results in separate sub-cultures, such as those of the teenagers, or the black

Americans, or the very-poor-or, in another sense, that of the intellectuals.

The use of language, then, rests on assumptions which are shared these are present in all of the members of a particular group. Since everyone belongs to some types of in-group, how can the influence of closed groups be modified or destroyed? Aranguren, in Human communication, p 140, suggests that this is the special social function of the intellectual: 'A intellectual is someone who is capable either of emerging from the social group to which he belongs or else of criticising it from within', This is way intellectuals are usually only partially dntegrated in society. At a further extreme, this is why, in Aldous Huxley's words in Literature and science, p 13. The elements of experience which are unique, aberrant, other than average remain outside the pale of common language.

It remains to note that in open or pluralistic, societies these groups are partly an abstraction, since individuals may belong to several different ones. But the result in cultural terms is the same, and from the point of view of the individual, conflicts between groups will naturally be reflected in his mind-which is not necessarily a bad thing, since it helps to ensure social progress.

Promotion of Science

Meredith, in Instruments of communication, stresses the social elements in scientific information work: 'Social communication among scientists is an essential condition of their work'. He claims further that because of the limitations of the printed word, it is more important in science to talk to people than to read books. Noting the traditional classical concept of oratorical argument where, because uncertainty prevails, emotive techniques can be used, he points out that there are not only depths of emotion which traditional rhetoric recognised, but also depths understanding which it failed to distinguish. It follows that communication problems are rooted in social and technical changes which go far beyond the realm of language studies. From the more narrow point of view of librarianship, the implications have been recognised by many of those engaged in the retrieval of scientific imformation. A number of investigations have indicated that scientists use information retrieval systems and library information service far less than might be expected, and that social factors are largely responsible.

There are, therefore, or there should be, as many types of spoken and written language as there are types of readers, and bad writing is simply that which is inappropriate for its purpose, and which fails in the full sharing of understanding. When one considers that the most effective means of communication in modern physics, for example, is often the use of mathematical symbols alone, but that the results of its researches must also be presented to the understanding of the layman; the extent of the problem becomes apparent. Kapp, in 'The presentation of technical information' has indicated the main difference between functional and other kinds of writing, by noting that a good functional style maintains receptivity in the reader: it should not be 'creative', since receptivity cannot be stored. But as far as scientific research or discovery is concerned, there is obviously a 'creative' element, which means that scientific activity is by no means as wholly objective as sometimes alleged. The creative aspect in science includes subjective insights, and in consequence there are often accidental features in research and discovery. The information scientists have also had to recognise this element, hence the increasing attention which has been paid to 'serendipity', or random selection.

Apart from these factors, language in itself often fails as an instrument of communication because of the rapidity of change. There is in fact a language crisis now, because the old association been words and the things they represent becomes impossible. The older use of language was much more rhetorical, in the sense of the word used above: this rhetoric may now hinder contact with 'reality', which, at least as far as the material world is concerned, is increasingly scientific.

Within the field of linguistics itself, a number of authorities have studied the fact that our thinking is determined by the structure of particular languages. This work has been particularly associated with the theories of B L Whorf, who, in Language, thought and reality, claims that language actually organises reality. According to Whorf, the world is presented in a kaleidoscope flux of impressions which has to be mentally organised-and this is done not by classification systems, but largely by the linguistic structures in our minds. The pattern of our language imposes an obligatory codification.

Negative Side

Increasing concern has been expressed in many quarters that an outstanding defect in modern cultures is a failure in communication. The proliferating literature on communication studies exhibits the same use of specialists' jargon, incomprehensible to the layman, which characterizes other specialist topics: the communicators are talking to themselves. Seligman's Encyclopedia of the social sciences defines communication as a 'network of partial or complete understandings' one might equally well substitute the word 'misunderstandings'. What follow is a discussion of some of the possible reasons for this relative failure.

Power of Information

The increase in the quantity of information (and the speed with which it appears) is the factor which most librarians think of which considering how to control the flood of publications by bibliographical and library means. The first problem is to ensure that relevant information gets to users at the right time. As is indicated in my book 'Bibliography and the provision of books,' these matters are fundamental to library and bibliographic organisation. The same figures are constantly repeated for the quantity of publications, with particular reference to science and its exponential rate of growth. One authority (Professor Price of Yale University) has pointed out there if the present rate continues, there will soon be more scientists than people; another has calculated that there are more scientists alive today than in the sum total of the past.

The answers to the explosion lie in the field of social and bibliographic organisation. Yet even if solutions on this level were to be found, there is no evidence that real communication would be achieved. The fact that information is emitted or disseminated, and even received, is no guarantee that communication occurs. The transmission in itself has no meaning, and the informatiom has to be deciphered and interpreted, and as a result it is frequently not understood. There are, in fact, more fundamental barriers to communication, some of which we have already noted in relation to language.

Within the field of information flow as a social process it is evident that a modern society requires a far-ranging network of communications in order to function at all. It is only to be expected, therefore, that information often fails to circulate. The apparatus of the welfare state, for example, is so complex that many citizens (particularly those who need the services most) are not aware what actual benefits they might receive. State agencies, and all organisations within the state, organise information services, and this is an essential element in management technique. As a social process the free flow of information is wholly dependent on the existence of free democratic (*i.e.*, politically unrestricted) institutions at all levels, and on the absence of censorship or authoritarian suppressions. It is possible to have a free flow of some types of information within particular organisations and still not have a free society, because there is some overall control. The growth in size of modern organisations, particularly those engaged in scientific research, may also produce, and indeed is producing, a situation where individuals work on a specialised job without knowing for what purpose their particular operation is intended, or what the complete venture is. This is a further example of the dehumanisation which can occur. It follows that a man may be working, could be working on some totally anti-human form of research without even being aware of the fact.

One response to this and similar problems is the current demand for 'participation' in all forms of social, political and economic life. This amounts to a claim that information itself is not enough and a consideration of it would take us beyond information as such, and into politics.

It was suggested above that the use of language is often inadequate because it no longer describes reality. This seems to be part of a trend which has many facets. In Kafka's nightmares, the main protagonists never discover what is happening or why. The 'theatre of the absurd' is truly absurd on one level at least, because nobody can communicate at all, and Becket's clowns and tramps are primarily studies in the manners of non communication. The key factor in modern developed society, as Herbert Marcuse constantly proclaims, is that social structures seem to be wholly rational but rebellious individuals instinctively feel that this rationality does not satisfy human needs. As Daniel Bell states in Technology and social change, edited by Eli Ginzberg, p 59, 'The whole breakdown of the rational cosmology is imminent and will ultimately create the most serious problems for society because of an alienation of the modes of perception about the world'. Society is unable to find cultural terms for expressing what is happening-and twentieth country thought lacks confidence in the rational solution of social and cultural problems.

The implication can only be that the 'rational solutions' are inadequate. Many radical critics would dispose of the matter in the traditional Marxist manner by pointing out that capitalist ideology inevitably obscures the real nature of society. (It should not be forgotten that the word 'ideology' means, or originally meant, a system of beliefs which does not explain, but explains away reality, just as rationalisation obscures reality for the individual.) If this is the case, as it certainly is in the USA, it is probably true in the USSR also, where the official ideology corresponds even less with life as it is experienced-and furthermore any attempts to modify radically this discrepancy cannot appear above ground.

There is therefore a blockage in the communication of ideas. Traditional political or religious faiths provided an analysis of social reality which *inter alia* explained how society (and the universe) was believed to work. At one time the Christians, and the Marxists, explained everything to the satisfaction of millions of adherents. Up to the end of the country even the scientists provided answers whose implications could be understood by everybody. The gods have failed now because their analysis is irrelevant, and in consequence their panaceas do not help. As McLuhan has claimed, the overworked concept that God is dead really refers to the Newtonian universe that has passed away, and the ground rule upon which so much of the Western World is built is dissolved. Because of this we cannot control events, and 'nobody knows what is happening.' (Harrington deals with this at length and that is why he calls his book on our times the accidental century.) In many spheres where ideas are important, few people have anything valid to say, and for this and other reasons we stop listening to the message and there is a widespread growth of disbelief, scepticism and negative criticism but leaders seem to be more in the dark than anybody else, illustrating in a new guise Acton's dictum that power corrupts. A Bob Dylan has it, 'Something is happening but you don't know what it is-do you Mr. Jones?'

It is most noticeable in the case of the revolting young that they tend to use terminology-for example anti-capitalist slogans-which does not really express what they are trying to say. They are grouping towards a new language-a true communication-but, meanwhile, in adequate slogans from the past must serve. The millions of young people who stick a poster of the Guevera on their wall do not share either his beliefs or his language. Most of them are aware of this circumstance: they are also very conscious that there is this need for true communication, and the leaders of the pop world like the Beatles have frequently said so. This is why the trends in clothes and long hair are to them so important: they are fundamentally methods of communication. There is a Beatles song called 'All you need is love', which on the face of it is a banal and puerile statement, but they are not simply referring to the usual commercial concept at all. Sex as a basic form of communication was discussed above. On another level it is beyond doubt that without love, in the sense used by most of the great religious leaders, true human communication is impossible. If society as it exists does not allow for this act of communication, either because the structure is wrong or because of social injustice or because there is no freedom to express opinions, then the social consequences will be revolutionary.

The trumpet calls for human solidarity are based on a recognition of this, but what usually happens in practice is that the kind of solidarity which is based on human love only occurs temporarily within small groups (opposed to other groups), or where societies are at war or in times of revolution and crisis. Or else these human needs are perverted and rendered evil by false prophets like Hitler, who must base their movements on error. This brings us back to those radical opposition movements which fundamentally reject modern societies, since what they are fighting is hypocrisy in all its forms: where untruth prevails, communication breaks down. That is why this chapter is not about technical processes such as 'positive and negative feedback loops'. All the loops in the world cannot obliterate fabrication.

Case Study

The history of the press is at the same time a reflection of political history. Journalists are the chroniclers of their age and the results of their labours, the newspapers, reveal what problems confronted the different epochs in a nation's history.

Germany is the mother country of the modern press. It is true that other countries made attempts to provide information for the' population by means of periodic announcements on the part of the state or the state authorities. This was the case for instance in ancient China, where an official journal was published, being printed by the woodcut method. The official journal appeared from the ninth century onwards under the name of King-Po, and in the course of centuries, with a succession of titles, it developed into the precursor of the later official imperial gazette in the Celestial Empire. Before the Chinese however the Romans had also found ways and means of providing the population with information on the affairs of state in a kind of prejournalistic publication. This was the daily gazette which was published by

Caesar under the title of Acta Diurna making public the decrees of the Roman authorities around about the middle of the first century before Christ.

German Press

The modern press, which originated in Germany, could not really have been created anywhere else than in the land of Gutenberg.

Gutenberg was the first person in Europe to invent movable type and is thus the father of the modern art of printing, the black art, the art which is concerned with the colour black which has become the symbol not only of journalism but of the entire modern age. Gutenberg might however also justifiably be called the father of journalism. His efforts to create an instrument for circulating news rapidly and simultaneously in many areas corresponded even in those days to the journalistic flair which in Gutenberg was combined with the boldness of the inventor and the precision of the scientist. Gutenberg's name is closely connected with the German city of Mainz. "Golden Mainz" (the name which the first arcbbishopric of the Holy Roman Empire bore for centuries, just as Cologne for instance was known as "Holy Cologne" was Gutenberg's birthplace.

Gutenberg's real name was Henne Gausfleisc zu Laden, but he became more well-known under the name of Johannes Gutenberg. In the year 1854 his 42-line Bible appeard for the first time. Many copies of the Holy Scriptures, previously written out laboriously by hand on parchment by the monks, could now be circulated among the people. The art of printing with movable type, invented and perfected by Gutenberg in the space of about a decade, began its triumphant progress throughout the world.

The man whose invention of printing gave the entire 'population access to learning and knowledge, which bad hitherto been confined to the privileged wealthy few, did not however get any thanks for his invention. In order to perfect his printing machine he was forced to borrow money from a wealthy citizen of Mainz, Fust by name. Round about 1447 appeard the first Gutenberg publication, period at his parents' house, the name of which was "zum Gutenberg", and it was by this name that Henne or Johanes Gansfleisch was later known. This publication was a minor epic work by some contemporary, known as the Weltgerichts-gedicht (The poem of the universal court). A year later appeared the "Calender for 1448". But people did not yet display much interest for the new technique.

This did not happen until the printer came out with the idea of publishing the Bible. Now people in Mainz began to prick up their ears. The above-mentioned Fust lent Gutenberg so much money that after the publication of the work, on which Gutenberg had laboured for two years or so, that entire inventory of the Gutenberg printing works belonged to him. Fust later went into partnership with another wealthy burgher and created the Fust-Schoffersche Press. The inventor of printing however lived a hand-to-mouth existence. Relatives supported him and enabled him later to bring out smaller publications now and again. Thus the Catholicon which appeared in 1465, was probably printed in his workshop. Today no one knows where this was situated. The Bible was printed in living quarters where Gutenberg had some time before established a workshop, in the house "zum Humbrecht", a building which today in Number 18/20 in the "Schustergasse".

The Archbishop Adolf von completely impoverished inventor gave Gutenberg a place in his him by means of this board death. Nassau took pity on the in his old age. In 1465 he household, thus preserving and lodging from certain.

Later generations desired to make good the neglect which Gutenberg suffered at the hands of his contemporaries in Mainz. In 1837 Maim; erected a fine Gutenberg Memorial, designed by Thorwaldsen. The inscription-on the memorial reads:

Artem quae Graecos latuit latuitque Latinos Germani sollers extudit ingenium. Nunc quidquid veteres sapiunt sapiuntque recentes, Non sibi, sed populis omnibus id sapiunt. (The art which remained concealed from the Greeks and Romans Was brought to light by the inventive genius of a German. Now the knowledge of ancients and moderns is not confined to Them alone, but known to all the nations of the world.)

The Gutenberg Museum established at Mainz in 1900 and the Gutenberg Society set up in 1901 have kept alive the memory of one of the greatest inventors of all time.

The man who received such honour at the hand; of later generations died in 1467 or 1468; the exact date is not known. He was buried in the Franciscan Church, which was demolished in 1742. There is nothing to recall the last resting place of this great citizen of Mainz. With his invention he heralded the dawn of a modern age, and set in motion the mechanism that was to cause an intellectual awakening. In the same period, by some strange whim of fate an unknown man in far-away Korea was using movable copper type for making reproductions. In the Far East no one took any notice of this invention. Within a century however it altered the entire social and intellectual face of Europe, making education and culture the common property of all men.

One of the historians of the German press, Robertrot who published his Geschichte des deutschen Journalismus (History of German Journalism) in 1845, rapturously described journalism as the highest form of Gutenberg's art Journalism is the most perfect use to which Gutenberg's invention could be put; it is, so to speak, the press in its, most concentrated form the energetic quintessence and embodiment of all the effects produced by the art of printing.

The newspaper which appears regularly every day with the daily news have various names in different languages, which point to its characteristic features. In German the daily paper is called "Zeitung". In the fourteenth century this word was written as "Zitunge", a form which originated in Central and South Germany. The word "Zeitung" originally meant nothing else than "news". Thus the first journals, flysheets and pamphlets, which were only produced in connection with some specific event, were called "Neue Zeitungen" (or "Newe Zytungen" in the spelling of that period), meaning the "Latest news". The oldest printed work still in existence is a NeweZytung von orient und auff gange (Latest News from the Orient and the East), from the year 1502. Pamphlets of this kind were however already appearing in Germany in the last decades of the fifteenth century.

In time there also appeared what were known as serial issues of newspapers, dealing with a major political event il1 two or three issues. This scheme was also frequently employed for announcing some military event or other, an imperial proclamation or an event of religious and political significance.

As well as these serial issues there were also the so-called Messrelationen, published quarterly or monthly at the time of the Spring and Autumn Trade Fairs in Frankfurt-on-Main by the historian Michael von Aitzing at Cologne. These Messrelationen, journals which gave information about the trade fairs, may be described as the precursors of economic periodicals and also of political journals. Experts on the history of the press are not absolutely certain of the publication date of the first newspaper to conform more or less with the modern definition of "mass medium". Some take the view that it was the Historische Relation, printed by Samuel Dilbaum of Augsburg, and published by Leonhard Straub at Rorschach. A complete annual volume of this monthly journal from the year 1597 is still in existence. At that time, however, several journals must already have been appearing regularly. In 1587 for instance there was already a periodical with the following title: Newe Zeittung/Warhafftiger Bericht aus Nurnberg an einen guten Freundt geschrieben/was sich im Monat April dieses 1587. Jahrs zugetragen und begeben (Latest news/ Accurate report from Nuremberg, written to a good friend of the events and happenings in the month of April in this year of 1587.) Some German researchers cautiously describe these monthly journals as the forerunners of the weekly periodicals. The newspaper expert Professor Hans A Munster for instance has the following to say in an article entitled "The oldest Periodical Newspaper and Review" (Die alteste periodische Zeitung and

Schrift), which appeared in the monthly Die Deutsche Zeitung, Bielefeld, July 1953:

> 'There is thus nothing new in describing the old monthly reviews as the "oldest periodicals", and certainly there are good grounds for this assumption. For the longer gap between dates of publication in the case of monthlies as compared with weeklies is after all not a fundamental difference but only a relative one. The step forward from the "Newe Zytungen", which did not appear regularly, to the periodicals was taken by the publication of either the monthly reviews (in 1587 and 1597 respectively, or the "Messrelationen" (in 1588).

Most historians of press history however hold the opinion ,that the year 1609 is of special significance for the development of the press and that it was in this year that really modern newspapers came into existence. In 1609, for the first time, there appeared two weekly papers, and the complete annual volumes of them both are still in existence. These two papers were called Relation and Aviso respectively.

It is likely that the Relation was published at Strassbourg. It is a rather more Protestant journal, which made available information on political and economic affairs to readers in the former German imperial city. The full title of the journal was as follows: Aller Furnemmen und gedenckwurdigen Historien/so sich hin und wider in Hoch und Nieder Teutschland/auch in Franckreich/ftalian/Scbott and England/Hispanien/Hungern/Polen/Siebenburgen/Wallachey/Moldaw/Turckeyetc. Inn diesem 1609. Jahr verlauffen und zugetragen mochte. Alles auf das trewlichs wie ich solche bekommen und zu wegen bringen magjln Truck verfertigen will. (An account of all undertakings and noteworthy events/occurring in Upper and Lower Germany/as well as France/Italy/Scotland and England/Spain/Hungary/Poland Transylvania/Wallachia/Moldavia/Turkey/etc., in the year 1609. Everything having been edited and printed exactly in accordance with the news items as they came in.)

The geograpbical origin of the news items printed in the second newspaper, the Aviso, already reveals a bias towards American and Asiatic countries. The name of this periodical with the characteristic heading and long-winded title corresponding to the fashion of the time reveal the still close relationship of the periodical with the book. The full title was as follows: Relation oder Zeitung. Was sich begeben and zugetragen hat/in Deutsch: und Welschland/Spanien/Nieder landtjEngelland/Franckreich, Ungern, Oesterreich, Schweden, Polen und in allen Provintzen/ in Ost: und West Indian etc. So allhie den... angelangt. Gedruckt im Jahre 1609. (Journal or newspaper. The events and happenings in Germany and Italy/Spain/The Neitherlands/England/France/ Hungary/Austria/Sweden/Poland/and in all the provinces/in the East and West Indies etc. All items printed as they arrived, in the year 1609).

It has still not been definitely established where the journal was printed. It might have been Augsburg, but Nuremberg is also a possibility, while there are various reasons that would appear to suggest Wolfenbuttel as its source.

The significant thing about these newspapers was not that they attracted a large circle of readers but that were read by a small class of politically and economically important persons who now suddenly received regular information from a news paper. This then was the birth of the political press, i.e. the press of modern times.

Between 1618 and 1648 there appeared various new pamphlets, which for the next few years proved something of an obstacle to the development of periodicals. All the same, it was precisely in this early period that well-known publishers such as Andreas Aperger of Augsburg developed into prominent newspaper publishers.

Newspaper history reveals that the towns where there newspapers originated were not the political centres but the' famous merchants cities of the Holy Roman Empire. Thus an important weekly paper was published at Frankfurt-on-Main as early as 1615, while by 1617 this city already had two weekly competitors.

During the Thirty Years War a forerunner of the press in our own century appeared at Magdeburg; it was published in, 1664 by what afterwards became the Muller-Faber publishing house, later developing into the Magdeburger Zeitung which is published in the Federal Republic of Germany today; this newspaper is read in exile by the citizens of Magdeburg who have fled from the Soviet Zone.

During the sixteenth century a number of German book printers emigrated to other countries and, just as they had already been doing in isolated places for a century, disseminated the art of Gutenberg to an ever growing extent beyond the boundaries of the Holy Roman Empire. The first forerunners of the French newspapers developed as early as 163 Land some time later the first papers were also published in England. From the very beginning the English papers differed considerably from the continental ones in that they revealed differences of opinion, whereas the French government had some control over newspaper policy right from the start. The German press however reflected the attitude of the various German princedoms.

One of the old trade centres was Leipzig, the city where the traditional Leipzig Trade Fair is held. This city can claim to have published the first daily newspaper of modern times. The Leipzig daily newspaper appeared on I January 1660 with the following title: Neu einlauffende Nachbricht van Kriegs-und Welt-Handeln, (The latest news of events from the military and commercial sphers.)

A feature of the seventeenth century is the establishment of various prominent newspapers and journals, for instance the Frankische Kurier in 1673, or the Jenaische zeitung in 1674. The first German learned periodical appeared in 1682, entitled Acta Eruditorum. Six years later there also appeared the first learned periodical printed in German: Schertz-und ernsthaffter Gedanken uber allerband nutzliche Bucher und Fragen... (Humorous and serious thoughts on diverse books and questions, both amusing and instructive).

In 1693 we find a monthly journal appearing in Jena with the following title: Monatlich mutzspielende Lustfragen zu Gelehrter und Ungelehrter sonderbarer Ergetzung. (A monthly review of useful humorous matters for the amusement of scholars and others. This journal is a forerunner of the type known as "moralist weeklies", established for the political and moral instruction and enlightenment of society, which originated in Germany in the year 1713. The first genuine moralist weekly to appear in Germany was Der Vernunfller (The Sophist) in Hamburg. In 1725, with the publication of the weekly journal Die vernunfligen Tadlerinnen (The judicious-Faultfinders) which appeared in various places, such as Halle Leipzig and finally Humburg, the writer Gottsched bestowed a certain measure of fame on these moralist weeklies in Germany and the rest of the world. The journals themselves are based on English models, Defoe, Steele and Addison having. become models for German journalists. Already the press was growing aware of its international significance.

The beginning of the eighteenth century also saw the birth of the intellectual reviews which were to have such a stimulating effect on intellectual life in Germany. In the year 1703 the famous Wiennerische Diarium appeared, a review which still appears today under the same title, and is the doyen of all publications of this nature in the German-speaking world.

Another new type of publication were the so-called' "privileged journals". In 1740 the Koniglich privilegierte Nachrichten von Staats und Gelehrtensachen (Journal of affairs of state and scholarship, under royal patronage) appeared in Prussia. The King himself, Frederick the Great, was responsible for its publication. Later, as the Haude Spenersche Zeitung, this newspaper was to represent the old middle classes of Berlin. There was however an even earlier forerunner of these "privileged journals". A weekly periodical published in Berlin from 1691 onwards, called Allergnadigst privilegierte Curiosen Natur-, Kunst-, Staats und Sittenprasenten erster Jahrgang durch R. Oelven zum Nutzen und Ergotzen. (The first and annual volume of curious events from the realms of science, art, politics, and morals, published by R. Oelpen for the instruction and amusement of all).

In this period Frederick the Great, who was rebelling against the Empress Maria Theresia, founded the forerunner of what was later called the Schlesische Zeitung; it appeared in 1741 in the German city of Breslau, entitled Schlesisch privillegierte Staats-, Kriegs- und Friendenszeitung (Silesia, journal of state, war and peace, under royal patronage). Today the Schlesische Zeitung is read by all the German Silesians who were expelled from their homeland and do not forget Breslau or other towns in the territory of Eastern Germany.

One could compile a long chronological table giving the most important dates of foundation for German newspapers.

The most significant names to appear are the forerunners of the Bremer Nachrichten (1743), the Braunschweigische Zeitung (1744), the Saarbrucker Zeitung (1761), the Anhalter Anzeiger (1763), the Kolnische Zeitung (1763), the Elbinger Zeitung (1789), the Vogtlandische Anzeiger and Tagesblatt (1789) and the Geraer Zeitung (1795).

The seventeenth and eighteenth centuries thus displayed a welcome degree of initiative in the sphere of the press. At the same time however the newspapers were not without their critics. At Leipzig, as for back as 1672, Professor Otto Mencke had introduced a kind of historical and political study of the press into the university syllabus. Some years later Ahasver Fritsch published the first learned work on the press: Discursus de Novellarum quas vacant Neue Zeitunge Hodierno usu et abusu (Discourse on the Present Day Uses and Abuses of the Publications Known as Newspapers), which appeared at Jena in 1676. In the same year Christian Weise followed with a similar work. In 1679 Johann Ludwig Hartmann had a book published under the title of Unzeitige Neue Zeitungssucht. (Untimely Passion for Newspapers). This look is the first learned work on the press published in German.

Leipzig was also to be the place where the first treatise of the press was published. It was written by Tobias Beucer in 1698 and entitled De Relationibus Novellis (On Newspapers). Hamburg followed in 1695 with Kasper Stieler's Zeitungs Lust und Nutz (Amusement and Instruction from Newspapers), while in the same year the first treatise on press law, entitled Jus Novellarum was published by Friedrich Hagen at the University of Kiel. Thus the outlines for newspaper and press research were marked out. When Johnn Peter von Leipzig began to lecture on "The uses and abuses of newspapers" at the newly founded University of Halle in the year 1698, the study of the press bad already become a field of research taken for granted at the universities. It is astonishing bow the world of learning subjected the mass media to critical scrutiny during the seventeenth century revealing an admirable and instinctive awareness of the danger and advantages of the press.

During the reign of Frederick the Great, the government of Prussia as it was then was liberal and tolerant in its treatment of the press. This factor also had a decisive influence on neighbouring regions. Until the seventeenth and eighteenth centuries German journalism, that is to say the press in German speaking countries, had been the province of anonymous writers. Of course, as has already been mentioned there were a number of prominent writers contributing to journals of a high standard. But the type of journalist able to achieve a certain amount of power and consequently exercise a considerable influence on public opinion does not appear until later on in the eighteenth century.

Mention should be made here in particular of the statesman and writer Justus Moser (1720-1794), who published a journal called the Wochentlicbe Osnabruckische Anzeigen (1766-1782), which represented a note-worthy achievement in the field of journalism. Another scholar who combined a statesman like insight with a flair for journalism was August Ludwig von Schlozer (1735-1809), who was active in the field of journalism as Gottingen, his more important publication being the Staats-anzeigen (1783-1794), which provided information on events in Europe at that time and the rest of the world. The journalist

Friedrich Karl Freiherr von Moser (I723-1798) was active during the same period. In annual volumes entitled Patriotisches Archiv fur Deutschland, published from 1784 to 1790 and from 1792 to 1794, he created a unique documentation worthy to rank alongside the periodical documentary works of our time.

Similar to the link with politics, journalism was also even more intimately connected with art. The great writer Gottfried Ephraim Lessing, the German herald of tolerance, was for a period .of hour years literary editor of the Vossische Zeitung (1751-1755). During this time he created a critical journal that betrays the pen of the gifted writer that he was. Another writer Matthias Claudius (1740-1745), the editor of the Wandsbecker Boten (from 1751 to 1755), published a critical journal whose attractive style and responsible tone earned it a reputation that extended far beyond the local region and gained it subscribers all over Germany. Another of these prominent journalists was Wieland (1733-1813), who published a journal chiefly devoted to literary matters, whose political significance however cannot be overestimated; this was the Teutsche Merkur (1773-1810). The gifted but ill-starred Heinrich von Kleist (1777-1811) was publisher and editor of the Berliner Abendblatter (1810-1811). At the moment when Napoleon was taking steps to crush the press, Kleist was bold enough to show the nation, cautiously and cleverly, that national dignity and national aims were still possible. He was one of the German who fought against dictatorship and oppression. The Swabian Christian Friedrich Daniel Schubart (1739-1791) founded the Deutsche Chcronik (which appeared in Augsburg in 1794, in Vim from 1774 to 1777 and in Stuttgart from 1787 to 1791). In these journals we find over and over again a harmonious blend of revolutionary poetic enthusiasm and the prudence of journalists with a critical turn of mind. Other great journalists of the period were Ludwig Weckherlin (1739 to 1792), Moritz Flavius Trenck von Tonder 1746-1810) and Arnold M allinckrodt (1767-1825). It was the latter's dream, even in those days, that one day there might be a united Europe.

Apart from art, the book trade too now tried to establish -

closer links with press. Particular mention should be made ,here of Johann Friedrich Cotta (1764-1832) and Friedrich Perthes (1772-1843). During the period of Napoleon's despotism Johann Josef Gones (1776-1848) was the most prominent ;figure in German journalism to join in the national struggle, with his outstanding periodical the Rheinischer Merkur (1814-1816). The Rheinischer Merkur's contribution to the resistance against Napoleon and to the efforts at reviving the Empire was so substantial that the mighty despot regarded it as a kind of fifth columnist movement.

After Napoleon, Europe was the realm of experiment for journalists who either on a national or a European basis proclaimed their desire for one great state of Europe united in the brotherhood of nations. Here one should note the journalistic efforts of Johann Georg August Wirth (I798-1898), the publisher of the Deutsche Tribune (1 July-18 December 1831 at Munich, and until 18 March 1832 at Homburg).

In the struggle against Napoleon and in the post Napoleonic era there appeared a new phenomenon in the world of journalism: the party press. Journals advocating a particular idea or policy were founded in that period, and the birth of the party press represents at the same time the birth of public opinion in the party political sense. The newspapers claimed to be liberal, but had a general moral, Catholic or Protestant bias, so that their readers were always groups linked by denominational or political connections. These newspapers in the first half of the nineteenth century are regarded by the German political press of today as their legitimate predecessors.

The nineteenth century however also witnessed another phenomenon in the sphere of journalism the birth of the popular press. Even in those days the popular press employed telegraphic communications, receiving news from the telegrafic agencies and news services. In the year 1849 the Wolff Telegraphic Agency was established in Berlin. This is the oldest modern news agency in the world.

It was in Germany, the traditional home of the "Relationen" and trade fair journals, that one of the largest and most important news agencies in the world commenced its activities: Reuter's was set up two years after the establishment of the Wolff Telegraphic Agency. We know the exact dates of its foundation On 22 April 1850 the newspaper correspondent Julius Reuter arrived at Aachen, where he was met by the brewery and distillery owner Heinrich Geller. This Heinrich Geller owned one of the largest earlier-pigeon lofts in the old imperial city of Aachen. The two men diliberated for two days, and then, on the 24 April, they signed a contract providing for Reuter to establish a carrier-pigeon post for the conveyance of all kinds of news. This contract of 24 April represents the birth of a world enterprise which became a by word in the field of journalism. The first carrier-pigeons were dispatched on 27 April. Important items of news-particularly stock exchange quotations -were often reported in other places one or two days quicker than by conventional methods. A year later the great firm of Reuter's as Aachen, with its first branch at Verviers and connections with of the chief cities of Europe, had achieved such a reputation that it transferred its headquarters to London, the capital of the British Empire. There is 1865, Reuter's Institute, which had meanwhile expanded into an international undertaking, was converted into a limited company. Paul Julius Reuter, born at Kassel in 1821, died at Nice in 1899, having been created a baron by the Duke of Coburg-Gotha in the year 1871. Possessing German and British nationality, and at home too in France and Italy Reuter represented a considerable section of European thinking in the nineteenth century.

The nineteenth century was equally mindful of technical progress as well as intellectual activity. Thus in the year 1811 Friedrich Konig patented his invention of the mecbanical press. In 1814 this mechanical press was employed for the first time in the printing of a newspaper: The Times of London. The first newspaper on the European continuant to introduce the new invention in its printing house was the Haude-Spenersche Zeitung in Berlin, but this was not until 1823.

The result was that in 1824 the Haude-Spenersche Zeitung and the Vossische Zeitung in Berlin began to appear daily.

Stereotype offset was invented in the year 1829, and this invention acquired particular significance in 1872 with the construction of the first German rotary press at Augsburg. Then, in 1852, the German teacher Philipp Reis demonstrated the first telephone, an invention which was just as important as that of Daguerre, who invented the process of photography in the years 1837-38.

The circulation of the popular press received a further impetus through the reduction in price that resulted from a new paper manufacturing process. Then, in 1880, Georg Meisenbach made it possible for photographs to be reproduced on newspapers with the aid of autotype. In 1884 the typesetting machine was invented by Ottmar Mergenthaler, who how had just emigrated to America, but such machines were not constructed and employed in Germany until 1896.

The 1920's saw the development of radio as a rival to the press. The first German radio company was established in 1923. A few years later Herman Tolle broadcast from Cologne the first spoken radio commentary and the first leading article on German radio. The first radio pictures appeared in 1927.

The popular press is noncommittal in tone. It does not represent any definite polical point of view, but is for the most part only interested in increasing its readership by pandering to the popular taste. A typical example of a nonpolitical newspaper of this kind was the Tagliche Rundschau in Berlin. This publication was strictly non-party. It made its first appearance on September 1881, presenting itself as a "newspaper for nonpoliticians, as well as a supplement to the political organs of all the parties." In the year 1884 it described its functions as being a "newspaper for non-political politics". Its slogan, as declared in leading articles and other publications, was to provide happiness and harmonious griety for all.

To some extent it was a newspaper apart, for unlike other papers it claimed to be political without supporting any particular policy. Later however it modified its point of view a little, tending more in the direction of the National Liberal Party.

It is interesting for historians of the press to know that the first official organ published by the Sovier military authorities in the occupied zone of Central Germany bore the name Tagliche Rundschau. However the former non-political Tagliche Rundschau was published in the early years of the Bismarck state at a time when even a harmless family gossip magazine like the Gartenlaube could appear; whereas the Tagliche Rundschau published by the Soviet authorities commenced an extreme policy of communist indoctrination.

Here we may be permitted to look back for a moment. In the era of the popular press the "General an zeiger" also played a prominent part. This type of newspaper claimed to be more serious than the average popular paper, but still tried rather to gained the non-political section of the population as its readers. The leading promoter of this type of newspaper was Josef La Rouelle, who experimented with publications at Aachen in 1871 and Cologne in 1875, before publishing his Billigste Zeitung fur Arm und Reich (Cheapest newspaper for rich and poor) in 1882, thus producing a genuine type of "Generalanzeiger". Hermann Minjon was active in Frankfurt, while the name of August Scherl is eternally linked with the history of the Berlin press. Other men prominent in the general advertiser press were W. Girardet and August Huck.

German newspapers were particularly active in the political sphere, whatever their political tendencies. Shortly before the First World War there were around 532 Conservative and Free Conservative newspapers, 509 National Liberal and Radical Democratic papers, 419 newspapers supporting the party of the Catholic Centre and 85 Socialist newspapers, plus 61 publications representing the Polish, Danish and other minorities. As opposed to this number there were a total of 1,621 non-party newspapers.

In 1932 the numbers were approximately as follows:

596 newspapers supporting the Centre and Bavarian People's Party,

197 supporting the German Social Democrat Party,

121 supporting the National Socialist German Worker's Party,
81 supporting the German National People's Party,
50 supporting the Communist Party,
14 supporting the People's Party,
11 supporting the Economic Party,
8 supporting the German State Party.

Another analysis presents the following picture: 562 newspapers advocating more conservative views, 363 with progressive middle-class views, 64 with more liberal views, 58 with liberal-democratic views, 19 with progressive republican views, and 9 with general socialist views, while 1,814 papers claimed to be independent; 123 newspapers advocated varying policies, and 337 made no declaration of their views at all.

The long list of newspapers existing at that time, many of which were what was known as "Kopfzeitungen", *i.e.*, the political section on the first two pages was often taken over on matrices from a larger newspaper) presents a colourful and varied mixture a new and decisive event however was soon to compel the German press to take on a more gloomy and monotonous appearance.

On 30 January 1933 Hitler book office as Chancellor, and it did not take long before he usurped sole power in his position as Fuhrer and Chancellor, brusquely ignoring the promises he had given to the nation about allowing it the opportunity to criticise his policies at regular intervals. Dictatorship and dictators always proceed in accordance with a similar scheme. This period when the German press was in fetters has recently been the subject of particular study in quite a number of publications. General surveys have appeared of the process of concentration, throwing light on the National Socialists' control of the press. By the end of the Third Reich this process had led to 80 per cent of the newspapers and journals which appeared in Germany being in the possession of the party-owed Eranz Eher- Verlag at Munich. Today it requires considerable effort to get a clear picture of the mass of legislative and other measures taken by the National Socialists against the independent press in Germany. The result however was plain:

the elimination of serious criticism. Apart from the Minister of Propaganda, Goebbels, the leading figure in the compaign to bring the press into line was Max Amann, director of the Eber-Verlag; in his capacity as representative of his party he brutally expropriated leading publishing firms and brought them under the control of his own giant publishing house. The press policy commenced in 1934, when the Ullstein house was transferred into the hands of the National Socialists, and continued until 1944, when Hugenberg's Scherlverlag was taken over. The National Socialists' Pravda was the Volkischer Beobachter. This newspaper had its origin in the Munchener Beobachter, founded in I887, appearing for the first time under its title Volkischer Beobachter on 9 August 1919. This was the beginning of a troubled period of German history.

This period of German history has however been consistently continued in one part of Germany which is not yet free. This is the case in the Soviet-occupied Zone of Germany, which with a conscious debasement of political terminology has given itself the title of "German Democratic Republic". The Communist and National Socialist ideologies, based on the same intellectual source, *viz.*, a false interpretation of Hegelian philosophy, pursued the same policy in regard to the press, just as they also seized power in the same way. Their newspaper often bear epithets such as "free" or "national", or have tities like "die Wahrheit" ("The Truth"). But their newspapers are not intended to serve any human values, but simply and solely the aims of one party, a despotism represented by a minority in control of the state. The press in. the Soviet Zone following Lenin's oft-quoted dictum, which applies today as much as it ever did, gave itself the task of "being not only a collective propagandist and a collective agitator, but also a collective organizer." True to this formula the Soviet Zone press has agitated, organized and spread party propaganda in accordance with the example of the Soviet press. It praised Stalin extravagantly. And the same men and the same pens were just as indignant in their criticism of Stalin when the Party came out wita its condemnation of the men without whom three decades of Communist history would be unthinkable. It also criticized Krushchev in exactly the same way, in accordance with its instructions.

The only criticism against measures taken by the authorities and the Party in a communist state is found in "readers" letters'. The situation is exactly the same in the Soviet Zone as in other communist countries, as the London Times wrote of Isvestia on 24 February 1965 in a series of articles entitled "Newspapers of the World":

> "In a communist country a letter to the editor is one of the few channels open to the individual to appeal against injustice and bureaucracy."

In the postwar period the press has experienced a great change in what is today the Federal Republic of Germany. After the end of the Second World War the press, which until then had been controlled by the National Socialists, virtually ceased to exist. At first the occupying powers published their own newspapers, and later gave certain persons licenses to publish newspapers and magazines. In the American and French Zones members of the different parties combined to publish independent newspapers, whereas in the British Zone the preference was given to a definite party press system. In the same way the Soviets favoured a party press system in their zone of occupation-the communist press and the so-called "middle-class press", which is subject to communist pressure. The existence of the latter is intended to lead the rest of the world to believe that the press supports different political parties in the Sovietoccupied Zone. The licensed press continued until 1 September 1949; after which it was no longer necessary to hold a licence in order to publish a newspaper. As from this date, a large number of newspapers again began to appear under their former titles. In some cases there was a struggle, even carried out in public (for instance in the case of the newspaper Die-Welt), between these old papers, which called themselves local German papers ("Hdmatzeitungen") and the licensed press. Many of the old publishers' newspapers, which reappeared after 1 September 1940 suddenly failed to arouse the echo which they had hoped for, or they were unable to adapt themselves to changed conditions. The flood of expellers from the eastern territories of Germany, now under Polish and Russian Administration, and the flight of inhabitants of the Soviet occupied Zone to the Federal Republic of Germany also had a particular effect in that they wrought a considerable change in the composition (If the population. This change did not however make any difference for some of the other old newspapers which boldly took up the struggle against the licensed press and today, with an imposing body of regular readers, are again, playing a leading part in the sphere of the German press. The monotony of a twelve year long totalitarian regime had thus given way to a press which again reflected public opinion, in accordance with the tradition of the press in the mother country of the press. In addition there are of course also news-, papers, which take no definite political line, adapting them selves to please tastes, or rather the alleged tastes of their readers. In the modern industrial state the popular press plays a prominent part in every field. As in every state which believes in free competition, there is rivalry among the publishers, who compete for the favour of regular subscribers. By and large the press in the Federal Republic is still supported by regular subscribers, the newspaper being delivered to the reader's house every morning. There are however also a few large popular tabloids which are sold at newspaper stalls and in the streets these are holding their own. With the popular tabloids there also came the illustrated magazines, of which a variety of types are available.

A gratifying large section of the press was concerned with publications for young people, ranging from school magazines to the younger readers' section in the weekend magazines. Many of these publications had a particular political bias, or follow a cultural or religious line. Unlike the totalitarian systems in the Third Reich of the National Socialist and in the communist Soviet Zone there were also a number of denominational newspapers and magazines in the Federal Republic, which commented and criticized as they please and meet with a positive response from their readers. It is true that there were newspapers which call themselves religious in totalitarian states too, but their influence is confined to the affairs of the parish, while the majority of the other papers, on the other hand, were free to attack religion and religious institutions with political means.

Journalists in Germany, have their own local associations and their German Press Association. In some cases they cooperate with the International Journalists' Federation, which endeavours to arrange a regular exchange of ideas on certain matters affecting the journalists' profession; it also investigates the position of journalists in all the countries of the world, considers salaries and wages, examines the development of radio and television and their effect on the printed press, organises international conferences on the subjects of vocational training and measures for the protection of journalists in the exercise of their profession, and generally deals with all matters connected with journalistic activity and the relationship among one another of journalists from different nations. It is also fosters good relations among journalists' and journalists organisations, and among the newspapers and publishers of different countries, as well as devoting itself to the struggle for the geniun internal freedom of the press.

In the early days of printing Gutenberg's new invention rapidly conquered the world. The most imaginative offspring of his invention was the regular periodical, the newspaper or magazine, .read by millions every day. Millions of people who arc prevented from reading themselves, by reason of their age or their youth or other adverse circumstances, get others to read aloud to them. The newspaper is the link between events all over the world and the individual, and for this reason its task is considerable.

The most essential function of all newspapers however should be the eternal theme-to ensure that the nations of the world live in peace and harmony, to try to educate people in freedom and respect for other people's views, though rejecting totalitarian and ideological one-sidedness; the press should help to build such a world along the path of peace. The newspaper serves the printed world. In the Holy Scriptures of the civilized nations and the great religions, both Christian and non-Christian, in the Bible and in the ancient Veda scriptures of the Indians, the World has become a concept of a divine power which can reach the height of perfection. Christians speak of the World, the logos, which brought the world salvation. Christians and non-Christians understand the power of the Word: "And the World was made flesh..." The true Word is wedded to true reality, not the slogan or the political phrase. Let us repeat once again the Christian Word, the truth librates, and the words from the Upanished, which became the motto of the Republic of India-and there is no finer motto imaginable Satyameva jayate "Truth will conquer".

Journalists and pressmen from every era who have defended the nations right to freedom ought not to forget that every form of freedom begins with the freedom of the Word, the honourable Word uttered without haste or taint of propaganda.

Bibliography

Altschull, J.H. : *Agents of Power: the Role of the News Media in Human Affairs,* Longman, New York, 1984.

Baehr, H. : *Women and Media,* Pergamon, London, 1980.

Berelson, B. : *Content Analysis in Communication Research,* Free Press, Glencoe, Illinois, 1952.

Bhattacharjea, Ajit : *Emergency and Media,* Mainstream, 1999.

Carey, James W. : *Communication as Culture: Essays on Media and Society,* Routledge, New York, 1992.

Chaney, D. : *Processes of Mass Communication,* Macmillan, London, 1972.

Cohen, B.C. : *The Press and Foreign Policy,* Princeton University Press, Princeton, N.J., 1963.

Cohen, S. and Young, J. : *The Manufacture of News,* Constable, London, 1973.

Czitrom, Daniel J. : *Media and the American Mind: From Morse to McLuhan,* University of North Corolina Press, Chapel Hill.

Davis, Howard and Walton, Paul : *Language, Image, Media,* Basil Blackwell, Oxford, 1983.

Davison, W.P. : *Mass Communication and Conflict Resolution,* Praeger, New York, 1974.

Dube, S.C. : *Communication, Innovation and Planned Change in India,* International Development Institute, East-West Center Press, Honolulu, 1964.

Fiske, J. : *Introduction to Communication Studies,* Methuen, London, 1982.

Gerbner, G. : *Mass Media Policies in Changing Cultures,* Wiley, New York, 1977.

Hagen, E. : *On the Theory of Social Change,* Dorsey Press, Homewood, Illinois, 1962.

Halloran, J.D. : *The Effects of Television,* Grenada, London, 1970.

Hopkins, M. W. : *Mass Media in the Soviet Union,* Pegasus, 1970.

Innis, Harold Adams : *Empire and Communication,* University of Toronto Press, Toronto, 1972.

Keesing, F. M. and Keesing, M. N. : *Elite Communication in Samoa,* Stanford University Press, Stanford, 1956.

Klapper, J.T. : *The Effects of Mass Communication,* Free Press, Glencoe, Illinois, 1960.

Lakshmana Rao, Y.V. : *Communication and Development: A Study of Two Indian Villages,* University of Minnesota Press, Minneapolis, 1966.

McQuail, D. : *Towards a Sociology of Mass Communication,* Collier Macmillan, London, 1969.

McQuail, D. : *Mass Communication Theory,* Sage, London, 1987.

Mills, C.W. : *White Collar,* Oxford University Press, New York, 1951.

Narayan, Jayaprakash : *Nation Building in India,* Apala, Lucknow, 1990.

Natarajan J. : *History of Indian Journalism,* Report of the Press Commission, New Delhi, 1955.

Peterson, R.C. : *The Mass Media and Modern Society,* Holt, Rnehart and Winston, New York, 1965.

Pye, L.W. : *Communication and Political Development,* Princeton University Press, Princeton, 1963.

Singh, Yogendra : *Modernization of Indian Tradition,* Rawat, Jaipur, 1988.

Snow, R.P. : *Creating Media Culture,* Sage Publications, Beverly Hills and London, 1983.

Weiner, Norbert : *The Human Use of Human Beings: Cybernetics and Society,* Aron Books, New York, 1967.